THERAPEUTIC WORK WITH CHILDREN AND YOUNG PEOPLE

Also available from Cassell:

V. Varma (ed.): *Coping With Unhappy Children*
L. Winkley: *Emotional Problems in Children and Young People*
J. McGuiness: *Counselling in Schools: New Perspectives*
R. Best, P. Lang, C. Lodge and C. Watkins (eds): *Pastoral Care and PSE: Entitlement and Provision*
R. Best (ed.): *Education, Spirituality and the Whole Child*
R. Best, P. Lang and A. Lichtenberg (eds): *Caring for Children: International Perspectives on Pastoral Care and PSE*
T. Tarrant, S. Roffey and K. Majors: *Young Friends*

Therapeutic Work with Children and Young People

Beta Copley and *Barbara Forryan*

CASSELL

Cassell
Wellington House
125 Strand
London WC2R 0BB

PO Box 605
Herndon
VA 20172

First published by Robert Royce in 1987

British Library Cataloguing-in-Publication Data

A catalogue record for this book is available from the British Library.

ISBN 0-304-70010-X (hb)
      0-304-70011-8 (pb)

Typeset by BookEns Ltd, Royston, Herts.
Printed and bound in Great Britain by Redwood Books, Trowbridge, Wiltshire

Contents

To the memory of Martha Harris

Acknowledgements

We want to thank all those who made this book possible. Firstly, those upon whose work it is based: most of it was discussed in a course led by the authors which was held at the Uffculme Clinic in Birmingham and we thank course members for both their contributions and discussion, as well as Dr Roslyn Jamieson and Dr Linda Winkley for the provision of the framework and support. We are grateful for our own training in the child psychotherapy discipline of the Tavistock Clinic in London and for the influence on our thinking of many colleagues and ex-colleagues, in particular that of Mrs Martha Harris. We also thank Mrs Rolene Szur for her kind reading of our manuscript and her helpful suggestions. They do not of course commit her to agreement with the views expressed, which are those of the authors. We are also grateful to the Undershaft Annersley Trust for their support, and to Kate Copley for her typing.

NOTE ON CONFIDENTIALITY

We have made changes in the case material and in the observations of babies and young children in order to protect confidentiality.

NOTE ON TERMINOLOGY

In the cases we describe, more of the workers involved were female than male, so we refer to the worker or therapist as 'she' and the client or patient as 'he' unless the sense demands otherwise. The term 'client' includes 'patient' where appropriate, and also the other way round; the same applies to 'worker' and 'therapist'. The word 'client' has some unsuitable connotations, but it seems to be the best generic term available. We avoid using the term 'child' in a general sense, because we want to make it clear that we are referring to a wider age range than that would imply.

Introduction to the Second Edition

We describe a psychodynamic approach to work with children and adolescents. Central to this is the relationship which develops between a child or adolescent on the one hand and a worker or therapist on the other. We think about this in the context of the everyday experience of professionals in health, education, social and other services. The content of the work may vary with the context, but the interactive processes between worker and client are relevant to them all. Gaining insight into the client's feelings not only helps the worker to understand what the client is bringing: it also enables her to understand how he responds to what is currently happening between them and to make therapeutic use of her own response. Insight into the dynamics of the relationship also serves to develop understanding of what, in the course of the interaction, brings about change.

The work we describe is concerned with trying to understand what is happening in the present rather than laying major emphasis on possible historical 'causes' of problems. Primitive feelings and states of mind exist in all of us; they may have roots in early experiences, but changes can only be effected in the context of our lives now. Toleration, exploration and understanding provided within the relationship offered by a worker may – perhaps for the first time – give a child, or an adolescent, the experience of an adult who accepts and tries to understand his feelings. The bearing of anxiety, and the ability to think about and recognize mental pain, are central to the work described here.

The application of a psychodynamic approach will of course vary with the professional task and the service in which it takes place. In some instances the provision of therapy is itself the purpose of the encounter; in others, professionals, such as teachers and social workers, carry wider responsibilities. The importance of the relationship between client and worker may be obvious in long-term work in which some form of ongoing personal interaction takes place, but less immediately apparent if the worker's role is brief or linked with some kind of control, as, for example, with disturbed children in an institutional setting. We think about the specific requirements of the work in different settings, but show that by listening, and trying to understand the client, within the framework of a consistent and dependable relationship, it is possible to provide far-reaching help to children and young people in a wide range of circumstances. Even within quite brief contact it may be possible to use oneself in a way which allows the client to feel that certain emotional needs are heard.

Our approach is founded on insights gained from psychoanalysis, but we hope that this book will be readily comprehensible to people without previous knowledge of psychoanalytic theories. Our main debt is to Klein and the post-Kleinians, such as Bion and Meltzer, who have developed areas of thought relevant to the human needs experienced within the professional settings about which we write. We do discuss theory, but the emphasis of the book is not on theoretical knowledge for its own sake, but on the understanding derived from it which is of use in the everyday fieldwork undertaken by members of the caring professions.

We want readers to feel as close to what we are trying to convey as possible. This has led us to base our book on case material drawn from a wide range of settings. Most of this was brought for discussion to a course led by the authors.

Children and adolescents in need of help may sometimes remain silent, but usually they talk, draw or play. They also communicate by arousing feelings in the adult who is working with them. It is not always easy for a worker to recognize the source of such feelings. Our detailed discussion of individual sessions may enable readers to deepen their capacity to be receptive not only to the overt problems of their clients, but also to their implicit messages.

We have not singled out what could be thought of as 'successful' cases. On the contrary, several of the sessions are the first of workers new to this approach, and show their hesitations and uncertainty. Some of the questions and doubts voiced by seminar members when the sessions were originally discussed have been included since the issues they raise are likely to be of interest to anyone new to this way of working. We have chosen this method of presentation so that readers are able to think about whether they find our way of working useful.

We do not limit our discussion to work with 'co-operative' clients. Many children and young people come at the behest of parents or others; some may not actively seek help, some may feel that the proposed contact is intrusive; others may not believe that any kind of help could be available. Willingness on our part to accept and try to understand their negative emotions, starting perhaps with the referral itself, may enable children and young people to make use of what we can offer.

The experience of individual therapeutic work needs to become alive for the reader before the underlying concepts become meaningful. In order not to detract from the vivid 'here and now' impact of the material, we have not overburdened the chapters in which cases are presented with detailed discussion of theories and concepts. Terms drawn from psychoanalysis, such as transference and containment, are useful to workers in deepening their longer-term understanding of their work. We use them only in the earlier part of the book when they contribute to the understanding of case material under discussion. A fuller exploration of the concepts themselves takes place later.

Part 1 of the book introduces our approach. We convey what it feels like to work in the way we describe and what the contact could mean to the children and young people concerned. We also give some indication of the demands on the worker that this kind of approach may make.

In Part 2 we consider the context in which the work takes place, including the relationship of the worker with families and colleagues. We draw on material from staff working in institutions – such as residential homes and schools, hospital wards, nurseries and hostels – who want to understand more about the needs of the children and young people they care for and their own relationship with them. This incorporates some investigation of the functioning of the institutions.

Part 3 centres on the kind of change that takes place within a longer-term contact and how it occurs. The most problematic areas of therapeutic work, including the 'difficult' client, are discussed at some length. The ending of the relationship is explored. We discuss the criteria for deciding to finish, the need to prepare for an ending and the significance for the client of a premature or abrupt closure.

In Part 4 detailed descriptions are given of events drawn from the lives of babies and young children, mostly observed in the context of their families. These observations have something in common with the detailed case material discussed earlier in the book and may help readers with their own work, especially non-verbal communication. They also illustrate some of the major concepts on which our approach is based and serve as a bridge between the case material and the more theoretical part of the book.

The major development of concepts and themes has been left to Part 5. These concepts will already have begun to become alive since they have been linked with actual events between worker and client. The more formal discussion of them here again makes links, this time with the observations of babies and small children as well as with the case material.

Since the first edition of this book was published in 1987, new legislation has led to changes in some of the services from which our examples are drawn. This does not directly affect the actual relationship between worker and client – the central theme of this book – although it does affect the provision of services and the manner in which they may be implemented. We comment on these changes. Recent legislation may lead to some increased provision of facilities for early intervention. Brief work, if it is able to relate to a client's emotional needs, may provide sufficient response to certain kinds of problems or may clarify the need for further help. With this in mind, we have included a new chapter on brief interventions.

We also provide an updated bibliography, a discursive reading list and directory of further learning opportunities.

Part 1

A General View of the Therapeutic Approach

Chapter 1

Process and Setting: Some Introductory Examples

This chapter contains examples drawn from the work of different professionals who have found the psychodynamic approach helpful. We use these examples to introduce some central themes related to the therapeutic process and to the work setting, which will be developed more fully in later chapters.

FEELING 'HELD' IN THE WORKER'S MIND (AN OCCUPATIONAL THERAPIST AND JERRY)

Jerry was two and a half when he was referred to a child psychiatric department in a general hospital. The paediatrician referred him in conjunction with the health visitor for a number of severe behaviour problems. He was uncontrollable, hitting, kicking and biting other children and adults. He was repeatedly cruel to the family dog; he also threw food all over the floor, tore up plants and pulled wallpaper off the wall. He ate the dog's excreta; he wiped his own excreta over the wall and up his nose. His parents said he showed no fear, and did not like being shown affection. He often appeared not to hear and would go completely blank, or else parroted other people's speech if they talked to him. Father admitted to hitting him on the legs, and had wondered whether to lock him in a cupboard to control him. A playgroup had been tried but he had been excluded from it because of his destructive behaviour. The health visitor had wondered if he was autistic.

Jerry and his parents were seen by the consultant psychiatrist who then asked the department's occupational therapist to see Jerry fortnightly under his supervision; the social worker saw Jerry's parents at the same time. In the first session Jerry was initially reluctant to do anything. Eventually he made some tiny dolls fall repeatedly from a roundabout. Then he made plasticine 'sausages' as he called them, broke small bits off and then threw them across the floor. The occupational therapist encouraged him to talk about what he was doing, and told him about the times she would be seeing him.

When Jerry, towards the end of the session, began moving larger objects, the worker explained the limits she was setting, and the reasons, for example that the windows were not to be broken nor were either of them to be hurt. At the end Jerry agreed to help put everything away; he crashed the toys into his box from a height.

In the second session Jerry began talking, apparently to himself at first and rather incoherently, about naughty boys, and eating dinner; he ran across the room a great deal, jumping on chairs; the occupational therapist had a feeling of confusion and chaos. However, Jerry was keen to put his toys away carefully at the end. In the third session his play centred around making dinners, tea, cookies and milky bars for the worker, and he came and sat on her lap to play.

The family began noticing great changes in him, and he was accepted into a small sheltered playgroup. His young inexperienced mother was able concurrently to discuss with the social worker her unrealistic expectations of Jerry, and her own difficulties faced with critical neighbours. She gradually began to play with Jerry and listen to him at home, and found new ways of handling him. After six months Jerry's parents felt he no longer needed help; mother continued seeing the social worker, though less frequently.

In discussion in a seminar group, one member asked why the worker allowed Jerry to throw bits of plasticine all over the room. Would it not have been better to train him out of this chaotic behaviour, since that was what he was referred for in the first place? The occupational therapist said she had been very aware of feeling confused by what he did, and had tried to put this into words with Jerry; she had also suggested to him that perhaps *he* felt confused and lost in this big building. Someone else wondered if Jerry was throwing things at the worker, as if at a dog, because he was frightened of her. We thought about this suggestion. Someone asked the worker to describe in detail the throwing of the 'sausages'; she said that although it was difficult to be absolutely clear, it seemed that the emphasis of the roundabout play was on the dolls falling off, and the plasticine being scattered all over the place. What about the ones that actually came in her direction? Someone else wanted to know. The worker said she did not actually feel they were specifically directed at her and did not feel treated as if she were a wild animal. It was agreed that the detailed observation was important, but whether the worker's feelings were relevant, or should be ignored as unscientific, was the next area of discussion. Could one tell what was relevant to Jerry and what wasn't? In any case, someone commented, was it not simply the worker's job to 'mirror back' what Jerry was doing? The leader commented that workers might not only be able to observe the children's play, but also try to look at their own feelings, trying to distinguish areas relevant to the interaction with their clients.

Someone else pointed out that the worker had in fact set limits appropriate to the setting and had explained the need for them to Jerry. Perhaps she came across to him as someone who did not act on impulse, as he did, and did not respond to him with anger and more actions in the form of punishment, as his parents had done. A teacher in the group asked how this differed from the playgroup experience, which had not been a success.

It was suggested that Jerry needed the experience of an individual relationship with someone who gave him a set time and place, with understandable limits and boundaries, and who tried to understand his chaotic, confused experience and put it into words. Jerry found that the worker remembered him from one time to the next and that she was not overwhelmed by his difficult behaviour but was prepared to carry on seeing him. Perhaps he felt 'held' in her mind safely, unlike the toy children flung from the roundabout. She was clearly not primarily concerned with the externals of behaviour, but had space in her mind for Jerry's feelings, however chaotic. Although she could not completely understand what he was doing, she did not react with the distracted anger he had experienced from other adults; she was prepared to wait and try to learn from what he could show her. She also tried to convey her understanding to him in a thoughtful manner.

This approach can be described as a thoughtful and potentially 'containing' one and is central to this book. The term 'containment' as used here derives from the work of Bion (1962a, 1962b). Bion draws on a mother's capacity for 'reverie' in relating to her infant and helping him with his otherwise unmanageable feelings. He indicates how a frightened or otherwise distressed infant can convey by his cries or other means this part of himself to his mother, so that she really experiences this aspect of the baby within herself. This communication makes use of the mechanism of 'projective identification' (Klein, 1946), a somewhat unattractive and clumsy name for a brilliant insight into how a part of the self carrying particular feelings can be 'projected' from one person and felt to be located within another. In the case of the infant and his mother, the mother attends inside herself in 'maternal reverie' to what the infant has conveyed to her. She experiences and reflects on the troubled aspects of her infant. Then, if all goes well, she is able to return to him the troubled aspect of himself, but now in a form which has been given some meaning and made more bearable. In Chapter 10 ('Maternal function and reverie'), we describe such a process taking place in infancy between baby Gita and her mother. We also, in the description of Kevin, include a less happy example, showing how the process can go wrong. The mechanism of 'projective identification' is discussed more fully in Chapter 12. The theme of containment recurs throughout and is reviewed as a whole in Chapter 13.

Jerry's response to the containing experience of the early sessions was to draw closer to the worker and begin to relate to her as someone who had the qualities of a mother (a lap to sit on, and someone with whom to share a feeding experience). In this piece of play, he was the one who was going to feed her (with cookies and milky bars) and it sounded as if he were idealizing what he could give the worker, just as it sounded like a denial of the mess he was making when he called the plasticine lumps 'sausages'. It did however seem to be a move forward from the earlier chaos and confusion. The possibility of understanding and further development could depend on the child himself, the length of therapy and what the worker was equipped to offer. Idealization, and the risk a worker runs of colluding with it, was referred to in the seminar however, and will be discussed in Chapter 8 under 'Idealization and negative feelings'.

Jerry's own mother meanwhile was being helped to appreciate and understand him, and it seemed that this double experience they both had enabled mother and son to renew their relationship with each other on a better footing.

THINKING ABOUT WHAT HELP CAN BE OFFERED: PAINFUL DECISIONS (A FOSTERING OFFICER AND WAYNE)

Jerry and his mother both appeared to need help, and were able to receive it from the two workers concerned. The clinic in which they were seen provided a stable setting for the work to proceed and there was also outside positive support from the health visitor and paediatrician. It is not, however, always easy to locate who needs help, what this help is to consist of, and who among the various professionals who may be involved is to offer it. Nor is there necessarily a supportive framework of a clearly defined setting available. Such areas may require clarification in order to allow therapeutic work to take place.

Miss J, a foster placement officer for social services in a small market town, brought for discussion a case where she was required to supervise the foster-parents in a short-term placement. Wayne, aged twelve, had been living with his father who was over seventy and suffering from a progressive disease. His mother, who was much younger, had always shown very little interest in the children and been frequently away from home even before a divorce and final break-up of the marriage the year before Wayne's referral, and was not in touch with Wayne. While living with his father, Wayne was said to be 'running wild' and was thought to be involved in various minor thefts along with some other boys in his neighbourhood. Father complained that he never knew where Wayne was because he stayed out as often and as long as he liked, and his school attendance was poor.

Wayne was admitted to an assessment unit run by social services, and showed no behaviour problems in the unit. His father was tired and ill, and unable to keep pace with his boisterous, active son. He could exercise little or no control over Wayne, often resorting to bribery. He said he would welcome a short break of a couple of weeks from the boy.

The field social worker allocated to Wayne discussed the child's needs and future at a case conference, where it was decided that Wayne should be placed in a temporary short-term foster-home; this should inculcate regular routines of school attendance and stabilize his behaviour so that he would then be suitable for long-term fostering. The temporary foster-home would also introduce him to substitute parenting, and prepare him for a permanent placement. It was thought he should stay in the temporary foster-home six to nine months.

Wayne was being looked after by the local authority, defined at the time as being in care on a voluntary basis. Father had spoken of it to him as 'giving him a two-week break', and indeed that was how it had been put to father himself. The social worker planned to 'feed them the idea of permanent separation' gradually, once Wayne was in the foster-home. This work took place before the implementation of the Children Act 1989. Had its provisions been in force professionals would presumably have attempted to ascertain the wishes and feelings of Wayne and his father and relate to them more openly before making their decisions under section 22 of the Act.

It was at this point that Miss J became involved as foster placement officer. She had worked with a couple, Mr and Mrs Dare, who had fostered children for the department before, and it was felt they would be suitable as foster-parents for the anticipated six- to nine-month period. They were told of the social worker's long-term plans for the boy; they were also told that Wayne was not to know of this yet.

In the few days that Wayne had been with the Dares before Miss J told the course about her involvement, he had said to Mr Dare that he was only staying a fortnight and that his 'old man' would get him out and they'd be one happy family together again. Wayne visited his father every day after school. The plan at the weekend was that his father should have come to see him at the Dares' but father refused and insisted the boy spent the weekend with him instead. However, father complained to the field social worker that Wayne was as usual out of the house all the time, refusing to come home when told, etc.

Mr and Mrs Dare reported to Miss J, who called to supervise their management of the children, that Wayne insisted to them that he was in care because the field social worker had put him there, and not because his father could not manage (Wayne never spoke of his father's illness). The Dares replied, 'You're here at your Dad's request.'

The field social worker had been in touch with Miss J a number of times, ringing her at home as well as at work, in considerable anxiety over whether he had taken the right decision over the child's present and future placement. It was clear that he was very concerned about Wayne's welfare and hoped to act in his best interests.

In the discussion that followed, it was some while before members of the group could understand the roles of the different people involved. Who was responsible for making the decisions about the fostering? Who had what legal rights? It was plain that Wayne, and perhaps the Dares, must have felt similarly quite at sea. It was also not plain to the group what father himself really wanted; did he say one thing and mean something else? Here again the same doubts must obviously have been in Wayne's mind. How much did Wayne realize about his father's illness? If he knew of it at all, did he know it was progressive and incurable? One group member suggested that when Wayne called him 'my old man' this could be conveying a hint of his worries about his father's age and ill health; Mrs Dare had responded by telling Wayne he was to refer to his father as his father, and not as his old man. Wayne's vagrant behaviour might itself have been some reflection of his anxiety about his broken home and about his father's ability to care for and control him.

Wayne was very insistent that it was the field social worker who had taken him away from home and that it had nothing to do with his father; he was also very insistent that he was going back home at the end of two weeks. It might well be very painful for him to feel rejected and unwanted by his father, and very difficult for his father to be open himself about his real wishes. It did seem that nowhere was there any possibility for Wayne to talk about, explore or face his fears, anxieties, and perhaps guilt. The adults seemed to be colluding in blurring the facts and leaving everything unsaid for as long as possible. This was presumably done with the intention of sparing the child and father pain. It was suggested in the group that this was like concealing the diagnosis from a patient, when there were plenty of clues for the patient to guess at the truth. Evading pain makes it the more difficult to deal with. Wayne's own solution seemed to be to run away from intolerable situations. The group wondered if he should not be helped with this.

Miss J's quandary was that it was not easy to apply this sort of insight gained from the seminar when the constraints of her job and her limited role in this case did not always allow it; nevertheless the field social worker had repeatedly asked her advice so she felt it might be possible to bring about some modification of things here. It became feasible to think about the need for someone to gather up the confusion surrounding Wayne's placement and future fate, and help him to recognize both the sad reality of his father's age, illness and failing competence, and his own feelings about this.

Children who are being moved away from home need to find one adult who is able to set aside the need to make decisions or to find practical solutions, in order to listen and talk to the child. Decisions can be made over the children's heads as a result of a mistaken view of the child's best interests, and the child finds changes happen in his life which he is emotionally quite unprepared to digest.

This example illustrates the link between setting and process, and how there can be a preliminary task for the professionals concerned to make a setting available where an ongoing process of listening and talking can take place. Wayne would need the framework of a containing relationship if he were to face some of the painful truth. This implies a degree of thoughtfulness in the worker, with a depth component greater than might be indicated by the term 'mirroring back'. In Jerry's case, the boundaries of a session seemed to be important in helping him to feel 'held'. Although the specific setting would be different for Wayne, he would also need to feel that an adult was willing to grapple with his problems. This would need to include reliable meeting times. Wayne needed help in talking about and accepting his situation rather than running away from it.

FINDING A PLACE FOR DIFFERENT FORMS OF COMMUNICATION (AN EDUCATIONAL PSYCHOLOGIST AND LEN)

Len was eight years old, the eldest of five children born in fairly rapid succession. The parents lived in difficult social circumstances, and both Len and the sister born about a year after him suffered from severe eczema as babies. Len was described as quiet and no trouble as a toddler. But when he started school at the age of five, it was recognized that he had a speech difficulty, and his teachers over the following years found him to be 'switched out', withdrawn, and unable to make any progress educationally. Mrs A, an educational psychologist, had assessed Len when he was six, and had arranged for him to attend a special unit where he could have more individual attention from the teacher, and he began to respond to this. But two years later Len had again become severely withdrawn at school. This followed the birth of a sixth baby, a little sister to whom Len was reported to be devoted.

Mrs A had met Len's parents on a number of occasions and they were now again anxious for her to try and help him with his problems. They said he was always 'the quiet one' at home; in fact they wished he stood up for himself more with the younger children in the family. Mrs A was asked by the school to reassess Len and make a recommendation; she decided, after careful discussion with the head teacher and with colleagues, to offer Len a limited series of twelve individual sessions to see if she could help him explore what was troubling him. Len seemed to welcome her offer to see him regularly.

This was an extension of her role, and it required courage to set aside the security of a familiar way of working and embark on a new approach. Some careful preparation needed to be done beforehand with colleagues to clarify the nature of the work that was to be attempted, and also to create a setting where this sort of work could take place in privacy.

She needed first to find a suitable room that would be free each week at a time that was suitable for her, and also suitable for Len (something she discussed with his class teacher). The school was able to make a playroom available for her on the same day each week for an hour. It had large internal windows overlooking a busy corridor, and although the windows were above the height of the children, Mrs A decided to explore the possibility of curtains, to give a feeling of privacy to their time together.

It may not be immediately obvious why she needed to have the same room each week, nor why it was important that other people should not come into the room during Mrs A's time with Len, or even why it was preferable that other children could not look in through the windows. The importance of setting is discussed in Chapter 3, and some problems that arise when no suitable room is available are outlined there under 'A clinical medical officer and Tim'.

When she came to consider what she wished the room to contain, she found that there were a lot of toys and play equipment that were needed during the rest of the week, and there was no room (or time) to put them away before Len's sessions, so Mrs A had no choice about some of the play material that would be available for Len. But she decided also to have a box with a few individual things kept just for his use.

Mrs A decided to allow Len to use the session in his own way, rather than investigating or directing him to talk about problem areas highlighted by the history, or revealed by recent contact with the school or social worker. She told the seminar group that when she started using this more open approach in her sessions with Len, she found it easier to think about her own feelings in response to those conveyed by him.

She gave him the box of toys for his own use and told him the times of his sessions. She spoke a bit about the help she would be offering him, and that they would be meeting once a week for the twelve weeks of that term. He soon set out some soldiers in lines talking rather quietly as if to himself about what he was doing. 'This one goes here . . . the baddies go there.'

When this was discussed in the seminar one of the group thought the worker should direct the boy what to do, otherwise he would just waste the time in pleasant games. Someone else thought the provision of soldiers was provocative, 'like all these TV programmes'. Another member thought it would be a good idea to lay down the ground rules at the outset; for example that she would not let him break the windows or attack her. Someone else thought playing with soldiers was 'just conventional'; he was doing it just because boys always did this kind of thing.

After Len had set up the soldiers in lines he pointed to a soldier with a hand-grenade and said, 'He'll start it off.' He made a throwing gesture, and a sound like an explosion, and flattened some of the khaki soldiers. He used a tank, winding the gun barrel up and down, to kill some blue soldiers. A blue soldier with a machine-gun came out and gunned some khaki soldiers down at point-blank range. Len continued back and forth firing, exploding and gunning down and toppling the soldiers over until all the soldiers on both sides were lying down. He then said, 'They're all killed,' and started to pick them up and rearrange them.

He put the two opposing forces in the same positions as before. While going through the rest of the figures he came across a lamb. He stuck its hind leg into the gun muzzle of the tank, saying, 'It's stuck.' Then he fired the cannon. The lamb shot off the end. Len said, 'It's killed,' and removed it.

Another battle took place, even more violent than the first. The muzzle of a tank was put through the windscreen of an enemy jeep; the occupants of the jeep were blasted, and the jeep keeled over. The jet plane dropped a bomb on the tank, overturning it, then the jet plane itself crashed to the ground. All the soldiers ended up lying scattered and dead on the ground. Through all this Len continued, talking calmly in a quiet voice, not seeming at all perturbed.

In the seminar, one member suggested a lamb was something soft and vulnerable, both traditionally and also in the Bible; could this piece of play link with this timid, withdrawn, over-good boy's feelings towards his baby sister? Another said it could be just chance; the lamb's leg was the nearest thing that would fit in the canon, so it had no significance. The worker said that she herself had felt disturbed and upset in the session at what was happening to the lamb, although Len was speaking in a quiet, detached, flat voice about all the destruction that was taking place.

In everyday life Len is described as being devoted to his baby sister and concerned about her welfare; he is also described as being withdrawn. But if we are to take the killing that takes place in the play throughout the session seriously, we must also impute some aggression to him. Yet he seemed to show no concern at all about all the killings. We saw how the worker reported his detached attitude and how she felt disturbed and upset. Using this information, we are in a position to understand that not only lambs and missiles can be fired from tanks, but that feelings of disturbance and upset may be able to be passed, with some similarity to projectiles, from Len to the worker. This, as with Jerry earlier in this chapter, is an example of 'projective identification' in action.

Here, then, the worker experienced not only whatever anxieties she may have brought herself to the first session with this boy, but also seems to have been in receipt of others from Len. Len's anxieties may have had some connection with his softer, more concerned, upset feelings for his sister which he was not able to keep inside himself alongside the activity of his firing, battling self. The worker did not 'fire' his anxieties back, but was attentive to what was happening. It seemed that by passing some of his feelings to the worker in this way he had succeeded in conveying something to her about what was a difficulty for him.

When he was enacting the murderous battle scenes he seemed quite out of touch with any gentler, more tender aspects of himself. He made a fleeting reference to them with the lamb, and Mrs A was aware of feeling concern herself. It would have been helpful if she could have put into words for him how, when the lamb was being killed, he could not bear to feel sorry for it at the same time, but would like her to do this. In this way she could have helped him to be aware of and hopefully gradually take back into himself his own feelings, potentially made more tolerable as a result of her thoughtful attention.

We may surmise that Len needed help to be able to bear feelings of hostility and concern together, but there was no evidence that he was directly seeking help in the sense that he knew something was wrong with him; it might be more accurate to say that he strove to see himself as a loving brother, and that it was the parents and the school who were aware that something was amiss. One could say that he was not as happy as he might have been, and that the potential strength of his personality was diminished by his need to keep aggressive and loving feelings apart. It is not difficult to imagine that a boy who expressed aggressive impulses in a flat way and without overt concern might have difficulties in actively addressing himself to learning and making good school progress.

Returning to his contact in the first session, the initial work with his parents may have been useful in preparing the way for therapy. Len himself may also have felt some potential relief in the approach adopted by the worker. Her offer of time and equipment for himself, together with his experience of her thoughtful attention in the session, may have helped him to feel that this was a place where he could express himself meaningfully, which in fact he did in his play. In a seminar the following year Mrs A reported briefly on the outcome of her term's work with Len. Len was 'coming out of himself' more and had formed a good relationship with his teacher in the special unit, who reported that his work was also showing progress.

THE CLIENT'S INITIAL PERCEPTIONS OF THE WORKER AND THE SETTING

We need to be receptive as to how we are being perceived by the client, so that we can respond in a way that is appropriate to the setting in which we work. It is of course important that we should not fall into enacting what we may be felt to portray, such as some hostile or frightening figure, and thus confirm his fears of us. By using ourselves to give thoughtful attention to resentments and anxieties we may be able to do what we set out to do, to help.

The development of a working relationship may be impeded by anxieties directly related to the worker herself being in some way perceived as frightening or hostile. The anxieties on the other hand may relate more to her in her role as a representative of an institution or as a function of the setting, about which there may be negative feelings.

Satvinder, an adolescent taken to a child guidance clinic by his parents because they thought he had been involved in some theft, was initially surly and uncooperative. Not until the worker recognized with him that he felt he had been brought to a court rather than a clinic, with the worker acting as prosecutor on behalf of his parents, was it possible for the interview to come to life.

Lena, a 19-year-old adolescent, had referred herself to a counselling service situated in the premises of a clinic which also treated psychiatric out-patients. Despite her self-referral and wish for help, she found it difficult to participate in the interview, until the worker explored her possible feelings about the place she had come to; only then was she able to recognize that feelings she had previously joked about concerning being mad held some real fear for her.

It is also possible that the client may have such high expectations of an idealized person, institution or service that there may be a risk of his withdrawal if he finds no immediate resolution of his difficulties. Luke, nine years old, was substantially behind in his ability to read, but bragged to his classmates that it was 'easy peasy' to learn and that he could do so whenever he wanted. It was difficult to get him to accept further help when, after the first remedial session, his reading skills had not improved dramatically. Some of the initial contact involved acknowledging his disappointment at the lack of immediate results; this was necessary before work on his underlying problems could take place.

Myra, an 18-year-old adolescent, came to an adolescent counselling service saying she wanted help from a counsellor about problems she had with boys, and went on to pour out how upset she was about her relationship with her recent boyfriend, in particular about the way he had left her. The worker listened attentively and made some comments, finding it quite difficult to find space to do so, as she was worried about being felt to be intrusive by her client. Myra seemed relieved after their first meeting, and said how useful she had found the interview. They agreed there were further issues to be explored together, but Myra did not return for her next appointment.

On reflection, the worker thought she had been 'too good' a listener, so that Myra's troubles were largely evacuated into her with the consequence that Myra herself may have felt initially relieved, but may have also found it difficult to return and face what she had left behind.

From the above example we can see it is important for the worker not only to be receptive to the client's preconceptions of her or her setting. She needs also to think about the use the client may be making of the proffered relationship. If the wish to offload, for example, is not recognized, the worker can be experienced by the client as a kind of dump; there can be no real containment without some distillation to the client of the worker's reflective processes. But in this particular instance, for the worker to have been able to do this she would have had to resolve differently the feelings about intrusiveness she was experiencing within herself during the session. She needed to be clear whether they really came from herself or whether they originated with the client. We shall return to the question of feelings experienced by the worker in the next chapter.

Some of the themes introduced in this opening chapter are central to the approach outlined in this book. The importance of the setting and the need for a secure framework both physically and professionally were implicit in each case. The examples also highlighted the need to listen to the child or client and reflect on and attempt to respond to what he is saying. It was also apparent that there are various ways of communicating: through words, through play, and through the evocation of feelings in the worker. Perhaps the examples themselves also suggested the possibility of change occurring for the client as a result of the therapeutic relationship.

Chapter 2

The Worker and the Approach

In this chapter we give an example of the psychodynamic approach in the wider setting of a nursery and go on to discuss, in the context of a one-to-one relationship, what demands are made on the worker and what help and professional support she needs to do this work. The particular way a worker uses herself, how much she says and in what way will necessarily depend upon factors such as the length of contact, the nature of the setting and whether she has other roles to carry apart from the therapeutic contact. We get a glimpse of such issues here, and they arc further discussed in Chapters 3 and 4.

OFFERING HELP IN THE IMMEDIATE CONTACT (A DAY-NURSERY WORKER AND JUDY)

Thinking about here and now relationships can be helpful in settings other than individual therapeutic work. Playgroups and nurseries, for example, offer a great deal to a child as they often provide his first sustained relationships outside the family home, and many families have had first-hand experience of the emotional development their child has been able to achieve there. In the following example, however, the staff perhaps missed an opportunity to help a little girl work through some of her jealousy and rivalry.

Judy, who was four years old, was in a day-nursery. The staff knew her mother had just given birth to a baby boy. A little boy in the day-nursery, Philip, felt unwell in the course of the day and lay on a camp bed in the room in which Judy and others were playing. Judy noticed that he was getting extra loving attention and care from the staff, and murmured softly that she was going to be ill too when she got home. Later she brought a soft toy to Philip's bed, followed by some bricks she had picked from the floor, saying 'Look, Philip, this is for you.' A worker told her she was kind. Judy then asked a little boy to give her a toy stethoscope he had so that she could 'examine' Philip, and tried to take it forcefully from him when he refused to give it to her. When one of the senior staff intervened Judy banged into her, and thc staff member tried to turn this into a game. Judy then gave Philip more bricks, asking if he liked her. Later she went back to banging into the senior staff member and kicked the doctor's set of which the stethoscope was part.

Judy seemed to be struggling with feelings that were presumably related to the birth of her little brother. She evidently wanted to be looked after like Philip who was lying down and helpless like the new baby. Later she apparently tried to get the 'new baby', Philip, to like her by bringing him gifts. At first it was a soft toy, which suggested feelings of gentle concern; when Judy then gave him bricks which she had picked up at random from the floor, perhaps some of her angry jealous feelings were beginning to emerge. The worker's praise for being 'kind' did not take account of the negative feelings which were also there. For a while Judy tried to be Philip's doctor. The nursery staff saw how she related to Philip and heard her remark about intending to be ill too. One of them said to Judy she did not have to be ill if she wanted to be with her mother, and perhaps she could help to look after the new baby. The worker was suggesting to Judy how she could *behave*, but it might have been more helpful if she could have talked to Judy about how she was *feeling*. Judy had shown that she felt Philip was getting more loving care than she was, so the worker could have acknowledged this feeling with her and perhaps spoken in general terms about what it feels like to have a new baby at home. After all, she could not be sure that Judy was really capable of giving helpful care to the new baby at home; nor could she be sure that Judy's mother would welcome the offer. Rather than giving prescriptive advice about an unknown setting outside the nursery, the worker might have helped Judy more by speaking from the standpoint of her own relationship with her and the experience of feelings within that little group. This would be on the basis of the worker having taken in Judy's communication about her rivalry and thinking about it with Judy.

Of course nurseries are busy places with many children to look after and staff cannot always attend to the details of a child's feelings at the moment they occur. It seems important, however, that Judy's feelings about Philip and her hostility to the staff member should have been noticed in some way and not just deflected into being a game or treated as if they were only part of some conflict located in the home situation. An approach in which the reality of what a child feels ('psychic reality') is attentively noticed can help a child feel that she and her feelings matter and can be thought about. If this does not happen, a child in such a situation could be left experiencing a nursery equivalent of 'Run away and play. Can't you see that mummy and the doctor are busy with the new baby?' with no place to put her feelings of rivalry and feeling left out. Some nurseries find it useful to give one worker a particular role in relation to specific children; this could encompass not only her own direct contact with the child, but thinking about the child's experiences in the group as a whole.

It may be difficult for staff whose relationships with children are obviously much less central than those of the parent-child relationship to believe that what they offer is of value; on the other hand non-interpretative yet containing conversation is an everyday feature of many playgroups, nurseries and day-care centres and can help children through some of their struggles with painful feelings. Such contact seems especially useful when there is a major event in the family such as a new birth; the older child will then have an additional opportunity to work on some of his feelings. Thoughtful relationships within day-nurseries and day-care centres in which children may spend fairly long hours apart from their families are clearly particularly important.

The worker, then, it is suggested, can use her own observation and experience of the child to relate to his current feelings and try to think about them appropriately with him. To that extent her work shares a common approach with the individual sessions we are about to discuss.

THE IMPLICATIONS OF OFFERING A CONTAINING RELATIONSHIP (A NURSING SISTER AND EDWARD)

This piece of play therapy from a hospital out-patient setting was brought to a seminar early in the year. It was Edward's second session. He had been referred on account of difficult behaviour at home and at school, with aggressive outbursts and temper tantrums. He had a little brother aged two and was described as being 'difficult' around the time of his brother's birth. Father was described as a disciplinarian, and mother as feeling worn down. We were told that the team making the diagnostic assessment had recommended counselling for the parents as well as play therapy for Edward with a nursing sister.

After the seminar had heard a description of Edward's session, the members spent some time talking about the parents, and it was difficult to turn to considering the contents of Edward's hour with his worker. Noticing the details of a child's play, and seeing any meaning in it, is not necessarily easy at first. The succession of events can be bewildering and hard to relate to any familiar frame of reference. It can be much easier to turn with relief to a discussion of family problems and family relationships, and that seemed to be the case here. Whether we could look at the material in detail seemed to be the first problem for us; this involved leaving the 'second-hand' presentation about the parents and taking the risk of trying to see if we could relate directly to Edward himself.

The worker had told Edward that he could play with anything and that she would join in if he wanted her to. He immediately went to the garage which was new since his first session. He arranged the cars, vans and trucks in separate groups in a line and 'walking' with his fingers, 'got in' one, saying 'This is a robber'. He made it move and said that the police had seen robbers in the van and were going to arrest them. A graphic 'cops and robbers' chase followed, in which Edward pointed out that the robbers were faster than the police.

After the chase Edward changed the van to a refuse collection truck and asked if there was rubbish to collect. The worker made some scraps of paper and he collected them up.

Edward then turned to the doll's house. He pointed to a piece of furniture in it and said his little brother would like to have that. When the worker asked if his little brother had stayed at home that day Edward laughed and said that his little brother had cried because he had wanted to go out with 'my mummy' that morning, and he continued laughing as he spun a toy roundabout faster and faster.

Edward then set up the railway track, asking the worker to help him. After keeping the engine on the tracks for some time, he made it turn off at right angles, saying it was 'magic' and smiling at the worker. She agreed. As the train went round the curve he deliberately made it crash, then drove it on the tracks again for a short period. A little later he talked about how he got angry when sent to bed by his mother for being naughty, but claimed he didn't mind, because he had new toys in his room. As he was saying this, he hid the train in the tunnel and asked the worker to guess where it was. He then said he sometimes hid in a drawer with a friend.

When told there were only five minutes left of the session, he went to the sand tray and spun some sand through the wheel in it. Looking under the sand he found two boats and asked if they would float. The worker demonstrated how they could be made to move along in the water and he instituted a race with her, looking at her, laughing, and splashing more and more. He sounded pleased that he could come back the next week. After the session his father asked him what he had been doing, to which he replied, 'Just playing'.

The seminar discussed whether Edward was in reality doing something as trivial as his words 'just playing' suggested; or could his play have had any meaning in it? Edward himself may have told his father it was just play because he felt the need for privacy in his involvement with the worker. The group members themselves found it difficult to see any significance in the play they were hearing about. Someone said that cops and robbers was such a common theme in boys' games, Edward was just doing what all boys do. Someone else said if his play was important it would be better to film it and get a more accurate record.

Edward had said the robbers were faster than the police, and he seemed to take some pleasure at the robbers outwitting them. Some of his behaviour at home that he described to the worker also seemed to have echoes of a defiant 'naughtiness' (laughing in triumph over his crying little brother, and being angry and defiant when sent to bed, for example). It seemed possible the robbers represented a 'naughty' part of himself being chased by a policeman-like daddy. There was also some implicit anxiety about the outcome.

The van then changed to something more useful: a refuse collection service. Edward may have felt that while the worker was listening to him and following his play, she was also coming to understand something of the conflicts within him that it represented. Perhaps she could hold some of the conflict like the van collecting the paper.

Experiencing the worker as being able to hold on to the feelings he was communicating may have enabled Edward to risk letting her know something about his feelings towards his baby brother. He said his brother would have liked to have the piece of the doll's house furniture, and then told her that he had taken his nice mother away from his little brother, leaving the latter in tears. He had first shown behaviour problems at the time of his brother's birth, and his play could be seen as a form of working through his anger and possessiveness.

The train going off the tracks seemed to link with his doing something naughty at home; he claimed that he did not mind being punished, just as he claimed that the train was being magic when it went off the tracks. While he was hiding the train in a tunnel, he told the worker that he sometimes hid in a drawer. Perhaps he was conveying his belief in his powers of stealing inside, like the earlier robber in the car, and creating bad magic when he felt excluded from a relationship, as when he was sent upstairs by his mother. But he also showed that the dangerous magic was followed by disastrous crashes. In only his second meeting with the worker, Edward was therefore giving her insight into the behaviour problems which had occasioned the referral: he was making a link between his aggressive outbursts or temper tantrums, and his feelings about his little brother and his mother.

This sequence of play could be seen as a communication within the session and thus available for 'work' there, with more safety than in the outside world. If we accept this, it follows that we have to consider how the worker could best use herself as an important recipient of such communication; could she in this instance for example try to think with him about what happens if he uses 'magic' as a way out of painful feelings of jealousy and rivalry instead of just agreeing that it *was* magic? 'Magic' to Edward seems like a magical way of avoiding unpleasant consequences. She could show him that it led to crashes, that is, to more anger and turmoil inside him and between him and his mother. If the child feels the worker is giving a pleasurable assent to this sort of magical omnipotent thinking, he may see her as colluding in his construction of an inner world based on falsehood, where the 'cops' do not know what the 'robbers' are up to and where the robbers are allowed to win. In the long term collusion (even if unintentional) is obviously not going to help him.

When the worker warned Edward about how little time was left, she was sensitive to the feelings he conveyed that something might be wrong. 'Will the boats float?' sounded as if Edward did not think they were reliable. He may have been wondering if the worker could be relied on to keep him in mind till their next session. The worker here decided to show him that the boats would sail along as well as float. Someone suggested in the discussion that she wanted him to have a cheerful experience at the end of the session; but this would mean avoiding any painful aspect of the ending. It is true that Edward left looking forward to coming again, but it is not really helpful to him to feel that an adult joined with him in covering over his anxieties. If we accept that play has meaning and can form a communication, the worker could have put into words here Edward's wish to carry on coming to see her, and also his fear that she would be unreliable about it. We discuss the inner world, the phantasies within it and the meaningfulness of play in Chapter 12.

The relationship between the client and worker is the keystone of therapeutic work. The worker offers herself as someone who will think about what the child shows her, and try to 'contain' his thoughts and feelings however disturbing or socially unacceptable they may be. The purpose of the session is not just to provide a happy experience; the worker needs to avoid colluding with the child in masking painful feelings. So she has to consider whether to join in any activity which would interfere with her basic task, of thinking about what is happening. She will also need to concentrate on what the child does in the session (as Edward's worker did) rather than lay the blame on his parents for bad management. Of course, it is not always possible to understand all a child's play. What seems important is that the worker should notice, listen and think about what he does and face the painful elements in it.

It is hard to see children suffer, and the positive wish to help that may have led us to take up work with children may than make us wish to spare them pain, as with Wayne (Chapter 1). But there is no way of avoiding the truth of a child's painful experience, or the violence of his jealousy, for instance. If the worker can at least give space in her mind to recognize and acknowledge these, it may in turn make it more possible for the child to integrate them. The worker provides this sort of mental space by her regular, attentive, thoughtful presence. This means also that she has to be open to what is projected into her by the client, as we saw in Chapter 1 where both Jerry's worker and Len's worker experienced feelings evoked in them by the child.

All this can impose a considerable mental burden on the worker. Offering therapy to a disturbed child is not something that should be undertaken lightly. If workers new to this approach are asked to undertake this sort of work, the senior members of their team or of their profession need to ensure that sufficient training and ongoing supervision are available.

BEING IN TOUCH WITH FEELINGS WITHIN A DEPENDABLE COMMITMENT (A NURSE AND AHMED)

The worker, a nurse, told the seminar that Ahmed had been referred to the psychiatric out-patient department nearly a year ago, he had been initially seen by a colleague who had left after working with him for four months. After an interval of several months Miss Z had started to see him herself. The referral had been on account of destructive and attention-seeking behaviour, stealing, and an incident of fire setting, apparently directed at other children. When he first met Miss Z he told her that he used to see the other lady and she left; was she going to go too? he asked. Miss Z told us that Ahmed was in care and his current foster-mother was quite critical about therapy; the foster-mother had, for example, poured out complaints over the telephone to her, from which she had tried to disengage herself as quickly as possible because she wanted to safeguard her relationship with Ahmed. The worker brought the fourth session to the seminar.

Ahmed referred contemptuously to the toys that were in the box which Miss Z had provided for his sole use, throwing out felt-tipped pens and asking if there were any paints. She told him they would be arriving soon. He then seemed willing to use the communally available rocking-horse, but his eyes alighted on a small child's toy and he asked sarcastically, 'Is this for me?' The worker replied that it was just in the room. He got on the rocking-horse, and said he guessed they would have to talk, and that he might as well get it over with. (It seemed clear he knew that his foster-mother had complained to the worker about him.) The worker told Ahmed that the time was specially for him and he could do what he liked. Ahmed then said that his foster-mother asked him after the session what they talked about. The worker acknowledged that this was difficult for him and he agreed and then said he didn't want to talk anyhow. She assured him that the contents of the session were confidential.

He then said he wanted to start the race, referring to the rocking-horse and something they had done before, and 'rode' fast, the worker holding a blanket as she had done in previous play. He said dismissively that he had 'hundreds' at home of the small cars that she had provided for him in his box. Later he complained that his chair was not the same as the therapist's; she offered to exchange seats which he accepted.

He kicked the chair, after involving the therapist in a game making loud banging noises. She commented on his anger. Soon he draped himself across the chair, nearly falling, and called out. The worker put her hand out and he grabbed it. She told him he had given her a fright and that she thought he would hurt himself. He laughed, reinitiated the banging game, saying he would move the rocking-horse so that the worker would not hurt herself.

He then went on to ask if he could water the plant on the sink and with the worker's agreement did so. He waved the can in her direction, and she commented that he wanted to wet her. Soon he had overfilled the plant with water and had put the paper toys they had jointly made and also a felt-tipped pen into the sink, after looking at the worker for her reaction. Ahmed remained at the sink, hitting and spraying the water. After angrily throwing the soggy paper in the bin he sat quietly in a chair with a troubled face.

Miss Z commented that he looked sad and he asked her to draw something to 'cheer him up' but was scathing about the farmyard scene she drew. 'Is that supposed to cheer me up?' he asked. She said she was confused about what he wanted her to do. He then added to her drawing but 'pretended to laugh' at her further drawing. Telling her to continue, he put a pen top in her hair and asked her if there was something different about her; she 'guessed' the pen top and he indicated that he wanted her to play at finding something hidden. She said she would like to, but that time was nearly up. He looked disappointed and she said they could do that next week.

This was one of the first pieces of detailed material talked about in a seminar group. Some account of the discussion follows, with additional reflections from the seminar leader. The discussion at first focused on the boy's history and family situation and the outlook for the foster-home placement which was the sixth one to be tried. The relation of the foster-mother to therapy was also talked about and we thought from the reported telephone conversation that she would really have liked the worker to give Ahmed 'a good talking to'. An attempt was made to think about the foster-mother's feelings and whether any way could be found to relate to these, if possible by another worker; this could help to keep Ahmed's sessions confidential and to set some kind of boundary around his therapy as well as providing an opportunity of help for the foster-mother herself. It was again quite difficult to leave the subject of parents and foster-parents and come on to what seemed to be formidable problems for the worker. It is not easy to be immersed for an hour in a child's puzzling and apparently random activity; here there was the additional problem of Ahmed's sarcasm and anger.

When we began to talk about the contents of the session the worker told us that unfortunately building work was going on in the clinic; this had led to a need to change rooms in an earlier session, and Ahmed had been upset to see the previous playroom in pieces. It had also not been possible to provide all the materials she had hoped to have available for him by the time this session took place. She had, however, been able to provide him with a box, so that he could have a definite and private physical space for the things she had made available for him to use week by week in therapy. The box could also serve as some indication of ongoing space in her mind for him. She had commented that he had in fact asked to carry the box into the room; so he had evidently been pleased at the idea of this box being just for him. He was disappointed that the promised paints were not there, and contemptuous about the felt-tipped pens and the few toy cars. He was also suspicious and angry about the small child's toy he spotted in the room.

So perhaps he was showing her his bitter suspicion that she did not, after all, have a really separate place in her mind for thinking about him and his needs. It can be bewildering for a worker new to this type of contact with children, and eager to offer all the help possible to a severely deprived child, to be confronted with such mistrust and cynicism. But from Ahmed's point of view he had been in and out of care and removed from several foster-homes, and had also had a change of worker (and change of rooms) at the clinic, so this suspicion and defensive bitterness was what he most needed the worker to think about, before there was a chance of his being able to use her help in a more positive way.

When we talked about the aims and objectives of the session, one seminar member suggested it could provide a one-to-one relationship to build trust. But then we had to remember that Ahmed had already lost one worker and had asked if the new worker might leave soon; it was possible also that the foster-parents might remove Ahmed from therapy. How could all this be reconciled with such a therapeutic goal? The worker said sadly that she did not seem to be in a position even to offer a regular room, let alone a permanent promise of her availability, although she hoped to stay in the clinic for a lengthy period. The seminar leader suggested the worker could acknowledge these facts and also let Ahmed know that she had noticed and understood his negative feelings: his contempt for the small child's toy, his rivalrous claim to have 'hundreds' of toy cars, his possible envy of her better chair.

We could see some change having taken place inside Ahmed in some way related to his experience of the session, since his anger had been followed by sadness. The worker was clearly sensitive to this change, and tried to respond to his demand that she should 'cheer him up'. This raises the question whether it is more useful for a worker to try and perform the role the child ascribes to her, and in this instance to introduce an artificial cheerfulness, or try to find some way of thinking about the painful feelings with her client. It can be hard for a child like Ahmed, who had suffered so many reverses, to risk seeking understanding with a new adult. In this instance to try and face the feeling of sadness and how it occurred could help him to feel understood. If a worker complies too readily with his insistence on being cheered up, the opportunity of finding an adult who could stay thoughtfully with his experience of sadness is lost. As we saw with Edward, it is not always helpful if a worker 'fits in' with a child's wish for her to perform a particular activity. One cannot lay down rules as to what a worker should do; it is important, however, that she should try and use herself in a way that allows her to stay thoughtfully in touch with a child's feelings, rather than let herself be used by the child to remove or deny them totally. The worker may feel impelled by the child to take some action; but this in itself may be a way of avoiding thinking about the problem.

This material provides many points for discussion. The link with the parents, the need for a firm setting and the nature of the setting are developed in Chapter 3. Here we discuss the need to be in touch with feelings in the session, and the need for a dependable commitment.

We can see from the sessions with Edward and Ahmed how a child or client can convey something to us in many ways, not just through talking or play. Changing from one kind of play to another also needs to be noticed and thought about. A client's bearing, tone of voice, and attitude to the beginning and end of sessions are important. So also is what he feels about the room, and how he uses it. The worker needs to relate to the whole range of communication, try and experience what is being conveyed, and think about it.

The feelings that arise in the worker in the course of a session are surprisingly also part of the raw material. She makes herself available as a friendly attentive adult, but may be treated differently. From this we may learn something about the child's conception of her, or of the setting. During the course of the session different feelings may be aroused in the worker by her client. Sometimes this may feel like straightforward communication, as when Ahmed wanted the worker to cheer him up. Sometimes it may feel as if a communication is 'projected into' the worker, without the client experiencing it at all; when the worker spoke of her wish to protect Ahmed from hurt, his response was to move the rocking-horse so that she would not hurt herself, as if he were the potentially protective adult and she the child needing protection. It seemed that the worker was to experience the feelings of a child. The feelings in *her* could be taken as a communication of how *he* found being a small child in need of protection unbearable. Hence by thinking about the feelings arising in her as part of the content of the session, the worker would be in a better position to try and understand something with Ahmed about his painful feelings of being vulnerable and unprotected.

When Ahmed met his new worker, his anxiety was that she would soon leave as his previous worker and other adults in his life had done. In other words he may have had an inner expectation that adults could be practically poised to go from the very beginning of the contact. We have already seen in Chapter 1 (under 'The client's initial perceptions of the worker and the setting'), how a client can bring to the session expectations about the worker, the setting and the process, which are not related to the actual external situation. Freud's concept of 'transference' lies behind the understanding of such manifestations. This concept is discussed in Chapter 15 along with the 'countertransference' feelings aroused in the worker through contact with the client. In the new relationship with the new worker the possibility arose of this pattern becoming modified for Ahmed. This would not be on the basis of gratification, because he and the worker would leave each other sooner or later, but hopefully after his feelings about being currently left and abandoned had been noticed by Miss Z, lived through, recognized and thought about, to the extent that they could have undergone some alteration and become more bearable for him.

Miss Z knew that she would need to carry on seeing Ahmed, and that such a disturbed child was not going to be helped by another short-term contact. The child psychiatrist to whom Ahmed had initially been referred supported her in this and had arranged individual supervision, a work discussion seminar and a training course for Miss Z. We were able to hear towards the end of the year that Ahmed had settled in therapy after this unpromising start and was making good use of it. The nurse's need for training and support, the importance of her commitment to what could be a long-term task, and the need to respect her work as a professional task, are not always recognized by her nursing seniors or by her medical colleagues. Sometimes a nurse or nursery nurse is asked to offer 'play therapy' without being given any additional training, as if it were an easy task, although the example of Ahmed shows that such a child may be too disturbed to 'play', and that the 'therapy' is not going to be straightforward.

WHAT THE WORKER OFFERS AND THE DEMANDS UPON HER

The worker is offering a professional adult relationship to the child where his feelings can be borne, thought about and talked about. Obviously, when ongoing work is undertaken, a long-term commitment is called for and thoughtful attention needs to be given to unavoidable absences, breaks or changes of job. A professional is likely to be subjected to uncomfortable feelings in the course of the work in addition to any feelings of diffidence of her own. Although seeking to offer help, she may be perceived in a very negative way, and these negative feelings have to be tolerated and worked with. She also takes the risk of feeling filled with varying degrees and kinds of pain, like the feelings of uselessness (with Ahmed) or of chaos (with Jerry, Chapter 1).

Listening to what the child says, as well as observing his non-verbal behaviour and play, are both important means of understanding; but so also are the feelings which are evoked in us by the projective identifications of our clients. We have to try and hold the painful feelings projected into us and, as Bion wrote, respond therapeutically like a well-balanced mother, helping the child to receive the fearful or otherwise troubled aspects of his personality back again in a form he can tolerate (Bion, 1962b). We can try to think with the child about the 'here and now' relationship of the session, as this offers a first-hand experience of being in touch with what hc is feeling. What the child brings to the session can be understood as something emanating from his inner world, but also as something existing in the present reality of the relationship with the worker.

When Ahmed found the small toy, he made it clear that he felt it was the other children connected with the worker who were intruding into the room and, by implication, into the space in her mind reserved for him. As we shall see in Chapter 7 ('Bearing hate, rivalry and jealousy') it is useful when an opportunity arises to take up such feelings directly in relation to the worker and the 'rival' children whom this child thinks are involved with her, so that they become a live issue in the 'here and now'. In this way feelings of jealousy can be brought right into the session where they can be worked with. If Edward's worker had acknowledged his anxieties about the ending of the session this might have enabled his feelings about being dropped (perhaps in favour of the next child) to come openly into their relationship; this in turn might have led to some easing of the relationship between him and his little brother at home.

Turning again to the example of Ahmed, we can see how the worker could usefully have shared with him how she really took in his feelings about her, however negative: and that she understood his feeling that 'she did not provide adequately, had others in her mind, kept a better chair for herself, was not good at cheering-up', and so on. It is in this way that the 'here and now' relationship can be used in the work we are describing.

Members of our seminars have spoken of anxieties accompanying taking up this new approach. Any new work is liable to arouse anxiety and in this field there is also an extra burden to shoulder. It is not easy to be open to feelings evoked in oneself by a client or to tease out what is relevant for the client in one's own response, or to relate to what a client is bringing if much of it is not understood. Doubts, for example, about not being good enough or not getting it right; feeling liable to be blamed; not knowing, not understanding, feeling helpless, feeling intrusive, or, perhaps in reverse, feeling intruded upon, feeling lost and confused, are liable to beset most of us at times when attempting new endeavours or in difficult situations. Such feelings can be particularly burdensome when there is the double task of relating to our own anxieties, and distinguishing them from the feelings evoked in us by the client. This is discussed further in Chapter 15 when we discuss countertransference.

THE LIMITS OF THE APPROACH AND THE NEED FOR PROFESSIONAL SANCTION AND SUPPORT

Most of the cases in this book have been discussed in professional groups of the kind we go on to describe. Gaining insight through group discussion into a client's feelings, and understanding how to use the worker-client relationship, can be helpful to workers from all settings, including Judy's nursery workers referred to earlier in the chapter. It is, however, the needs of those engaged in sustained individual work with which we are particularly concerned here.

There is certainly a need for extended work to try and help the number of distressed children that have been shown to exist (Rutter, 1970, 1975). Some professions are expanding their work to try and meet this need, and there are examples of the work they are doing in this chapter and elsewhere in this book. We aim to show the nature and application of a psychodynamic approach to this work. How the worker uses the communications from the clients, including her own countertransference feelings, to think about and talk about what is happening between them is a central theme. But it would not be appropriate in this sort of work to explore deeper levels of the unconscious. Individual work with children and young people based on the approach we describe, although it is informed by psychoanalytic thinking, is clearly different from psychoanalytic psychotherapy carried out by professional child psychotherapists. The latter of course required personal psychoanalysis or psychoanalytic psychotherapy, extensive theoretical knowledge and intensive supervision, which is provided within the framework of the professional training in child psychotherapy.

If someone in another profession is going to undertake individual therapeutic work with children it needs to be firmly anchored within her own profession, sanctioned and supported by it. Some professionals already work in the way we describe. Others may be changing their functioning from a more traditional role; this was true for the nurses who worked with Ahmed and Edward. They needed support from nursing seniors for this change, and clarification and thoughtful exchange with other involved professionals in the setting. Ahmed's worker, for example, wanted to provide a stable setting for ongoing work with him; she had to get agreement from her own seniors about this use of her time, and about her share in the duty and holiday roster; she also had to negotiate with others in the building about her use of the room and equipment.

Appropriate training and support are essential for those asked to grapple with the multiple demands of a new approach, especially as it involves extending their work into painful areas of the mind. Seniors in the worker's own profession, and the colleagues who refer children for individual work, need to ensure that training and support are available. There is also a limit to the amount of individual work with children as disturbed as Ahmed that young professionals, and particularly workers coming fresh to this approach, can undertake. Some responsibility to monitor this must lie with those who make the referrals, from whatever discipline.

With regard to the question of educational help, individual supervision is obviously valuable. We saw how the psychiatrist who had referred Jerry to the worker provided this support (Chapter 1). In some instances, where a worker is really covering new ground such as Mrs D's work with Nicholas which we describe in Chapter 8, supervision is essential.

Workers also need to develop their understanding of the approach. A work discussion group, in which members, often drawn from different professions, bring detailed accounts of interaction with their clients can provide such an opportunity. Members of the group, with the help of a seminar leader experienced in the psychodynamic approach, can discuss how the worker sees her role, what is happening in the session, what the client could be attempting to convey to the worker, what is evoked in her, and whatever else seems professionally relevant. (The task of normal professional supervision or of a work discussion seminar is not to examine feelings personal to the worker, but to help her to think about the material and recognize what may be 'put into' her by her client.) Such groups have in themselves a thoughtful and containing function in that the emphasis is not on finding an 'answer' but in helping the worker with her thoughts about the client and the material.

It is in such work discussion groups that much of the quoted material of this book has been presented and discussed. Parallel seminars based on infant observation are a valuable learning tool, and are more fully discussed in Chapter 10. Courses currently available on these lines are listed in the Directory of Further Learning Opportunities.

Part 2

Worker and Client in the Setting

Chapter 3

Framework and Boundaries

In a containing approach the therapist must have a place in her mind where she can relate to her client's feelings on a consistent basis. A necessary component of work of this kind is an adequate setting which can in itself portray something of the worker's mental availability.

A basic facet of the setting will be the time for which a client is seen, both regarding the length of each individual session and the longer time span of attendance. There will be a question of place; we saw in Chapter 1 how Mrs A had to work at providing an appropriate room in which to see Len. In working with children there is also the question of providing some equipment for their personal use. In many instances relations with colleagues belonging to or outside one's own service may be relevant (as with Wayne in Chapter 1). Beyond the immediate setting within which one sees the client, the function and task of the service in which one works is relevant and part of a wider setting. The worker may for example have some other role to carry apart from that of being able to offer a potentially therapeutic working relationship to her client. In this and the following three chapters we shall look at the requirements of an adequate setting, and the interactive processes within the worker-client relationship in the context of various working situations and their constraints.

LINK WITH THE PARENTS

Children are likely to come to a new institution in the first instance on the initiative of their parents, and the feelings of the latter are also likely to be relevant to the contact. In the case of a child, an appropriate member of the agency will need to meet the parents and explore with them their expectations in the light of what help can be offered. Sometimes as we saw in Chapter 1, there may be a hostile or frightening component in the meaning that a person, a place, or the nature of the meeting itself, may have for the client, the parents or both. In these circumstances the development of the contact may be at risk unless the negative feelings are recognized. Parents or children may for example feel under threat if their child is referred to a clinic or institution with psychiatric connotations which for them carry some kind of stigma; or the institution may have painful associations for the child himself. This could be the case with some of the children of whom we write who have had prior physical investigations (for example Andrew whom we discuss in Chapter 8 under the heading 'A silent child').

Harriet's school had informed the Jones parents that Harriet was having learning difficulties and was a bit troublesome in class. The family found this information difficult to take, and although co-operating in making the appointment with the child guidance clinic, once there they were defensive and unforthcoming. They maintained that all was well with Harriet, and the discussion could only be opened up after the clinic worker raised their feelings about attending the clinic. It seemed that the family were defensively allied with Harriet's learning difficulties, and they found it difficult to accept a point of view presented to them, as they felt, by the school and clinic. Before any work on the presenting problem could get under way, it was necessary for the clinic worker to take up the family's reservations about the clinic as a place that was felt to be pushing unwelcome knowledge at them. The family's defences were experienced as operating against the functioning of the clinic, rather than against the worker as such, although of course it was with her that they interacted. The worker helped them to become aware of their feelings about the clinic in a way that enabled them to use the contact constructively. This work with the parents (which could take place separately from or with Harriet) seemed to be a necessary precursor to Harriet's attendance.

When work with a child is undertaken, co-operation at some level is needed from parents or those in a parental role. Our comments here refer to instances where the child is attending a clinic or hospital but also have some relevance to work done with children in other settings, particularly schools, which we discuss later. The child may be too young to attend on his own, so it may be necessary for the parents to bring the child. Parents themselves may wish or be willing to receive some help for themselves. In order to preserve the feeling of privacy within the relationship for the child, long-term help for the parent is more appropriately provided by a different worker. Parents may however feel they need at least some initial contact with the child's worker in order to satisfy themselves that the kind of work, and maybe the worker herself, are, in their view, appropriate for their child. Parents may wish to understand something of the nature of the work and in so doing may be able to support it better. A parent may for example be anxious about the degree of expressive freedom, or mess, tolerated in a therapeutic contact, and may need help in understanding that certain things are tolerated in such work simply for the purpose of relating to the underlying conflicts. With Ahmed (see Chapter 2) we were aware of a degree of antagonism from his foster-mother towards his therapy, and the worker. This is a difficult area, but it seems important that some attempt is made to allow parents or foster-parents to express views on both the child, and the course of the therapy. The worker may understandably want to keep herself totally available for the child only, but she should bear in mind the needs of the parents. The boundaries of such a contact may need to be clarified with the child as well as with the parent or foster-parent. It might be that after a meeting with the worker and the possibility of some occasional further meetings if the need arose, the parent or foster-parent might be willing to see some other worker in the team in a more individual relationship. Providing individual time and space for parents may help to diminish intrusions into the child's time with his worker.

It will be clear how much emphasis we put on the understanding of the current relationship between the worker and the client, but it is of course likely to be from the family that we learn about the child's background, problems and history, and also, maybe through a colleague, how he is progressing once therapeutic work has started.

It may be questioned why we do not use the information obtained from the family more directly in our work with clients. We prefer to see the history as background information which can illuminate our work. We thus attempt to hold the setting of our current relationship with the child within tight boundaries. Within a session we may well hear something about parents, as we did for example with Edward in Chapter 2. But in fact what we are hearing about are liable to be a child's feelings about his parents, which may refer more to the 'inner parents' of his mind than his external ones. It is important for the worker not to get caught up in this material in the sense of taking it as a necessary face-value representation of parents, nor should she be in any way seduced into a competitive stance of being a better parent. It is more helpful if the worker makes full use of the 'here and now' relationship which can allow troubled attitudes and feelings a new chance to be expressed and thought about.

Nevertheless, there are instances when she has in some way to relate actively to the possible external situation. If the worker had reason to believe in the session that the child may have been physically abused by the parents, the issue of boundaries needs especially careful thought. Has a teacher or health visitor seen the same evidence? There will probably be a social worker or some other professional colleague working with the parents, with whom the worker will need to consult. Perhaps it is possible for the child's worker to continue seeing the child while a colleague carries responsibility for the parents, for any other additional monitoring of the child's situation, as well as deciding whether the child should be removed from the family setting on a short-term basis. Dilemmas facing the worker in cases of child abuse are discussed further in Chapter 4.

Sometimes we have to recognize that the child's environment at home, though not involving physical abuse, gives rise to continuing anxiety, and is not likely to improve, perhaps through the personality disturbance of one of the parents. Colleagues may raise doubts whether there is any point in continuing to see the child for individual therapy, if the home 'setting' is 'undoing all the good'. Sometimes it may be possible to bring about change within the child even though the home situation is not likely to alter. Whether individual therapy is helpful or appropriate needs to be thought about in the light of all the factors involved in any one case. The possibility of inner change and the nature of the therapeutic process are discussed in Part 5, where we examine in some detail what help the worker actually offers the client.

THE IMPORTANCE OF TIME

An agreed time for meetings between worker and client, and a carefully chosen place, are important in order to convey continuity of thought and the availability of space in the worker's mind. Thus the setting up of any relationship with an implied therapeutic content needs to make reference to a time framework, which is part of the containing process. In Chapter 4 under 'Working in a hospital team', we see the potential disaster for Bob were he to be discharged. It is clear that breaks and endings have to be anticipated and feelings about unforeseen interruptions such as illness also need considering. From a practical point of view we see how some workers give their clients, particularly small children, warning of the coming end of the session, enabling feelings about this to come into the room and become more accessible for understanding. Individual calendars can be made for young children to help them comprehend the length of a break and may help to bring their reactions to this into the open; sometimes the calendars may have to be replaced more than once!

If it is known that the contact is going to be a brief one, maybe lasting only a few weeks for the purpose perhaps of some form of investigation or exploration, this needs to be clarified from the outset. This serves to avoid any confusion about what is offered and makes it possible to relate to any feelings about the length of the contact and the ending. In brief work the worker would probably consider it inappropriate to try and make a very temporary relationship with herself a central part of her work with the child. While the worker remains sensitive to what is felt to be happening between them, she may comment on the relationship largely as an illustration of what is happening elsewhere, for example in the family or in the child's internal world. Ahmed (Chapter 2) asked the worker if she was going to leave as the other worker had done. If it had been a known fact that this for some reason was only to have been an investigatory contact (for instance some form of assessment for suitability for placement) it would have been important to have clarified this at the beginning. Within such a context some work might be possible without the worker being experienced as an example of yet another person who goes away, but it would not be appropriate to focus on details of their relationship as one might do in a planned longer-term contact. Problems of interrupted therapy and a premature ending are discussed in Chapter 4 (under 'Working in a hospital team') and in Chapter 9 ('Problems of a premature ending').

The question of frequency is a difficult one to discuss without accompanying evidence. Many workers may not be able to offer more than a weekly contact, or may simply see this as the norm. Sometimes it may be the policy or practice of the sponsoring institution to timetable say twice a week contact as part of an in-patient programme, and more work may thus be possible over a shorter period. This makes it even more important to pay attention to the 'time boundary' of the planned ending, since the relationship will be more intensive with twice weekly sessions, and the duration will be shorter.

A client tends to experience the regularity of his contact with the worker as an expression of her ability to give him reliable concern, without being overwhelmed by his problems. He begins to trust the worker to give him a dependable 'thinking space' within her mind. Sudden increases, as well as reductions, in the amount of time the worker spends with the client are likely to be experienced as disruptive. If a worker continues a session over the allotted time it may be taken as implying that she is in some way succumbing to the anxiety or to other feelings aroused in her by the client during the session. If a client arrives early it may seem natural to start the session early, if the worker is free. But then the client can no longer feel that he has a specific, recognized time reserved for him, nor that the worker carries responsibility for ensuring the regularity of their time together. He then loses the opportunity of feeling 'held' in the worker's mind and the security of feeling that she has a dependable space within it which is for him. If a worker increases (or decreases) the time she spends with a child, anxiety or hostility may be aroused in the family. If the setting is in a group situation such as a school, probation hostel or children's home, other children or residents are likely to have feelings about an increased contact with just one of their number. They may feel rivalry or jealousy at the beginning, and experience triumph (or possibly depression) when it ends. There will also be repercussions in the feelings of the child who is singled out. The possibility of such reactions to change are obviously not a reason for failing to make a change if it does seem necessary. But equally such change will need to be made with thought, and where possible be prepared for; and the consequences will need attentive 'working through' with the client.

THE PHYSICAL SETTING

The worker will, we hope, be able to have not only a clear mental space for her client, but also a regular, physical space with defined geographical and time boundaries, known to both parties and offering a safe framework for work.

A client needs a place where he can feel attended to without distraction. This is also a physical representation of a space in the worker's mind. The setting needs to be stable in order to provide a firm and regular foundation for the expression and exploration of feelings. When such a setting is provided, the worker has to be sensitive to the implications of any disruptions in it. In everyday life, in a school for example, young children might see rebuilding work in progress and in some instances be distressed by the derelict appearance of something previously intact, and may be helped by a brief discussion with the teacher. In a therapeutic contact, where the worker uses the relationship with herself as an aspect of the work, the impact and meaning of damage to a place that is intimately linked with her mental space can be very strong; it may imply to the client that there is something wrong with her ability to provide therapy.

We heard how Ahmed (Chapter 2) had been upset when he saw his usual playroom in a broken-down state during building work; it was for him seemingly not just evocative of distressed feelings about things in general being demolished, but an actual representation of the worker's currently broken-down world; and therefore it influenced his feelings about the worker. We shall see in Chapter 8 ('A controlling child') how Annabel was also disturbed by the breaking-up of the usual playroom into two, and preferred not to accept a discrete area for work; she also gave herself the choice as to the person with whom she was to be involved, preferring the secretary to Dr C. Despite difficulties in the environment, which there clearly were in this instance, it is important for the worker to hold on to a clearly bounded space for the therapy as an indication of space in her mind for the child, and of a willingness to hold on to and struggle with thinking. In Chapter 7 (under 'Finding space for envious feelings') we shall discuss a session with Betty who wished to leave early after messing the room. What had happened in the room was an aspect of what Betty had felt had happened with the worker. By holding the boundaries of the setting, involving both time and space, that is, by helping Betty to stay in the room until the end of the session, the worker was able to provide an opportunity for Betty to be aware that someone was willing to grapple with her difficulties, which included in this instance bearing the feelings about the mess.

Where work takes place in the context of a playroom, a child being offered more than just exploratory contact should have some form of physical receptacle for his toys and drawings which can be locked away. Having something set aside for his personal use serves as a reminder of his activities, thoughts and feelings in previous sessions and allows continuity of play. A selection of small toys, colouring material and Plasticine may be appropriate for a young child and perhaps drawing material for an older one. If these are kept together in a box or drawer which is kept exclusively for the child, it can become a concrete representation for the child of a private area in the worker's mind where she thinks about him and remembers him.

The more simply a playroom is furnished, with strong, plain, furniture the better. Flimsy structures and those requiring excessive care in their use will be liable to convey fragility in the worker's ability to stand up to what is brought to her. Water, preferably running, can be useful in helping a child to express his feelings. Whether or not there is other communal equipment in the room, such as a doll's house or sand tray, may depend on extraneous factors, such as whether much assessment work is carried out. Whatever the decision, it seems important that there should be consistency about this. We saw how Ahmed (Chapter 2) was upset by the unexpected presence of a toy for a younger child: an indication perhaps of feelings that the worker did not have individual space for him, kept separate from her other patients. If there is communal equipment it should if possible be limited in amount, so as not to be too intrusive or to provide encouragement for a child to be 'all over the place'. It also does not seem appropriate that the room should be furnished with pictures or posters that could be felt to convey some kind of message. Valuable equipment, perhaps for medical or office use, is particularly intrusive. It may evoke fear or active curiosity and the worker has to use some of her concentration to see that the child does not tamper with the equipment; it therefore intrudes into her mental space for the child. It also makes the child feel that the room is really not available for him even for the brief span of time for his session.

Some workers give initial sanction to a room and equipment being used as the patient wishes, perhaps with some provisions about hurt to the child or worker not being allowed to occur or that windows must not be broken. There may however be areas of potential danger (climbing on top of unstable surfaces, playing with electric sockets, for example), or a child may make use of the material in the room in a way which is harmful to others, for instance if water floods and seeps beyond the confines of the room: these hazards cannot always be foreseen. It therefore may be wiser not to imply a blanket acceptance of all potential uses of the room and its contents. Equally, however, it is wiser not to begin straightaway by talking about possible damage a child may do, without waiting for any evidence that it is likely to arise. It may be felt like a criticism ('I know you always wreck things'); it may convey an invitation to some form of excitement; or it may leave a child feeling unheld. If the worker bears in mind that the equipment and the room are intended to represent her space for the child, she may be able to convey something appropriate about their use.

We have talked about equipment in the context of a clinic or other institutional setting. Workers who see children in varied circumstances, for example in children's homes or hospitals, may also keep portable cases of children's drawings and other equipment. Whatever the sphere of work, if it is designed as a regular contact it normally needs to be carried out in a regular, stable setting.

When a child or client is seen individually in a hospital or clinic setting, his therapeutic sessions are usually his only contact with the worker. It is usually possible to establish regular sessions in the same room, and to have fairly clearly defined boundaries for the relationship; the worker's role is limited to the one established in the therapy room. All this can be very different for someone attempting similar work outside a hospital or clinic setting, as we shall see later in this chapter.

Sometimes a worker may need to see her client in the client's own home. This was the case for Mrs Adams's health visitor (Chapter 4) and Graham's social worker (Chapter 9). Some clients may never manage to keep regular appointments outside their own home, perhaps because they have so little expectation inside themselves of a helpful relationship, or perhaps because their own inner world is too fragmented and chaotic; but they may nevertheless accept a relationship that is brought to them. The worker will need to think about issues like intrusion into her client's privacy, the degree of the client's commitment to the work, and the possibility of maintaining her therapeutic role.

BOUNDARIES AND CONFIDENTIALITY

A social worker, new to this approach, had started to work with Anthony, aged eight. Anthony kept trying to examine the locked boxes belonging to other clients of the centre which were stored in the room. In the session she brought for discussion he had drawn a picture which he said was specially for her, and which he wanted her to take home and put in her bedroom.

The social worker asked for help in thinking about whether the presence of the boxes was an intrusion into the space she could offer Anthony, or whether his activities in relation to these boxes was an intrusion into her confidential relationships with the other children. Also, should she thank him for the drawing and take it home? One could see that Anthony appeared to be preoccupied with the other people that he felt were in the worker's life, both in the centre and at home; he also wanted (through his picture) to occupy a privileged position in her bedroom.

The worker needs to have psychic and physical space where there is room for feelings of rivalry and jealousy towards other patients to be expressed. Anthony was examining the locked boxes and it was not clear if he wanted to break into them. Any receptacles, such as locked boxes or chests of locked drawers, of course need to be really secure for the protection of their confidential contents and the space of those to whom they have been allocated. However, their very presence in the room, particularly if it is very obtrusive, may be felt to be provocative and inviting attack, with consequent time and attention in the session being taken up on this issue. Hence some workers may prefer to provide safe storage outside the room and bring the equipment to it.

Clearly care has to be taken about other children's materials, whether in the room or not. It may be difficult to decide about using walls in the room for the display of different patients's pictures, although this did seem to be managed in Rupert's therapy (Chapter 7). Attention spent on actually protecting such pictures, however, can be felt to take away from that available for the child who is there. The child may also feel the worker is colluding in allowing other children's possessions to intrude into his space and time. A picture kept in a child's receptacle may also be regarded as confidential to the child and worker, and thus more available for thought than one 'on display' on the wall. A child may wish to take his own picture home, and it may be possible to think with him about his feelings about this. Again, a drawing kept with his other things within the setting enables further use to be made of it there even if it should be subsequently destroyed by the child. Similarly, to return to the example of Anthony who wanted the worker to put his picture in her bedroom, it might be helpful if she talked over with him what this meant in terms of his feelings, rather than simply agreeing to take his picture home.

A worker needs to be able to recognize with a child that he has feelings about others in her life, whether clients at the centre or those at home. This does not mean that any actual discussion of other clients or her external life takes place. Working in this way, she may be offering an experience that she has bounded space for more than one relationship. A clearly defined setting helps the worker to explore the psychic reality of a client's feelings that extend beyond it, without physical intrusion into the space of others.

Returning to our earlier discussion on contact with parents, we can see how it is important that the details of a child's session remain confidential between the worker and the client. This does not, however, mean that one cannot be open to talking with parents about a child's progress, which is after all a matter of parental concern. It may he helpful for team members to think together about what it would be useful for them to share with each other about their individual work with members of the family and what it might be unhelpful to share. Discussions with other colleagues who have a professional involvement in the work may also best be restricted to factors relevant to their involvement, rather than extended to include what took place in a session. It seems important to think about both aspects; the professional and adult needs in respect to the child, and also the confidentiality of the relationship within the session.

SANCTION AND SUPPORT OF COLLEAGUES AND PARENTS (A SOCIAL WORKER AND IVAN)

A social worker was responsible for three siblings who were being looked after by the local authority and placed with a foster-family. Two, the eldest and youngest, had settled well, but the middle child, a ten-year-old boy, continued to cause concern. The foster-mother felt she could not get through to him; he had a continuous meaningless smile, and very little reaction when spoken to; he seemed unable to relate to people.

After careful discussion with the foster-parents and the school, the social worker decided to offer Ivan weekly sessions, and a room was found in a local health clinic. The clinic staff welcomed the plan but a lot of different professionals used the building, and in spite of notices on the door, sessions were frequently interrupted. If the social worker were based in that building all the time, this way of working and its need for privacy would have become recognized and accepted, and she would have been likely to get to know other staff there; with her brief once weekly appearance there, this was obviously much more difficult.

Again, although the foster-parents had asked for and wanted special help with Ivan, they usually brought him very late, or needed to take him away early. The social worker was very aware that the foster-parents might have mixed feelings about this new type of help, especially coming from her, since she had previously devoted her time to working with the foster-mother; and it had consisted of informal, unscheduled contacts in the home. She needed to continue her visits to the home as well as her sessions with Ivan. There was also the problem of Ivan's contact with his own father; the social worker was normally the go-between here, making arrangements and taking Ivan. Sometimes the foster-father telephoned to say the arrangements for taking Ivan to his session had broken down, and the social worker then agreed to fetch Ivan from school herself. At school the head teacher or a class teacher would expect to discuss Ivan's behaviour with her while Ivan was being sent for. In the room itself, equipment would be rearranged or missing; even Ivan's own box had been used by someone else, though it was labelled and kept in a locked cupboard.

In the first few sessions Ivan was eager to use his time and began to tell the worker about himself. However, both of the first sessions were interrupted by someone coming to fetch something out of a cupboard. Ivan said she had come in to see what he was doing because she was nosey. Each time he gave up what he was doing and did not return to it. After he was brought late he played with a puzzle but complained there were pieces missing; another time when the agreed arrangement to bring him broke down and he was brought late he said there was a hole in his coat. After further problems over who should bring him and after some changes of time, he complained that his pencil had been used. He began to spend most of the sessions kicking a ball across the room or asking to go out and kick it in the hall. He seemed to ignore whatever the worker said.

In the discussion of his sessions, course members said they were not clear whether the missing puzzle pieces and the hole in his coat referred to his feelings about himself, or whether they referred to the missed times and curtailed sessions. They were also not sure whether his accusation about his pencil referred to anything in his 'inner world' and arose from within or whether it just referred to other people's actual intrusion into his time.

This illustrates the difficulty of trying to gain any insight into a child's inner world of feelings if the therapy itself is not completely dependable and reliable. It then becomes impossible to tell how much a client's communications are about the one, or the other. Ivan could have felt that the permeable framework meant that the worker, or what she offered, was so useless as only fit to be kicked around, or that by her not holding the boundaries she was not really thinking about him. The discussions about Ivan highlighted the evidence in his play and behaviour that he found the interruptions and changes disruptive. It was clear that his worker had many problems to struggle with in trying to establish a time and setting for their sessions. She was well aware of the difficulties for Ivan and discussed with the group possible solutions to some of the practical problems.

Ivan's worker had no possibility of a colleague seeing the foster-parents while she saw Ivan; she was the worker for the whole family. If this has to be so, the problems arising when one worker fulfils both roles need to be carefully thought out and openly acknowledged with the clients.

Being able to 'listen' to a child or adolescent and being receptive to whatever he is able to convey to us, require a state of 'relaxed' attention which is impossible to achieve if the privacy and continuity of the sessions are not safeguarded, and if the therapeutic approach itself is not at least tolerated by our working colleagues.

CLARIFICATION OF BOUNDARIES (A CLINICAL MEDICAL OFFICER AND TIM)

The importance of reaching an understanding about the nature of individual therapeutic work can be illustrated by Dr E's work with Tim in a school context. The head teacher of Tim's primary school, after discussion with Tim's teacher and the educational psychologist, asked Dr E, the clinical medical officer, to see Tim, who was then six years old. Tim was causing a lot of problems at school by his behaviour – spitting, biting and punching other children, and being rebellious with adults. Social services and a child guidance clinic had been involved in trying to help Tim and his family in the past, but his mother and step-father, who had many problems of their own, had broken off the contact in each case. The head teacher suggested that Dr E see Tim individually at the school once a week for a term in the first instance; Tim's parents agreed to this.

The only room available which was not a classroom in constant use was a small room used as medical room and remedial teaching area; it also acted as a kitchen for the staff during their tea and coffee breaks. The room therefore had to contain equipment which could not be moved or locked away, and Tim, with his need to test or deny boundaries, was constantly trying to attack the contents of the room. The staff had been used to 'popping in' during remedial reading sessions to make their coffee and tended to carry on with this. When Dr E went to fetch Tim from the playground for his session, it was treated each time by staff and children alike as a 'special' event. On three days Tim did not come to school, and Dr E was never informed. Some liaison was necessary with the parents; who should carry it out? Although the staff were keen to have help for Tim, ongoing individual therapy had not been attempted in their school before. Dr E met with them frequently to try and clarify the nature of the sessions, but it did unfortunately seem that the difficulties in the way were too many in this instance.

Work as a visiting professional, as we saw with both Tim and Ivan, can be difficult. Therapy with Tim could never really get established because other people kept coming in, as their equipment was in the room but not to be touched. Ivan's sessions were also frequently interrupted, and his private box of toys was treated as available to all. On a purely practical level it is difficult to find a room that will always be available at the same time; the room may contain a lot of equipment: should the child be allowed to use any of it in the therapy session? There may be large windows giving on to other school areas so that privacy is difficult to establish. Some of these issues were relevant to Len's worker discussed in Chapter 1.

If the person working with the child is not a member of staff but a visiting professional, other staff may have to be consulted and also helped to try and understand the need for privacy, as with Ivan in the clinic. In a school the head teacher and class teacher at least need to give full sanction and support to this type of work. Questions like why this child and not others, how long should this one child be seen, and who should decide, need careful discussion. Some of these issues are apparent in Mr K's work with June, described in Chapter 4. If the child is difficult to hold within the session, or his behaviour on leaving the session is very disturbed, who should deal with this? Nicholas (Chapter 8) sometimes ran out of his sessions naked. He attended a special school, but nevertheless it was plain that his worker relied greatly on the tact and understanding of the teaching staff to help keep his sessions going. Alan (Chapter 9) obviously also subjected the teaching staff to considerable strain.

These issues are also relevant if the sessions are carried out by a member of the school staff; but in that case the worker will meet the child outside the therapy sessions unavoidably, perhaps at break or mealtimes; several children may be together all day knowing they share the same therapist and having to experience very strong feelings of jealousy, rivalry, curiosity. An example of this is given when we discuss the ending with Alan in Chapter 9. This also calls for co-operative, supportive understanding between the worker and the staff.

It becomes especially important to think about contact with the parents if a child is seen in the school setting. It needs to be decided who should discuss with them initially the possibility of individual therapeutic help for their child, and who should maintain ongoing contact with them and if necessary offer them support. Professional colleagues also influence the setting in other ways. We shall see in Chapter 4 under 'Working in a hospital team' how the question of discharge threatened the work of the occupational therapist with Bob. In such instances it is important not only that the anxieties relating to discharge are worked on within the therapy, but also that the consequences for the client are made known to those who take the decision to terminate. This means that the people concerned with the patient need to think and plan as a team in this respect. Professional conflict can arise from genuine differences of opinion, but also from ignorance of the other point of view. Colleagues with whom it may be necessary to liaise may be within the same institution or service (as with Wayne in Chapter 1) or more widely spread, as with June (Chapter 4), where different members of the social services and the school were involved.

Chapter 4

Wider Aspects of the Setting: Community, Hospital/Clinic and School

EXTENDED APPLICATIONS OF PSYCHODYNAMIC WORK AND ITS CONSTRAINTS

Child guidance clinics, originating in the UK in the 1920s, and child psychiatric departments in hospitals have been the main centres for any individual therapeutic work with disturbed children (apart from private practice); and on the whole this work has been carried out by child psychiatrists, child psychotherapists and psychologists only. Increasing recognition of the widespread prevalence of emotional disturbance in children following the work of Rutter (1970, 1975) has come alongside the knowledge that many more children need help than could be catered for in the child guidance or child psychiatric settings. The Court Report (1976) suggested that child guidance clinic staff should make their skills more widely available on a consultative basis. Many clinics now do this. Workers with varied qualifications are now seeing children individually outside the child guidance or child psychiatric setting and offering help based on a psychodynamic approach. This cannot of course be carried out to the same depth as psychoanalytic psychotherapy. In addition the help they offer is not always long term. Nevertheless a briefer contact, for example in a time of crisis, as we shall see with Robbie in Chapter 5, can be very valuable. In many instances the clients seen would be unlikely to attend a clinic and are most usefully and economically seen in a different professional context in the community. Some workers are of course able to offer long-term work, often with very worthwhile results.

Workers outside child guidance or child psychiatric clinics face a major problem, however, in that they usually have no framework or setting for this work: there may quite literally be no room available; their pattern of working may not lend itself to regular time commitments for any one child; they have not the support provided by a multi-disciplinary team where other staff members are available to work with parents; they may not have any opportunity to discuss this type of work with colleagues; and finally their ascribed role with the child or family may include statutory duties of supervision, placement and decision-making which may appear to conflict with the traditional uninvolved role of the therapist. Many of these problems were illustrated in the examples of Ivan and Tim in Chapter 3.

In this chapter we look at work carried out within these constraints. We have chosen examples that highlight the problems and we discuss some of the issues that need to be thought about. We hope to show that the view of relationships and of a child's mental life that we describe in this book is valuable also to professionals who are involved in a managerial or supervisory role with children and families.

A HEALTH VISITOR'S WORK WITH A YOUNG MOTHER (MRS ADAMS)

We have seen examples in this book of children still quite young but already disturbed and needing skilled help, so the question arises whether more preventive work could be carried out. It is always difficult to find professional time for this. Screening babies and young children for physical abnormalities and mental handicap is recognized as essential but may crowd out the equally important area of a child's emotional development and his capacity to make relationships. When there are seen to be problems it is often felt that the family must be referred on to a specialist agency. Some families are in fact unwilling to take up such a referral, in some instances for the reasons we have outlined in Chapter 1 ('The client's initial perceptions of the worker and the setting'). Sometimes, however, a worker in the community who may already have an ongoing contact with the family, or whose agency at least is familiar to them, can provide the right help.

A health visitor told a discussion group (on two separate occasions) about a young family she was involved with, who had recently moved to the district. The nursery teacher in a class which she visited had had to exclude Vincent (aged three) after just a few weeks, because he was so severely disruptive. Although the smallest there, he was constantly attacking other children, pushing them off their trikes, tying string round their necks, biting and kicking them and the staff.

When the health visitor called at the house, following a letter to the mother, the door was opened by Mrs Adams, who it turned out was herself only twenty, rather heavy-faced and sullen. Vincent, an alert, mischievous-looking little boy, small for his age, was peeping round his mother's leg, grinning.

Mother reluctantly let the health visitor in, and seemed very defensive. She said angrily that the nursery staff had maltreated Vincent and pushed toilet paper in his mouth when he used bad language, which he had certainly not learnt from home. No one understood him except her. Vincent meanwhile was leaning against her. The health visitor invited Mrs Adams to tell her a little about Vincent. Mother said he had never been out of her sight until he went to the nursery. He had cried a lot as a baby and she had always picked him up, because she had a 'rotten' childhood herself, mostly in and out of care and in a children's home. Now, she never went out of the house. Her husband did the shopping. Vincent never went out, because nobody could handle him. She and her husband had never been out on their own together since Vincent's birth, as she was not going to entrust him to anyone else.

Vincent by now had gone to a box of toys in the corner and was throwing them away from him without looking where they were going; a number went on or near the health visitor. Throughout the interview he interrupted the conversation with shouts; his language seemed very retarded for a three year old. Finally he rubbed the remains of a sandwich on the sofa arm. Mrs Adams, who had not spoken to Vincent before, now said sharply 'Stop that! You're not ruining this one for me!' She said she had had to throw the last one away because he had ripped it.

The health visitor felt she was getting very conflicting messages from Mrs Adams about wanting help/resenting interference. She suggested coming again. Mrs Adams said sullenly she could please herself; she (Mrs Adams) never went out anyway; she could not call her soul her own because of Vincent. The health visitor felt she should not come without an appointment as this would be an added intrusion into Mrs Adams's privacy, and they arranged a time for the following week.

After discussion with the group and with her colleagues at work, the health visitor decided to offer regular visits once a week for a trial period. This was a departure from her usual practice, and at first seemed impossibly difficult to arrange, because of her large case load of families and her commitment to clinics. Her seniors agreed to a slight modification of her schedule. It was felt that this could also be very helpful preventive work, since Mrs Adams was certainly likely to have more children.

The door was always opened by Mrs Adams with a unwelcoming 'Oh, it's you again', or 'I was just going to start my washing', or 'You can't stay long'. But the health visitor found that in spite of that Mrs Adams did manage to let her in, and there were never silences. Mrs Adams would sometimes give her an alarming piece of news – that she had threatened to hold a cushion over Vincent's head to stop him screaming; that she had made Vincent sleep locked in the dark, empty attic because he was so naughty – always told in a flat, expressionless way. A few minutes later, Mrs Adams would then tell her, and it seemed as if she was secretly pleased, that Vincent would not even let her go to the toilet on her own, he insisted on going with her; and he slept in his parents' bed every night (except when he was sent to the attic).

The health visitor felt an urgent need to take action on several occasions: surely Vincent could not be left with mother, he might be at physical risk from her; should the health visitor not arrange a place for him in a nursery group for disturbed children? Should she arrange for him to see a speech therapist? Should she involve social services? She put some of her anxieties into words with Mrs Adams. Mrs Adams seemed to live at two extremes: either Vincent was so bad he deserved the severest punishment, or she was everything to Vincent and they must never be separated. When Mrs Adams found the health visitor did not respond with actions designed to take Vincent precipitately out of her care, and was not herself acting the role of a punitive mother, she began to share some of her difficulties with her – her current relationship with her stepmother, and problems with her neighbours. The health visitor also discussed the situation with the appropriate officer in social services. After consultation it was decided that she should maintain contact with social services but that they should not become directly involved at that point.

After a month, Mrs Adams asked the health visitor what was the point of these visits, they weren't altering anything. She added rather defiantly that she had put Vincent in a playgroup. She made it all sound very negative, like her manner on opening the door. But the health visitor felt this might be her way of defending herself against a rebuff, or against anticipated criticism. Mrs Adams said she was pregnant again; she was very anxious how Vincent would treat the new baby when it came; she was sure he would attack it, as he had the children in the first nursery.

Apparently the new playgroup managed to handle Vincent, and his speech had improved. When the baby was born (a little girl) Vincent surprised everyone by being really tender with her. The baby herself proved to be a good sleeper and good feeder and Mrs Adams visibly enjoyed looking after her. The health visitor began to think of visiting less regularly and tentatively raised this with Mrs Adams.

But on her next call, Mrs Adams opened the door with a face of thunder and did not at first ask the health visitor in. She said she was having Vincent put away. The health visitor felt all the months of work were useless. She asked to hear what had happened. It emerged that when Mrs Adams went to fetch Vincent from his playgroup the leader had come over and told her that Vincent had taken the lamp off a helper's bike and smashed it. Mrs Adams said he was not going back to the playgroup and she was keeping him at home today, and going to social services to have him put away. At the moment he was with father in the kitchen. It was apparent that mother felt very attacked by the playgroup leader and shown up as being no good at bringing up children. She also said that now she had the new baby she could no longer cope with Vincent. Once again the health visitor felt confronted with a sudden action as the only way out of a fraught situation. It was plain that, for Mrs Adams, Vincent had suddenly become a totally bad child who must be got rid of. The health visitor remembered that Mrs Adams had said she had first been put into care when her younger brother was born. At least Mrs Adams was agreeing to sit down with her and talk about it. The health visitor said Mrs Adams may have felt her own plan to visit less frequently was also a rejection.

Mr Adams came in at the end of the interview and listened to some of the discussion. The heat had gone out of Mrs Adams's remarks, and now she said to her husband couldn't he go to the playgroup and offer to pay for the broken lamp? (She had told the health visitor that he had been in the slow learner unit at school, and she had always seemed to discount him as a force at home.) Mrs Adams and her husband were moving towards finding a way of dealing with this crisis and it seemed that the plan of having Vincent put away was forgotten.

In the group discussion it was suggested that the health visitor was offering Mrs Adams a different experience of mothering; that the health visitor was resisting her own impulse to action as a way out of a worrying situation, but instead was offering time to think it over.

Also, Mrs Adams seemed stuck with a view that Vincent was either all black or all white. At times he was so wicked he must be locked away, got rid of, and at these times she felt no affection or commitment to him at all. At other times he was to share in every moment of her life (bed, bath, toilet) in an idealized fusion. Mrs Adams also felt very persecuted by any suggestion of criticism coming at her from others, and dealt with it in turn by breaking off relations with the critical person. She seemed to be keeping her feelings about ideal, lovely relationships very far apart from those involving hatred and feeling attacked. This is an example of 'splitting' within the paranoid-schizoid position which we discuss further in Chapter 14.

The health visitor had managed to hold on to her relationship with Mrs Adams in spite of the latter's anger and rejection of her at times. Perhaps this was gradually enabling Mrs Adams to find a middle course with Vincent, and accept some responsibility as a parent for his occasional destructiveness.

The health visitor herself felt that her work with Mrs Adams had enabled her to be more ready to listen, and to feel less urgent need of coming up with a solution herself. She had found several times that if she held on to her anxiety and resisted the urge to step in and take over, Mrs Adams herself found a way through her problem (she found a suitable playgroup; she suggested they pay for the lamp). Mrs Adams was managing to find some resources inside herself and was beginning to cope with the mothering in its widest sense. The health visitor felt this was a justified use of her time.

Workers in the position of the health visitor here carry heavy burdens on behalf of the community in deciding how to intervene in cases where children may be at risk. In this instance the health visitor's careful monitoring of the situation and her work with Mrs Adams together enabled Vincent to be left at home in a developing environment.

She regularly discussed events with colleagues in social services, and they took responsibility for the decision not to place Vincent on the child protection register.

RELATING TO THE CHILD IN CASES OF CHILD ABUSE (PAUL, FRANKLIN, JEANNIE AND HARI)

The health visitor working with the Adams family shared her anxieties about the possibility of child abuse with colleagues in social services. Social workers are commonly required to carry responsibility for these children; their burden may be greater than is usually recognized. Legal requirements may not always be easy to reconcile with the emotional needs of the child. Public feelings of anger may be very strong and may carry with them the wish to blame someone for not foreseeing, preventing or stopping the abuse. The horror of what happened to the child may be experienced at an unconscious level by the professionals involved, in a way that perpetuates the trauma for the child. Concern to protect the child from physical injury may be so urgent that the feelings of the child may be ignored.

In the midst of the crisis, once child abuse is suspected, is it possible to think of offering a therapeutic relationship for the child? Many social work agencies increasingly refer these children for intensive psychotherapy. Inevitably, this is some while after the trauma; it may be as important to think about the child's relationship with the social worker, NSPCC officer, or other professional who is the first one to become involved.

A social worker told the group that she was to interview two children who had possibly been victims of sexual abuse. The older child was a mentally handicapped girl with severe speech problems, so it was necessary also to see her younger brother as well, who had in any case first raised the alarm. This younger half-brother Paul, aged three, had told his nursery nurse about sexual games which Uncle Jack played with Paul and his sister, and added that 'We musn't tell Mummy'. The social worker was to see Paul, possibly together with the nursery nurse, in the presence of a policewoman, and encourage him to talk or play. Some members of the group discussed what sort of things the three-year-old was likely to say or do, and would it be accepted as evidence coming from such a young child? Were dolls with sexual organs the best way to find out what happened? Another member of the group said that he felt there was a risk of doing more damage by persisting with questions about sexual events, especially if Paul proved silent or reluctant to talk. Was there a parallel here with investigations of rape, which many women found nearly as disastrous as the original event? It seemed as if the legal requirements for evidence could themselves be repeating any initial trauma. On the other hand it was clearly important to find out if the children had been sexually abused; to gloss over it would mean exposing them to further risk, but to act on it would quite probably mean breaking up a family (Uncle Jack was now living with mother), and obviously this should not be undertaken without convincing evidence.

The social worker voiced her anxiety about the court appearance, and especially about her evidence being torn to shreds when she was cross-examined. Someone commented that it sounded as if she were going to undergo an ordeal herself rather like a child being abused.

Another member asked if it was relevant that Paul had said 'We musn't tell Mummy' – not only his mother, but also social services and the police had by now been told. It sounded as if Paul needed help with his feelings about loyalty to Uncle Jack, conflicting with his guilt about secrets kept from his mother. The group wondered if space could be made for Paul's feelings, even in one or two interviews; this raises the possibility of brief work or assessment being combined with a therapeutic approach, which we discuss in Chapter 5. The social worker therefore needed to relate to Paul's conflicting feelings in the interviews. She also carried her own anxieties about being intrusive with her questions, of being attacked in court, and feeling responsible (and perhaps guilty) about the outcome.

The social worker could not know at that stage what the outcome of her involvement would be, whether Uncle Jack would be forced to leave the family for example; Paul might show some anxiety about the future, directly or indirectly, which she would need to acknowledge with him. Paul had been able to talk to his nursery nurse about what had happened, probably because he knew and trusted her. The social worker might well not know in advance what her own continued contact with Paul would be, and she would probably need to put this uncertainty into words with him. Even if her contact was limited to a few meetings, it might still be possible for Paul to experience her as someone concerned to listen and try to understand his feelings, rather than as someone preoccupied only with physical events.

If the social worker in a case of actual or suspected child abuse can be involved over a longer time, it is often thought best for the professional relationship to consist mainly in working with the mother, as in the case of Mrs Adams, or with both parents, to enable them to form a better relationship with their child. It can be difficult for the same worker to see both mother and child regularly on an individual basis. Conflicts over loyalty and confidentiality are always likely to be present (see Ivan in Chapter 3); but if a parent is actually maltreating a child this issue becomes central.

Another child, Franklin, was eight years old when the school reported that he had bruises; neighbours also reported hearing his screaming. Franklin's mother seemed co-operative and friendly when Miss W, the social worker, met her, but there were many discrepancies between what she told Miss W and what turned out to be true. Franklin's behaviour with Miss W was very controlled and apparently unrelated to events at home, until he said out of the blue 'Mum said, "Don't tell Miss W about belting you or she'll have you put away".' Franklin was conveying to Miss W the trap he was in; he saw himself as having only the two alternatives: putting up with ongoing cruelty or being 'put away'.

Miss W was thus made to experience the impossible emotional conflict Franklin suffered, which was perhaps even more destructive than the physical pain. Franklin had been able to communicate this conflict as well as to let Miss W know about the belting; Miss W's task was a double one, to relate to Franklin's tangled feelings as well as to think what needed to be done about the physical abuse.

Many children cannot express the facts of their maltreatment in words. The feelings it arouses are perhaps too chaotic and too extreme for the child to encompass. Physical details of abuse may only emerge after a long time, and after a great deal has been worked through in the relationship with the worker.

Jeannie's social worker, Mr S, was concerned about the quality of parental care Jeannie (aged three) was receiving. The social worker was aware that Jeannie had suffered physical punishment bordering on abuse and decided to see her in the nursery school setting. For several sessions Jeannie tumbled about the room, tripping over chairs, throwing all the toys out of her box, and making loud shouting noises. Mr S, the worker, felt his mind invaded by chaos and confusion. Gradually Jeannie began concentrating her activity on a little girl doll, who was thrown up at the ceiling, and when having her hair washed had her head pushed under the water, forced up into the tap or pushed down the plughole. Jeannie showed unremitting hatred and cruelty to the tiny girl doll, once running a toy car over her legs. She refused to acknowledge any link between it and herself, or indeed to allow Mr S to voice any concern at all, either about the doll or about herself as she balanced precariously on the edges of tables, windowsills, and chair arms. It was only after months of work in which the relationship with Mr S had been strengthened and tested that Jeannie showed him a sore place on her palm and told him father had held her hand over a candle to teach her not to play with fire.

If there is any suspicion of child abuse, whether sexual or not, it seems important to offer the child a relationship as well as to explore physical trauma. The effects on the child's mental and emotional life need to be thought about with as much urgency as the child's need for physical safety. Indeed, as in Jeannie's case, it is not always possible to learn about the physical events until attention has been paid to the child's emotional state. The attacks on the girl doll were not exact physical representations of actual attacks on Jeannie. They were her way of conveying her experience on life, of the disturbed adults around her. Until the worker had himself experienced that state of mind and managed to contain it for Jeannie, it was not possible for Jeannie to communicate the actual events, or even perhaps to remember and think about them. (We discuss in Chapter 13 how a mother and a worker can help in bringing meaning and thought to chaotic sense impressions and experiences.)

Professional workers are naturally concerned to act swiftly if a child is suffering, and to remove him to a place of safety. This does not in itself take account of the child's emotional state, not does it take away the emotional pain the child has been and still is suffering. It may in fact add to this; a sudden removal from home, however necessary, is likely to be experienced by the child as a trauma in itself.

There may indeed be an urgent need to act quickly to rescue a child. But this can concurrently be a way of avoiding the need to relate to the child's mental pain. We remember the first social worker's anxiety about gruelling court appearances. The whole paraphernalia of a court case may be necessary in the interests of justice, but it is not really related to the emotional needs of any of the participants. The trauma the child has suffered can sometimes invade the institutions set up to deal with it so that the professionals are re-enacting the trauma on the child and on each other.

A community psychiatric nurse described her involvement with Hari. A social worker had close contact with Hari's parents, and had asked the child guidance team of which Miss H, the community psychiatric nurse, was a member, if Hari could be seen individually. Hari was six years old and had been in care twice, subjected to non-accidental injury, and was now at home under a new care order. When in care previously he had had a foster placement which was, with hindsight, seen to have been disastrous; in particular there were many conflicts with both foster-parents over Hari's toilet training.

Miss H had been asked to tell a review case conference of her ongoing work with Hari. The social worker and Hari's teacher were clear that Hari was already showing benefits from this work. The sessions had been very difficult: Hari demanded to go to the toilet four or five times each session but never actually used the toilet; instead he hid, or dashed into other workers' rooms; when in the toilet he rammed new toilet rolls down the lavatory pan. After some weeks, Miss H noticed that he sometimes passed a motion while in the playroom with her, though he always strongly denied this; at times the smell of the faeces became quite invasive; once some lumps fell out of his shorts on to her carpet.

Miss H's response to all this behaviour and her willingness to think about and try to understand what Hari was communicating were beginning to have an effect; Hari was settling down at school and much of his problem behaviour at home had gone. He had recently shown Miss H a round sore on his leg and told her it was a cigarette burn, although he at once contradicted himself and said that was 'only pretend'.

However, Miss H got in touch with Hari's social worker after the session and learned that the school had also reported it. She met with Hari's social worker and the team leader, and the implications for Hari's continued stay in his own home were carefully discussed. The decision not to remove Hari from home again on this occasion was taken by the social worker and her senior. But in the conference this was the one aspect of the community psychiatric nurse's work which was picked up. To her distress, Miss H heard senior workers at the conference, who had administrative roles in social work and education, dismiss her therapeutic relationship with Hari. They felt it was pointless for her to carry on her work if Hari was still being physically injured. Indeed, by carrying on her work she was, they felt, ignoring, denying or condoning the injuries and colluding with parents in implying that it was all somehow Hari's fault. They also felt that she should have simply picked him up, cleaned him, and given him toilet training, rather than 'just talk' while he carried on dirtying. Miss H was somehow made to feel as if she had made a childish mess of the work and was being heavily censured for it. Miss H had in their eyes become invested with the offensive qualities of Hari's symptom (surely the only way he could at first convey his mental state).

The administrators focused on the physical assault (the cigarette burn), and it was difficult for them to accord any value or significance to Hari's developing relationship with Miss H and the insight this gave into his feelings. It seemed as if Hari's feelings, his mental pain and chaos, were unbearable to the other professionals who focused therefore on the need to take action; the primitive nature of the conflicts and anxieties in a case like this can only too easily affect the professional workers themselves at an unconscious level. We refer again later in this chapter (under 'Relating to colleagues in the school setting – a specialist teacher and Clare') to how workers can feel 'split' and divided, and return to this subject as a group phenomenon in Chapter 6.

CONFLICTING EXPECTATIONS OF COLLEAGUES AND PARENTS (A SOCIAL WORKER AND JUNE)

Social workers are often required to carry the expectations of other professionals as well as of the family. Mr K, a social worker in a child guidance clinic, was asked to see June, a fifteen-year-old, at a professionals' liaison meeting at the school. The head teacher said June's mother was also anxious that June should have this help. June was said to have no friends at school and to be sullen and unresponsive; she complained that other pupils talked about her, and had run out of school because of this. Mr K met mother and June together at the school by arrangement the first time. Mother said June might be better off in care; she was at loggerheads with everyone at home, bullying her younger siblings, stealing, refusing to do chores, and also threatening to take an overdose. ('In care' is used here to refer to what is described in the Children Act 1989, as 'accommodated and looked after by the social services', that is on a completely voluntary basis.) An older sister had recently been taken into care. Mr K then saw June on her own. He saw her again the following week; she was very upset by some trouble with her home economics teacher which she had not been able to sort out; she was also dreading the start of the summer holidays in a few days' time as she had no friends, and said she had nothing to do but stay at home and row with her mother. She asked if Mr K could not get her away for two weeks; last summer she had been in care for a short period and she wanted this to happen again.

The following week a case conference was called to discuss whether June should be taken into care. June and her mother were asked to join the conference. A decision was reached to offer June two weeks' involvement in a youth camp, another worker would be allocated to the family as a whole, and Mr K should offer further interviews with June. After the conference finished, mother wanted to see Mr K on her own to talk about trouble with her husband (Mr K dealt with this by introducing her to the new worker, giving reasons); and June then asked to see Mr K on his own. Mr K had tried to clarify the issue with the home economics teacher at school, and although June said it had been very helpful, she had also resented Mr K repeating what she had said to him outside the sessions; she had found the conference very upsetting for the same sort of reasons (though Mr K had not discussed in detail anything she had said).

The next week Mr K called to see June and take her to the camp. June refused to see him as she did not wish to go to the camp, but she agreed to see him the following week. In the school holidays the problem existed of where to see June; at her home, her younger siblings frequently interrupted.

When the school term started, Mr K saw June at the school. This had its problems, as June had to be fetched from her lesson, and (as with Ivan) the headteacher wanted to use the time to let Mr K know about June's continuing problems in the school. A review conference was called to consider taking June into care (as she herself seemed to wish); again, June found this very difficult and felt Mr K must have betrayed her confidence. He continued seeing her at school. Once the school was closed and Mr K had not been notified. He went to June's house, saw both parents, and then June.

In the seminar, members discussed in turn the many expectations Mr K was trying to meet; June's mother seemed to have given up trying to cope, and was passing the problem on to him. The headteacher wanted him to know about things that went wrong at school, as if he might somehow have a solution, and yet the headteacher did not help

Mr K set up reasonable working conditions. (He did not tell him in advance about the school's closure; he did not take responsibility for having June ready at the start of her agreed time.) June wanted him to help her get away from home, and the two case conferences seemed to support her view that this was his role, or at any rate could be. There was also the anxiety about June's suicide threats. Mr K was being saddled with a lot of disparate demands. He was also being expected to solve a long-standing and very unhappy family situation for June by some form of action.

One member said it seemed impossible to set any boundaries – was Mr K to be available only for June, or also for her mother, and occasionally her father? Could he combine a managerial role of taking into care, arranging holiday activities, with a role of offering to help June explore her feelings? Should he limit their meetings to one place and one time, even if that meant not seeing her just when a vital case conference was due?

It was clear from the discussion that Mr K's role needed to be clarified. In his description of individual sessions with June, June herself had made it apparent that she found his multiple role hard to accept: she resented his contact with the home economics teacher, and his talking about her at the two conferences; she refused to see him when he arranged to take her to a holiday camp; she resented other members of her family intruding when Mr K visited her at home.

Another worker had already been allocated to the family as a whole, so that Mr K did not need to be involved with the parents. Mr K said he could discuss the disturbing question of June's suicide threats with the clinic's child psychiatrist, who could then be in touch with the family doctor if appropriate. A member of the group suggested Mr K could explain to the headteacher that it was difficult for June if he was seen to act as liaison with the school staff. He could offer necessary time for discussion with the head teacher at some separate occasion when June was not present. A teacher in the group said Mr K could also stress the need for regular sessions and see what arrangement the head teacher could suggest to have June ready at the right time. At the end of the discussion Mr K decided that he would offer June a number of further individual sessions and negotiate their privacy along the lines suggested in the group. It remained to be seen whether June really wanted and could use this help.

BOUNDARIES IN THE COMMUNITY

Dilemmas similar to those of Mr K face many social workers where there is a possibility of a child or adolescent needing to be accommodated and looked after by the local authority, or for some other action to be taken. Mr K was under pressure from many people to bring about some sort of change, and too much was left to him. We talked about such issues in our discussion group, where the membership is drawn from a variety of professions and services. Someone drew a parallel with the tasks of the residential schools which we discuss in Chapter 6 (under 'Headteacher and care worker in a residential school') and said that some workers or services seem to be expected to carry an extra large share of the burden in caring for the suffering of some children and adults. Another comment was made about the sometimes unrealistic expectations of apparently well-meaning colleagues about the capacity of such workers to effect change. (This seemed to be the case in regard to Mr K, the social services and June.)

Someone else suggested that at times such services seemed to be asked simply to tidy away the problem. There was general agreement that workers in these services could be lumbered with being perceived as being 'at the end of the line', in conjunction with their clients.

Workers can feel that too heavy a burden has been imposed on them by clients and by other agencies. They will need then to think about how they and their services are being perceived; it may not always be a realistic perception. This is an aspect of countertransference which is discussed in Chapter 15 (under 'Countertransference and the setting'). The worker may then be able to work out what sort of appropriate response she can make; it may not be the one for which her clients or colleagues have been pressing.

We also discussed in Chapter 3 (under 'Clarification of boundaries') the need for careful professional discussion and clarification where there was a possibility of overlap or confusion of roles or failure to act, in that instance in a school setting.

It is worth thinking about the fact that a client or family can behave in a way that provokes conflict among professionals, making it difficult to establish and maintain clear roles and boundaries. This is often outstandingly apparent in family therapy in which therapists may have very different feelings 'put into' them by members of the family. (Family therapy, mainly with adolescents and their parents, with a similar conceptual approach to that of this book is explored by Box *et al.* (1994).) There are also examples of similar projections in this book. We shall see for instance how Liz (discussed in Chapter 6 under 'The containing function of the institution') 'spun off' some of her confusion into staff members within the school, to the potential detriment of the setting, not only for herself but for the wider group. We also see later in this chapter (under 'Relating to colleagues in a school setting') how staff may have to take care that they are not turned against each other by an individual child and how they may need to ensure that the way their school is run does not itself foster this sort of divisiveness.

In the case of June, the school, the social services, including a specifically designated worker for the family as well as Mr K, the family and June herself were all involved. Some of the difficulties affecting the professionals may have arisen because aspects of June and her family's problems may have been passed on to them by projective identification. It seems that the professionals did attempt to communicate with each other; the school was apparently anxious for help and case conferences were instituted by social services. Some of the disorganization and contrariness within the family about communication may have 'got into' the school, affecting their responsiveness to making appropriate arrangements. In such an instance some appraisal and monitoring of the possibly out-of-character malfunctioning of workers and institutions could have been useful; Mr K could also have considered whether he was being used to 'mop up' at 'the end of the line'.

Such a review among professionals may be called for if the family's own difficulties are not to be in danger of re-enactment by them. This can be a latent danger when there is a marked tendency to large-scale projective identification within a family and a network of professionals involved. Britton (1994) gives a vivid account of family anxieties being passed into the varied professional network by means of projective identification. The anxieties were not recognized for what they were and it was therefore not possible for the workers to think about them; instead they re-enacted the anxieties themselves. The passing on of anxieties to others in a wide range of settings is also addressed by Obholzer and Roberts (1994).

Mr K's proposal to establish some boundaries to his work with June may have provided more chance for her anxieties and feelings to be thought about as opposed to widely projected. It needs to be recognized, however, that if such a boundary were to be instituted, the further task of struggling with the practically inevitable breaches would follow.

WORKING IN A HOSPITAL TEAM (AN OCCUPATIONAL THERAPIST AND BOB, AN IN-PATIENT)

Bob, aged ten, had been referred to a paediatric department for severe problems of soiling. His mother had placed him on a pot from the age of ten months to toilet train him but this had never been achieved. He now refused to go to school because he was called smelly.

Although Bob had never left home, his mother had had many problems and anxieties through his earlier childhood, and said he often 'had to fend for himself'. Her own health had never been good; Bob's sister suffered from chronic illness and two of his other siblings had had a series of minor illnesses. His father lived at home but worked shifts; his mother also worked, and there was considerable discord in the marriage. The family lived at some distance from the hospital.

Bob was admitted as an in-patient and the consultant asked the occupational therapist attached to the children's wards to see him twice-weekly for individual help. Bob's soiling stopped soon after this, though it recurred at home when he went home for weekends.

It was not clear how long Bob would be kept in the unit. Regular frequent contact with him as an out-patient after his discharge from the hospital would not be possible because of the long distance; therefore the occupational therapist's work had to be limited to the duration of Bob's stay as an in-patient.

The occupational therapist described Bob's fourth session with her. In his previous sessions he had used the little train layout in her playroom. This time, again, he set up a large track system. He arranged it so that the train could run straight on to a ferry-boat, cross a large empty expanse of carpet, and run off again on to tracks on the other side. Bob ran the train on and off the ferryboat several times and smiled, saying perhaps he would play this again on Friday, when his next session was due. He carried on sending the boat and train from 'Britain' to 'France' and back across the large expanse of 'water' and looked contented and absorbed.

Then he suddenly pushed the train off the ferryboat and said it had sunk in the middle of the deep sea. He got an older wooden train and decided to make that be the 'sunken' one, not the new train he had been playing with.

The worker commented on the deep sea and said it might be hard to get the train out. Bob agreed; he said the train would not be rescued and had to stay at the bottom of the sea. He also said someone accidentally pressed the release button which had caused it to be ejected. He moved the 'sunken' train away and said he did not need it any more.

He lay on the floor listlessly in the centre of the track. He got his little piece of 'comforter blanket' out of his pocket and held it while he sucked his thumb. After a while he put the blanket back in his pocket and said the train had to collect some freight.

He chose two tigers from among the animals, saying they were stuffed, and placed them on the station for collection. He then said that a bad man cast a spell on one tiger which had made it come to life. The worker said she 'reflected back' to him what he had said, but he ignored her. The 'live' tiger prowled menacingly around the station. Then he put it on the train and pushed the train around the track, but the tiger fell off after a few seconds. He put the tigers back and stood up, asking if he could play something else. The worker said it was up to him.

He left the toys and went over to another part of the room, asking the worker to go with him. He asked what he should play. She said the time was his and he could play with any of the toys he wanted. He decided to play shop and started to organize this. But then he got out his blanket again and sucked his thumb for a while.

Eventually he took on the part of the shopkeeper and sold the worker items in a repetitive and stereotyped manner; individual items were named and paid for, all very cheaply. He then said the shop was closing down and that the worker could have all the remaining items for nothing; but even though the shop was closing down she could still visit him.

When the worker told Bob that there were only five minutes of the session left, he said he would play with the doll's house. He crammed a lot of activity into these last five minutes. First of all a mother doll was named and set in the kitchen cooking dinner. then a grandad was in the lounge watching TV. One baby was covered in a cot; another was placed in a wardrobe, hiding, because of not wanting to have a bath. A dad was then placed in the bath. The worker asked if the dad got into the bath. Bob said 'No, he's been thrown in.' He agreed with her when she said that perhaps the dad didn't like the bath either. Another male was then placed in the shower, and a baby was placed on, and then in, the toilet. He then said there was only one room in the house and placed table, chairs, cooker and mother in the bathroom. He added an auntie doll who was helping her mother with the cooking, putting her feet in the oven. He agreed emphatically with the worker's comments that it was a busy, crowded room without much privacy, saying it was very, very, crowded. He placed a grandmother and uncle downstairs with grandad and moved the TV around. Time was up; he left the session easily saying he would like to make a little doll like the doll's house people. He also asked when his next session would be.

In the discussion, several members of the seminar thought the relationship with the worker carried meaning for Bob. He remembered their last session together and wanted to carry on with the same play, and at the end he asked when his next session would be, so he explicitly showed that the relationship had a value for him. But they voiced their distress at hearing that as the boy lived at some distance the work would have to stop when he was discharged. The occupational therapist said it was also possible that his discharge from the unit could be made suddenly, leading to a precipitate end to her work with him. It was suggested that the train layout in the first part seemed to refer to links and continuity; the falling train and the falling tiger seemed to suggest fear of the opposite – of being dropped. Many members felt that his play reflected his relationship with the worker, and above all how long his sessions would be able to continue. Perhaps the sinking train signified the 'sinking' of a potentially useful relationship. It is worth noting that it was the old ship that was sunk, not the new one, so perhaps there was a glimmer of hope that something new does not necessarily have to be sunk.

Someone also wondered if the material linked up with his symptom of soiling, as if faeces dropped out by accident because nobody was thinking about what they were doing. We were reminded that mother had sat him on the pot from ten months on, too early for him to have acquired any control over his motions. Was this leading to some mindless, automatic action inside his body depriving him of the chance to think about the contents of his rectum and be aware of them, before deciding to release them? One member suggested that when he retreated to the curled-up position with his comforter, perhaps he was feeling that nobody could or would keep him in their mind. The dangerous tiger also got dropped off the train. Perhaps he felt his 'tigerish' violent impulses were what people could not cope with, which could link up with the disastrous early years of his history.

In his later game of shops, Bob seemed to be showing conflicting thoughts. On the one hand perhaps he was suggesting that the worker was the kind of person who kept her playroom 'shop' simply for her personal reward, and Bob may have been accusing her that her work was just 'automatic'; on the other hand he seemed to hint at his desire for a home visit from the worker.

This material seems to illustrate many points. Perhaps the most outstanding one is the importance of the relationship with the worker which needed clarifying in the session. There would otherwise be a risk that the 'sea' of Bob's mind would be littered with one more sunken wreck. Perhaps Bob actually recognized the worker as someone who could help with his anxiety, when he asked her to come with him into a different part of the room. It seemed important for him to be enabled to think about his feelings of anxiety when he broke off his play following the sunken ship and the dropped tiger. Maybe it was the worker's attention that was of primary importance for him at that time, rather than a choice of play material; that may have been why he asked her what he should play with next.

Endings and change were clearly fraught for Bob, as he showed in his retreat to his comforter blanket. Situations too could change very suddenly for him: the ship dropped off the boat; the bad man cast a spell on the tiger; the last five minutes of the session started with a mother cooking in the kitchen but became rife with whirlwind movement. The worker had put a boundary of a set time around the session, which could help her to hold the events in it. But a wider boundary is also important, so that there would be a framework within which she could help Bob explore feelings about endings and breaks. It would have been useful to have open and shared knowledge about the likely timing of Bob's discharge from the unit. But if this was not possible, Bob had shown in this session how important it was for this very uncertainty to be spoken about with him. What he feared was the occurrence of sudden, mindless change like the accidental pushing of a release button. So it would have been helpful to talk to him about how long he had been coming, how he thought his 'release' was decided upon, and if there was any possibility of contact after the 'therapy shop' closed. This seems important even if eventually no future contact proved possible, because it could have helped him feel that the therapist was thinking about him. This would be more than a reflecting back, it would be a form of holding and 'containment' based on the worker's taking in and bearing his pain and trying to relay it back to him in a meaningful way.

A worker in such a situation clearly has a double task. One part lies in struggling to work with her client's anxieties about his feelings. The other part lies in her relationships with her colleagues, where she will be struggling to convey the meaning of the kind of work she is attempting to do, and the stability of setting required for it.

RELATING TO COLLEAGUES IN THE SCHOOL SETTING (A SPECIALIST TEACHER AND CLARE)

Mr Q worked in the support unit of girls' comprehensive school. The school had high standards of work and expected somewhat formal behaviour from its pupils. There was considerable emphasis on achieving good examination results and participation in sport. The support unit was attended for a number of hours each week by pupils who had problems of one kind or another. Some had learning or behaviour difficulties; a few had physical handicaps, some of which were quite severe. Mr Q, in working with those who attended the unit, operated more informally than the classroom teachers, and it was accepted in the school that his work included an element of counselling, although this was not formally defined. He saw the pupils mainly in small groups or occasionally individually.

We shall discuss in Chapter 6 how in any institution there may be a tendency to set up a defensive structure to avoid pain and conflict. In an institution such as the school in question, where a sub-unit such as the support centre operates in what might loosely be described as a 'softer' manner than the main body, it can lend itself to being seen as a repository for projections of being a 'soft option' for the whole institution. Such projections would, for example, remove the painful need to think about the degree of achievement that might be striven for from pupils with difficulties without much indication of the possible outcome. (Readers may know of units that have been 'landed' with imputed functions over and beyond their institutional tasks. For example, a withdrawal unit within a school may be seen as a 'sin bin' for more extensive problems than those for which it was constituted.) Mr Q was aware that such a tendency seemed to be present from time to time in the school, and strove to avoid enacting such anti-task projections. He tried for example to encourage the pupils he saw to participate in the ordinary school activities as much as possible, and liaised with their class teachers and year heads, the latter having responsibility for pastoral care.

The possibly incipient tendency for this kind of institutional splitting to take place may be influenced by those attending the unit. Clare, aged thirteen, originally attended the unit at pre-arranged times, on account of her learning and social difficulties. She started however to leave her classroom whenever she felt under stress in class, sometimes asking to come to the unit and sometimes going to the library. Her class teacher became increasingly worried about Clare's performance in class. Clare herself, as well as having difficulties in her work, tended to be denigratory of her class teacher. Mr Q had to contend not only with the potential dynamics of the setting, which could lend itself to work with him being seen as an easy option, but also with Clare's active involvement in 'splitting' the class teacher and himself into 'bad' and 'good'. This made it more difficult for him and the class teacher to relate constructively to each other, having been 'programmed' by Clare into a position of expected disagreement. The projection of 'goodness' and 'badness' into a couple has of course a parallel in home life, where parents may be 'wedged apart' by a child, with a consequent burdensome task of extricating themselves from that which is projected on to them. The situation is of course more complicated where the projections make use of some real difference: it was in fact true that there were more pressures on Clare from her class teacher than from Mr Q.

We talked about what Mr Q could do. It seemed necessary to think about the role he held in the institution aside from support teacher and counsellor, which seemed to be the one that Clare was wanting to see him in exclusively. He decided that he would need to discuss the situation in some detail with the class teacher, which did not feel easy to do when they were both recipients of Clare's projections. Prior to this he also needed to clarify with Clare what belonged inside the boundary of their counselling relationship and what were more general school matters. He was after all a teacher in the school. This may seem an obvious point, but perhaps not easily accessible to Mr Q when he was under pressure from Clare to feel himself solely as her special counsellor. In the discussion with the class teacher it emerged that she had wondered if at least some of Clare's absences in the library had been sanctioned by Mr Q, which was not the case. They were in fact able to have a discussion in which they thought together about Clare's problems and what would be reasonable expectations from her in the school setting. They decided together that there were a number of worrying features about Clare and that it would be useful to have a meeting with her parents to try and understand what was happening so that the school could respond most appropriately to her needs.

We can see here how an institution, by the apparently necessary and useful provision of special facilities for the care of pupils with difficulties, can lend itself to potential splitting and how such splitting can be influenced by those within it. We can also see how countertransference problems can exist for the staff: in this case it is necessary for those involved to think about how they may have been split. It is clear that individuals (in this case Clare) for whose benefit the institution was set up could in fact fail to benefit from it if the staff did not try and work together to try and heal the splits and understand what was happening.

We further discuss institutional dynamics throughout Chapter 6. Here we want to emphasize the interaction between the individual teaching/counselling work done with Clare in the immediate setting of the support unit and the wider setting of the school in order to encourage those extending their psychodynamic approach into a wider area to be aware of the attention that needs to be given to the maintenance of the setting.

The naming and function of specialist teachers as well as of the units in which they work can vary from school to school, and it will always be necessary to think about what responsibilities such teachers carry for various tasks in the school. Do they for example carry teaching, disciplinary and counselling roles or only some of them? They will also need to think how they function alongside other teachers. The function and responsibilities of Mr Q and the way he could use himself in his work, for example, differ considerably from that of the specialist teacher, Mrs V, who undertook the individual work with Colin which we discuss in Chapter 7. The issue of interaction among professionals which we discussed in Chapter 3 (under 'Clarification of boundaries') is also relevant here.

EMOTIONAL DISTURBANCE AND SCHOOL-BASED PROBLEMS

Some schools, like Clare's, have a support unit. Others have teachers who are also trained as counsellors and who are available for individual consultation by children. In other schools the educational psychologist or the clinical medical officer is able to offer individual help. (For example see the discussion of Len in Chapter 1, Tim in Chapter 3 and Lindsey in Chapter 5.) The children who are seen as needing this sort of help may often be showing behaviour problems, being disruptive in class or at break-time, stealing, or soiling. But it is increasingly becoming recognized that educational difficulties may also have an emotional base. Learning itself is not something that takes place divorced from feelings, unless it is merely memorizing facts and learning by rote. The sort of learning that involves mental growth, the ability to think for oneself, and to use knowledge in an imaginative way, is inseparable from emotional experience.

The extent to which this is recognized is likely to depend on the climate of opinion within the school. The setting is therefore of importance here. There is always a risk that terms such as 'dyslexia' or 'specific learning difficulty' become labels, and then become a way of packaging and disposing of the bewildering or disquieting failure to learn in an individual child. Used in this way, these terms can function to block off the anxiety and concern of the teachers involved.

Even where physical illness or disability exists and has been diagnosed, it is important not to prejudge the nature of the child's problems (see the example of Lindsey in Chapter 5). Emotional disturbance may coexist with physical factors and may need help in its own right.

The emotional basis of thinking is explored further in Chapter 13. It is relevant here to note that in observing babies it is often possible to see how intellectual growth and the mastery of physical skills are linked with feelings and relationships. When Dean, aged about three months, was learning how to make talking noises and use his new rattle (in Chapter 11 under 'Developing feelings of identity') he was clearly doing it with and for his much-loved father. When Emma (Chapter 11) was puzzling out something about her mother's two ear-rings, this was linked with her struggle to reconcile two quite different aspects of her mother. These were babies who were learning and developing as the corollary and outcome of emotional relationships.

Len when he was referred to the educational psychologist seemed to show the opposite; he was 'stuck' in his lessons and making no progress, just as he seemed stuck in an artificially sweet relationship to his baby sister at home. His first therapeutic session suggested that this was linked with his difficulty in knowing about his aggressive feelings; obviously the worker would need to wait for more evidence from his later sessions for any confirmation of this. Annabel's repeated play sequences making the psychiatrist into a stupid child who always got his maths wrong, which we discuss in Chapter 8 suggested that for her learning (or rather failing to learn) maths was linked with feeling stupid and humiliated. Here too, further experiences in the therapy would be needed to explore where these feelings came from.

Damon, aged eight, was another child referred for a general learning inhibition and more specifically an apparent inability to tackle even the simplest arithmetic. After some months of therapy he began writing columns of numbers on the blackboard and then whipping them with a wet floorcloth. He explained that a wet cloth hurt more than a dry one; he had learnt that from a film about Jewish people being whipped by the

Nazis. It was obvious that to him numbers were imbued with an emotional significance. Since they were the little victims of his hatred and sadism they could not be allowed the freedom to multiply and divide according to their own laws. Within a therapeutic relationship he had the opportunity of having his aggressive feelings experienced within the sessions, and of a possible link being made with other aspects of himself. The work with Rupert and Sam discussed in Chapter 7 is also relevant here.

Sadhna, also eight, spent her sessions being 'mother' – cooking and writing shopping lists or being a café owner writing out long menus. These were always written in what she called 'grown-up writing', an indecipherable scribble that imitated joined-up script, although she had not in fact learned to write. She had three younger siblings at home and it seemed as if she had discarded being a struggling child herself and become instead a superior adult who knew it all. Her feelings about her mother and the new babies were making it impossible for her to be a child herself and go through the slow, difficult task of growing up. Such feelings would need to be experienced and thought about in the relationship with the therapist. If the therapist can bear what is 'put into' her by projective identification, and relate to it, the child in turn may be able to develop his or her own capacity to tolerate stress and emotional pain.

It is also true that teachers in the group situation of a class can, by sensitive understanding of emotional relationships, help the children in their care work through many of the normal problems associated with growing up. The structure, ethos and dynamics of the particular school where they work is likely to be important here; the influence of the institution in this connection is discussed in Chapter 6.

Chapter 5

Short-term Work

OFFERING LIMITED HELP

In much of this book we explore extended work with children and young people. This allows time for a therapeutic relationship to develop so that even severely deprived children can experience hope and the possibility of change. However, brief work can also be effective in bringing help. It is often also a good way to discover if more help is needed. In suitable circumstances it could be the treatment of choice.

LEARNING TO LISTEN (A CLINICAL MEDICAL OFFICER AND LINDSEY)

This example comes from a clinical medical officer's experience in a secondary school. The school was one of a number Dr G visited regularly to offer assessment and short-term help for pupils and their parents. He was asked to see Lindsey, aged twelve, who was causing problems at home and at school by losing her temper and being very moody; her parents thought this was because, although Lindsey was wearing hearing aids, she was not able to hear other people properly.

The first time Dr G saw Lindsey, he followed a fairly precise medical format, using a directive approach, questioning Lindsey about her hearing aids, and focusing on her actions and behaviour at home. Lindsey gave very negative replies. In the group discussion of the interview, members began to explore what Lindsey's feelings might be (on meeting a stranger; on being singled out for referral to the doctor; on being seen because other people were complaining about her, not because she was asking for or being offered help) and they were interested in what indications Lindsey had given about her feelings in the interview.

Dr G felt he would like to try to relate to Lindsey in a different way at the next interview, and to give her a chance to show him what *she* might feel the problems to be. He offered Lindsey a limited number of interviews together. Lindsey began drawing glasses (Dr G wears glasses), then featureless, blank faces with glasses, Father

Christmas with glasses, and so on. Dr G recognized that he was still being directive and asking questions, and sensed that Lindsey was experiencing this as attacking. He explored with the group what Lindsey's perceptions might be, and noticed that as he became less directive, the glasses theme disappeared.

Lindsey began talking to Dr G about her interests and her Sindy dolls. Lindsey had always given everyone the impression that she had to lip-read because she could not hear with her aids; and her parents had thought her inability to hear was the source of her difficulty in making relationships. But during this long conversation she had not been watching Dr G's mouth at all, and yet had obviously heard everything he said. Dr G had a feeling of closeness to her throughout this conversation. Lindsey had seemed relaxed and eager to talk with him. Lindsey stopped, and seemed to realize that she had been responding to Dr G and that there had been no barrier of not-hearing between them. She turned suddenly away and began quietly crying; she said 'So you know'. She meant that Dr G had just then seen proof that she could in fact hear very well with the use of her aids, and had only been pretending not to hear.

When Lindsey found that Dr G could listen, and did not know the answers from the start, she let him see that it was not the aids that were a barrier to communication; it had been her choice to cut herself off from other people. While she was crying, Dr G said gently that it was very frightening for her now to be without the protective barrier of 'not-hearing' between herself and other people. Lindsey smiled, and returned to her conversation about her Sindy dolls, but with a new warmth Dr G had not seen in her before.

In the group discussion several members with similar functions to the clinical medical officer's said how frustrating they found it when their work was limited to just assessment. They wished they were able to offer long-term help. Several others said their own work could only consist of short-term contact with clients or children by its very nature, and they felt this ruled out individual therapy. But another member pointed out that even in these assessment interviews with Lindsey, her relationship with Dr G had evidently been crucial; Dr G had tried to make himself available as a listener and Lindsey had eventually responded to this. Dr G agreed that he had started to think about Lindsey's silence, and the feelings behind it, rather than countering the silence with a barrage of questions. The leader suggested that once he had done this, his interviews with her became not just assessment; Lindsey was able to let him see that she could hear him adequately, and found relief at having someone understand that her real difficulty in getting on with other people lay in her feelings, not in any hearing problems. Although her time with Dr G was brief, it enabled her to be aware of the possibility of relating to someone without the protective barrier of the hearing aids.

Dr G had only been able to offer Lindsey a limited number of sessions; he planned to see her again in a few months' time and review with her how she was getting on, and whether she might need further help. By his increasing use of himself as a listener and sensitive observer, he had made it more possible for Lindsey to find some 'containment', in the sense we have used it above, for her troubled feelings.

A DEATH IN THE FAMILY (A THERAPIST AND ROBBIE)

Robbie's parents went to their family doctor in despair because Robbie, although aged only five, was about to be excluded from primary school. His teacher described him as beyond control and unreachable. He would poke the sharp end of a pencil into other children's faces or throw chairs at them without any provocation or warning. His aggressive behaviour carried on relentlessly throughout the day.

The family doctor referred them to the local child guidance clinic, where a social worker met with both parents. She learned from them that six months before Robbie started school, his baby brother had died – a tragic example of sudden infant death syndrome. They were a young, kindly and very concerned couple, naturally still struggling with their grief over the loss of their much loved second baby. They said Robbie had been openly jealous when the new baby came, but not abnormally so, and the family had been happy enough until the tragedy. Since the death, however, Robbie had been moody and irritable in the day, and suffered nightmares and screaming attacks at night. The social worker offered the parents further meetings, and with their agreement, she also arranged for a child psychotherapist to see Robbie for a consultation.

When the therapist, Miss S, went to fetch Robbie from the waiting room, she found an alert, intelligent-looking little boy, who gazed at her with friendly curiosity and readily came with her to her room. Once in the room, his eyes lit on the box of toys put ready for him on the table. He gave the therapist a quick conspiratorial grin, and then crept towards the table, miming a burglar bent on secretly exploring a forbidden store of treasure.

Miss S introduced herself and said she had been asked to see him because his parents thought he seemed upset and might need help. She and Robbie would meet this one time, then she would see his parents. Robbie, while exploring the toys in the box, started to tell her who was in his family, naming the people and pets. At the end of the list he mentioned that they had also had a rabbit and a stick insect but both had died. Miss S said the family had had a baby boy as well, hadn't it, who had died, his little brother? Robbie said 'No'. After a few seconds he said 'Yes'. He added that his tooth had come out last night, Mummy had told him to put it under his pillow and the tooth fairy would collect it. He looked at Miss S anxiously and asked if she believed that. She said he was perhaps also not sure about what had happened to his little brother. Robbie said with indifference, 'Oh, I know that, he went to heaven'.

He started drawing a picture. It developed into a landscape with a green dinosaur with sharp teeth and a row of spikes on its back. It was gazing across a lake to the far side where the end of another dinosaur's red tail could just be seen disappearing off the page. Robbie explained that the green one was chasing the red one away from the beautiful lake because he wanted it all to himself. Miss S commented that he might sometimes have felt like that, wanting his Mummy all to himself, when the new baby came. When he was miming the burglar creeping up on her toys, perhaps he was also showing her about a possessive Robbie who wanted those to be his and his alone.

Robbie had started a second picture which just consisted of the red dinosaur, now inside a black cave. The first picture had been quite colourful, with a large yellow sun, blue sky, and green hills. In contrast the second picture was very bleak – just an otherwise empty black cave with a huge red dinosaur inside. This dinosaur was enormous, with sharp teeth like daggers in his gaping jaws and huge spikes along his back. It indeed looked like an illustration of a terrifying nightmare. Miss S said the green dinosaur must be very frightened that the red one was going to attack him back for being driven away, and that the red one looked enormously more dangerous. She added that sometimes babies did die. But if Robbie had sometimes felt very angry with their new baby, it might feel inside him now as if the baby had turned into a dangerous monster. He might be having bad dreams which made him feel very frightened. Perhaps he was also frightened of other children; they might seem threatening and dangerous like the red dinosaur.

Robbie asked Miss S if she would keep his pictures when it would be time to go. Perhaps he was hoping she would be able to remember him, along with the problems they had explored together. He had found that both his destructive jealousy and also the anxiety underlying his nightmares had been listened to and understood. There was in fact not much time left of their session. Miss S again explained she would be seeing Robbie's parents and thinking with them how Robbie's frightened feelings could be helped.

Miss S was aware that she had, during this consultation, found herself wondering very much about all the circumstances surrounding and following the sudden death. In the later meeting with the parents and the social worker, she realized that she wanted to ask a great many detailed questions about the circumstances surrounding their baby's death: what happened after they realized he was dead; where Robbie was during the panic and the emergency rush to hospital; was the baby buried? Had Robbie known anything about the ceremony? She was also not sure that it would be right to ask these questions. Would it be intrusive? Would it be taken as nothing more than curiosity? She shared with the parents her feeling that Robbie had a great need to know about these sad events too, but also that he might not feel able to ask. In this way she was able to use her worried feelings constructively in helping the parents explore what could be Robbie's unvoiced questions. Perhaps Robbie had felt his need to know, his 'curiosity', was wicked and intrusive, like a burglar's.

His parents said they had protected him from all that had followed the death to spare him. There may indeed be times when it is appropriate to shield a child from knowledge. Another seminar group heard about Dora, a 16-year-old girl in care who was struggling to come to terms with her stepfather's sexual abuse of her. She was also trying to restore a relationship with her alienated mother. In one of their meetings, her mother told her she herself had been regularly abused by her own brother (Dora's uncle). This plunged Dora further into despair and led her to a renewed suicide attempt. Whatever her mother's conscious motives were, this seemed like a gratuitous exposure of Dora to yet more trauma.

In Robbie's case the tragedy directly involved him; his parents' silence was motivated by love for him, and the wish to spare him pain. However, Robbie had to endure severe anxieties and nightmares, and was in effect being obliged by his parents' silence to carry these alone. The father of Wayne (Chapter 1), his foster-parents and the professionals involved had also preferred to leave everything unsaid for as long as possible, hoping to spare Wayne hurt and anxiety. Robbie's parents had been greatly helped by their meetings with the social worker; it can never be easy for parents to take up issues which relate to their own sorrows, but they were able now to think together that they would like to go over the events surrounding their baby's death with Robbie. They planned to drive with him along the ambulance route, and then the route to the chapel where the service was held, and decided that they would answer his questions as best they could.

When Robbie's parents were discussing their future meetings, they said they would like to see the social worker again after six months to let her know how Robbie (and they) were managing. At this meeting it turned out that Robbie was settling in very well at school and making friends. Re-experiencing together as a family the events of the death, and being able to talk together about the little boy they had lost, had become an ongoing healing process.

CRITERIA FOR CONSIDERING SHORT-TERM WORK

There were a number of elements both in the first encounter with Robbie's parents, and in the only meeting with Robbie, which suggested that he would be able to respond to limited help.

He was in a nurturing family setting with thoughtful parents who were well able to help him once they had explored the way with the clinic workers. This is very different from the family backgrounds of Rupert, Colin and Sam (Chapter 7). A child who had never experienced positive, reliable family relationships would not be able to seek so quickly for the help he needed, and make use of it, as Robbie did.

His behaviour in school was reported as mindless destructiveness. It could sound reminiscent of Jerry's behaviour (Chapter 1), who was also described as being out of control, hitting, biting and kicking other children. However, until Robbie was four and a half when his little brother died, he had functioned as a normal, lively, responsive child. It was clear from his parents' description that he had been progressing well. When Miss S met him, he came across as likeable, outgoing and friendly. The long period of disturbed behaviour which had brought about the urgent referral was the outcome of the disaster that had struck the whole family.

Robbie was well able to use words to talk about his family circumstances and he readily used drawings to convey his guilt and anxiety. This is in marked contrast to Jeannie and Hari (Chapter 4), Andrew or Nicholas (Chapter 8) and Alan (Chapter 9). They were able to communicate only by mindless, chaotic behaviour. Similarly Ahmed produced only 'puzzling and apparently random activity' in his session (Chapter 2).

Robbie's two drawings were rich in symbolism. As well as enabling Miss S to explore his feelings of guilt and fear of retribution, they also opened the door to exploring his fears about death and its aftermath. His drawings thus immediately gave access to his preoccupations, unlike the apparently meaningless chaos shown by the other children. A child's ability to use symbolism in drawings or play, and a wish to help the worker explore his underlying feelings and anxieties, would be relevant in deciding whether short-term help could be offered.

Many of the children described in this book needed a sustained relationship with someone able to gather in the violence and fragmentation in what they conveyed, and slowly find its meaning and the feelings linked with it. To give them a limited number of sessions would have felt like yet more cruelty, tantalising and then withholding. Further, if a severely deprived child who had never had a warm relationship with a caring adult were offered brief help this might only add to his bitterness and mistrust, as Ahmed conveyed so poignantly to Miss Z (Chapter 2).

Short-term work would be unlikely to be of use if there were a history of long-term disturbance within the child. It would therefore be important to explore if the child had been able to develop normal relationships before the onset of the problems that led the family to seek help. The child's family background itself would need to be considered.

Central questions would be whether his parents were likely to be able to give him emotional support in the future, and whether they themselves were capable of change.

Holmes (1994), reviewing approaches to brief dynamic psychotherapy with adults, suggests that similar criteria would be relevant in deciding to offer short-term help: 'high motivation for change, a circumscribed problem, evidence of at least one good relationship in the past and the capacity for "psychological-mindedness"' (see Coltart (1992) for a definition of this term); Holmes also emphasizes the need for supervision of the work.

Patton and Meara (1992) suggest that the worker needs to explore whether her client is capable of a working alliance with her. Although they discuss work with adult patients, many of their criteria are also helpful in brief work with children. They suggest noting whether the client can welcome and make use of any comments or interventions from the worker, and whether the worker finds herself feeling negatively towards the client in their first exploratory meeting. If so, she would need to think about what was causing this, and whether it was something that would mean the client would not be likely to benefit from short-term help. In Chapter 8, 'Working with negative feelings and behaviour', the children were experienced as dismissive, contemptuous and disruptive, and many of the workers acknowledged the feelings of despair, irritation or anger that were provoked. This sort of behaviour can be seen as a communication, perhaps the only way distress and damage could be conveyed. However, for such a child to build up trust in the worker requires a longer-term commitment. Short-term work with a limited purpose can still be of use in appropriate professional settings, as in the case of Paul (Chapter 4).

A GREATER AWARENESS OF CHILDREN'S EMOTIONAL NEEDS

The Children Act 1989 has contributed to a climate where families and professionals are increasingly looking for help with children's emotional problems. The needs are not new, but they have not always been noticed. A medical social worker in a hospital setting gave a moving account of her work with a 10-year-old girl, Tina, with terminal cancer (Hinton, 1980). Tina brought her teddy bear with her to the hospital and her talk and play with the teddy enabled Hinton to understand and help her with her feelings and anxieties about herself and her family in relation to her approaching death.

When our seminar group first discussed Wayne (Chapter 1) there were a number of comments relating to the sad consequences of both a failure to notice and to follow up his needs. Many children such as Wayne need help in accepting the break-up of their families and actual or impending bereavement. Longer-term work may have been indicated for Wayne from early on, but a worker often has to start from a position of not knowing whether brief or longer-term work may be required. Paul's social worker (Chapter 4) needed to use herself in an active exploratory role dealing with painful issues; but she also needed to acknowledge that they might have very little time together. As we saw in Chapter 3, 'The importance of time', it needs to be made clear at the start if brief work is being offered, so that a sudden ending does not feel like a betrayal, or come as a shock.

The health visitor who saw Mrs Adams and Vincent (Chapter 4), offered regular visits for a trial period. This can be thought of as a form of exploratory brief work of a certain kind, but taking place within an ongoing relationship which carried a different focus. Here the worker needed to monitor the boundaries of the work with her colleagues, as well as to be resilient to Mrs Adams' response.

Many family doctor practices are now moving towards offering a wide range of help at the earliest stage for families in their care. This is an area where short-term work, undertaken when a problem is first suspected, can be both beneficial and prophylactic. This obviously applies to problems with direct medical connections, for example the acceptance of a diagnosis of a chronic or long-term illness. Brief help, offered promptly in a familiar setting, can also be very valuable in relation to wider problems, such as bereavement. Some practices now employ counsellors who work with individual parents, couples and children.

The example of Robbie has enabled us to think about indications which may suggest a child may be able to use short-term work as the primary means of help. His family had been referred to a child guidance clinic at a time when few counsellors were working in GP practices. It is worth considering whether Robbie might appropriately have been referred to one when his disturbance began. The counsellor might have have found that she was able to help the family and Robbie directly. If his quite severe symptoms had persisted, she could have explored with his parents whether further help was needed.

In other settings too, the worker's role may include helping the child or family to think if further help is needed elsewhere. Some counselling services exist for adolescents who can refer themselves and are seen quickly. Both Lena and Myra (Chapter 1) were seen in such a setting, and knew from the outset that the meetings would be limited in number. Brief work with adolescents is described and discussed more fully in Copley (1993).

PRESSURES ON THE WORKER

We have already seen the importance of skilled selection of suitable cases for brief work. The requirements of workers' settings may however pose difficulties. It may be that only a limited number of hours is available for any one child or family. Longer-term therapy may be viewed by some colleagues and administrators as unjustifiably expensive. There may be a risk that pressure could be placed on practitioners such as clinical medical officers and practice counsellors to see all children briefly. In such instances an agreed opportunity to refer selected children on for specialist help could provide a necessary safeguard.

We explored in Chapter 2 the demands made on workers offering individual therapeutic help to children and young people and the need for professional sanction and support. A relatively new field of work, such as counselling in a GP practice, brings its own challenges. There may not yet be any locally organized professional group to which the worker can belong, and there may not be any colleagues doing similar work with whom she could talk over her concerns. She may in reality be professionally isolated, without status or support. Working as a member of a team in which actual interviews by colleagues could be very brief, could lead to being asked to justify the length of her own sessions. A worker might lack both a professional identity and a group identity. The need for supervision is especially important in such a new development.

Chapter 6

The Individual and the Institution

PROBLEMS OF THE INDIVIDUAL IN AN INSTITUTION

In Chapter 4 we discussed problems of therapeutic work in a variety of settings. Here we move on to discuss dynamics within an institution in relation to individuals, and how this affects the care given to the patient or client. The institution itself has a powerful influence on our clients, and one which is often overlooked; its functioning needs to be thought about as an extension of the setting.

How is the client or family first received? It may be by a busy secretary, immersed in her own 'busy-ness', or one who has been led by the team to think of herself as 'just' a receptionist. She may unwittingly already make clients feel demoted, classified as somehow a lower class of citizen by being on the receiving end of help. Do the professional members of the team include the secretary or administrator in team meetings? Perhaps the professional team unwittingly demotes the secretary; or does she feel demoted in being at the end of the line in an institution that deals with underprivileged or less well-endowed members of society? (We discuss this point further under 'Headteacher and care worker in a residential school', later in this chapter.) Unspoken and unconscious attitudes are all the more difficult to recognize. A hierarchy created in the institution will affect the client who comes for help too.

Secretaries and reception staff may need help in thinking about what part they might be able to play in the therapeutic team. One child, Annabel, discussed in Chapter 8, chose at times to relate to the secretary rather than Dr C and in such instances the secretary's response becomes relevant to the therapy. With professional clarification and support, reception staff may be able to increase their contribution to the work through their handling of telephone calls and relationships with waiting patients or parents. Parents wishing to speak with a worker might, for example, be attended to by the reception staff in a way that enabled them to forgo waylaying the worker on her return to the reception area with the child and accept a more appropriate contact.

Some institutions, including communities providing for disturbed children and adolescents, are specifically set up and designated as therapeutic communities. These, however described, recognize that they have a containing function in relation to the anxieties entering the institution, from whatever source, and are likely to have some internal structure within which staff and residents can examine the current dynamics. Others, such as schools catering for children and young people with emotional problems, day or residential, may also provide some containing function and structure, whether or not this is formally recognized. In fact any institution with a caring function for its clients, such as a hospital, school, children's home, hostel or clinic, can serve something of the same purpose. Thus workers in all the caring professions need to think in what ways they can develop or need to protect the caring potential of the institutions in which they work. An institution is always liable to be invested with feelings stemming from its clients, and can of course have a particular significance for them, which needs to be acknowledged. 'Breaking-up' at the end of term may, for example, for some children have a literal feel of the containing school structure breaking; it may then be useful if the staff can give some thought to the 'break', rather than going along wholeheartedly with the more apparently popular and sometimes manic end of term jolliness which may mask distress.

DEFENSIVE SYSTEMS AGAINST ANXIETY

The work of Jaques (1955) and Menzies (1988) demonstrates how anxiety can be widely projected and defensive structures built up to avoid its impact in a way that such anxiety is merely avoided rather than modified. Underlying the apparent formal structure and functioning of an institution there are unconscious collusive processes maintaining shared beliefs which act as a defensive system against the anxieties within it. Menzies describes the massive projection of anxieties, which so entered the fabric of the hospital which she studied that distribution of responsibility and the content of roles and boundaries became very obscure. This projection of anxieties has a parallel to that induced among workers which was described in Chapter 4 under 'Boundaries in the community'.

Menzies describes the division of tasks among nurses, and their strictly hierarchical organization in the hospital, together with the consequences. She points out that hospital staff are faced with seeing many tragedies, and that the institution develops systems like task division and hierarchy as a way of avoiding what is felt to be unbearable pain. She exemplifies for example how nurses tended to work to a task list which did not allow for sustained contact with individual patients. She also describes how nurses 'split off', and dissociated from themselves the more irresponsible, impulsive parts of themselves which might be hard to manage, and attributed these to staff below them in the hierarchy, whilst locating their own more critical aspects in their superiors. These psychic manoeuvres, carried out by projective identification (which is discussed in more detail in Chapter 12), she considers to be part of a social defence system geared to avoiding individual experience of anxiety, guilt and uncertainty. The experience of anxiety within the institution may indeed have been largely evaded, but the primitive defensive system of splitting and projecting to avoid pain cannot contribute to personal development nor to the performance of the task. Menzies goes on to hypothesize that the success of a social institution is 'intimately connected with the techniques it uses to contain anxiety'. Although commenting on the institutional aspect of behaviour, she makes it clear that the defences are operated by the individuals within them. We describe in Chapter 10 (under 'A young mother in a maternity unit') how a young mother had hoped for help in establishing breast-feeding her new baby, but was always made to feel it was someone else's job. Obholzer (1994) addresses the many defensive structures currently present in public sector organizations which are inimical to the fulfilment of their primary functional task and which also affect their capacity to contain social anxieties.

THE GROUP AND THE INDIVIDUAL (GINETTE AND DOMINGO)

The disturbance caused in us by seeing mental illness can arouse defences perhaps even more readily than seeing a physical illness. A teacher described how a 10-year-old girl who was thought to be psychotic was dealt with on a hospital ward. The teacher had been allocated to a children's ward in a hospital for three mornings a week to give lessons. There were three children on the ward; she was only to occupy herself with two of them as the third, 10-year-old Ginette, was 'still under assessment'. In practice this meant that Ginette was left to her own devices while two or sometimes three student nurses carried out tasks round the ward. Ginette was preoccupied much of the time with a helter-skelter for marbles; she dropped the marbles in at the top and watched them come out at the bottom. Sometimes she giggled or whispered to herself or made a tic-like movement with her head. The occasional interactions with the nurses were a negative experience on both sides: Ginette did not respond to their offer to play Ludo, and they grew irritated by her occasional outbursts of repetitive questioning, for example 'Can I see the library lady?' (They explained to the teacher that the library lady came once a week and Ginette always ignored her). Different student nurses were on duty at different times; they took it in turns at the end of each week to write up the 'Nurses' Observation Notes' on Ginette.

The teacher was given the feeling that the nurses occupied a low rung in the hospital hierarchy and that, although the nurses were with Ginette all day and the sister or doctors were not, nobody thought that a nurse might be given a special role with regard to Ginette and be asked to offer her an individual relationship. Here again the institutional system seemed to intervene between the people who wanted to be carers, and the person who needed care.

The teacher described the nurses as being very gentle and caring to the two children she worked with and to other new children as they were admitted. But she described one instance when the three nurses, a visiting laboratory technician and two nursery assistants were grouped at one end of the ward having coffee. Ginette interrupted them with her repetitive questioning, a nurse answered her in a jokey way that was also mocking, and the others joined in; together, they seemed to form a hostile group with Ginette as the victim-outsider. These people who individually were caring and kind, even if baffled by this child, had become at that moment like a hostile force united against her. Bion (1961) has described how a 'basic-assumption' culture can arise which is out of touch with individual needs. This is discussed later in the chapter.

Staff in children's homes and residential schools also work under great stress, and develop various ways of dealing with it. Domingo was always annoying the other children in his residential school by demanding to be the centre of attention. The staff explained to his visiting social worker that they could not let him get away with it because that would not be fair on the other children. They operated a reward system which meant that Domingo failed to earn the right to go on weekly trips to the library, or to the sports hall; he soon got on to a downward spiral where eventually even the right to leave the building when a visitor came to see him was forfeited. The defensive rules of the place seemed to take precedence over the task of understanding its clients. Dartington (1994) movingly describes how basically caring nurses may at times feel like responding with denigration to the ruthless demands of 'disturbed, frightened, angry, dependent patients'. Such emotionality may also be evoked in staff in institutions where workers may have low status and work with demanding clients with whom it is difficult to effect positive change. The staff working with Domingo unfortunately retaliated in a way which did not promote his welfare. Their emphasis on the 'unfairness to other children' may reflect issues of differential treatment of staff within the same institution where often the 'care staff' carry great burdens but get the lowest salaries and the least say in policy. This may evoke feelings of rivalry among staff members, together with a call to have them suppressed.

We have on the other hand, also examples where the institution itself functioned as a helpful 'container'. The school that Colin (Chapter 7) attended was flexible enough to encompass and facilitate individual work with some of its children; the staff also managed to provide a firm framework for their disturbed behaviour. We now look at further examples in this chapter.

HEADTEACHER AND CARE WORKER IN A RESIDENTIAL SCHOOL (HARMAN)

A residential school for children with emotional difficulties can be a very taxing place to work. The school is sometimes regarded by referring agencies or educationalists elsewhere simply as a means of 'disposal', somewhere a difficult child can be sent and regarded as 'dealt with'. There is often no real hope that the school will do any good; referring psychiatrists sometimes say specifically 'nothing can be done for this boy'. If the staff at the school try to understand, and help him find some meaning in his disturbed behaviour, they can feel they are ploughing a very lone furrow.

The children in these schools have usually been to a number of other special institutions – special units in ordinary schools, home tuition or child guidance clinics for example – and have possibly been in and out of children's homes and foster-care. Many now feel themselves to be beyond help and many have developed a defence of cynicism, mistrust and apathy.

In these circumstances the staff themselves may have a struggle to cling to a belief in the value of their work. It may be difficult to find support for themselves within the education system or outside it. There may not be enough resources to allow for any one member of staff to work individually with disturbed children. Such institutions may sometimes be used then as a 'dump' by society for its unwanted elements, in a similar way that a client can attempt to dispose of unwanted feelings in a worker. We saw in Chapter 1 ('The client's initial perceptions of the worker and the setting') how Myra evacuated her feelings into her counsellor. If the workers are used as a dump in this way it must always be a struggle for them to gather together their capacity to function in a containing manner. This would involve accepting what is projected, at least temporarily, but retaining the potential to work actively with it.

Harman was eleven, in a residential school for children with emotional difficulties. He had been placed there because he had been out of control and failing to learn in primary school. He was one of the youngest children in a large immigrant family. His father left home soon after he was born but returned for occasional visits which involved violence. His mother, although she had moved to England eleven years ago, still spoke no English. The children were left to run wild; an older brother was now in prison. In so far as Harman was brought up at all, it was by three older sisters; all complained that he was out of control at home as well. On first joining primary school, he was found not to be speaking at all, either in English or in his mother tongue.

In the residential school, his persistent stubbornness wore out both teaching and residential care staff. In lessons he sat on the periphery, dropping words here and there, causing trouble. He interrupted games, apparently in order to provoke conflict. He said 'No' to every request and at every bedtime refused to go.

He had been at the boarding school one term, spent the Christmas holidays at home and been back at school a few days when the following incident occurred, after lessons were over. The children were playing skittles. Harman wanted his go out of turn. He told Mr F who was running the game that someone else had taken his turn. Mr F disagreed. Harman went upstairs and started shouting 'White bastard, wanker'.

The school had been run on fairly authoritarian lines, with the emphasis on control of behaviour. The new head was introducing a different approach, one that was new to staff as well as children. He described the events to the discussion group:

> I heard cries of 'White bastard, wanker' and, on going out to investigate, saw Harman on the stairs. I went up to him and suggested he stop shouting as it disturbed others.
>
> Mr F was at the bottom of the stairs and said, 'I'm the white bastard in question.' Harman was now quiet and still standing on the stairs. Mr F went into the lounge. I walked away; the shouting started again. I went upstairs and took Harman by the hand. He said 'Piss off'. I said that if his anger was directed at Mr F he should go down to the lounge and face him with it. He went readily enough. I took him up to Mr F and said, 'I think you should work this through.'
>
> Mr F took Harman by the hand and led him across the lounge. They talked. I left. Mr F took Harman out into the grounds where they walked around. I saw them go outside. Twenty minutes later I went again to the lounge. Harman was standing stiffly near the door. Mr F was sitting down. Mr F and I spoke for a few moments. Harman, confident that we could see and hear him, started to say out loud 'I'm running away.'
>
> Another member of staff said, 'What will that prove?'
>
> Harman said, 'I'm running away like Chris and Sam did.'
>
> I said, 'But they did not go anywhere; they just stood on the drive for ten minutes.' This had happened weeks beforehand.
>
> Harman said, 'I'm going. I want to be in Jim's bedroom not in Mike's.'
>
> I did not reply but said, 'It's very cold out tonight, you'll freeze.'
>
> Harman replied, 'Don't care'. I started to talk to Mr F. He said quietly that when he was out with Harman some strange, possibly significant things were said and

done and he wanted to know from me what they meant and what line he was to follow.

I said he should continue to work through with Harman possibly in Harman's bedroom and follow his feelings and instincts about what Harman was actually communicating.

Harman was now in conversation with another boy, and responded to this other boy's challenge to run away at this point by declaring that he was going and leaving the room. The other boy had actually said, 'Don't go out. It's too cold', but he had said it knowing Harman's contrary nature.

I advised Mr F to walk after Harman, pick him up, take him to his room and work out the difficulty. He did this and at 10.15 p.m. we discussed what had occurred.

Mr F said that when Harman had been taken out by him on the first occasion he, Mr F, did not have the faintest idea what to do. His immediate thoughts were to practise saintly indifference and let Harman do or say what he wanted, or to dominate him physically and shake him into submission.

In the end he did neither, but took Harman by the hand and walked around the snow-covered drive for some time. He began to notice inconsistencies between Harman's words and actions. While shouting 'Let me go' he was clinging very tightly to Mr F's hand.

He said that he did not mind being outside, so Mr F said that they could stay out for hours if necessary.

Harman then said that he did not want to go in but complained of the snow and cold. Mr F insisted that they then come in.

When they went up to Harman's bedroom, Mr F felt that Harman did as a rule say the exact contrary of what he wished and proceeded to act on this assumption. Harman has difficulty at bedtime because he says he does not want to go to bed. Mr F felt strongly that Harman really wanted to be held safely until he was near sleep. Harman did not like stories at bedtime, he said. He did not listen. Did Mike who shared his room like them? Yes. Yes, he liked them a lot – but he, Harman, never listened to them.

By now Harman was undressed and in his pyjamas. There had been tears. The only thing he liked in the world was cricket.

Mr F asked again what the cause of his sorrow/anger was. Harman said, 'Can't you see it's flooding everywhere?' Mr F considered this reply and reverted to talk of cricket before asking, 'Is it flooding in the classrooms? Is it flooded here?'

Harman affirmed the first, then said, 'You can see, you are here, aren't you?'

Mr F, not wanting to say, 'What's flooding?', said, 'How deep is it?' and Harman gestured with his hand a foot from the floor. After a pause he said, 'It's mad. The whole school is flooded with mad.'

Mr F asked me what I thought this meant but I suggested his closeness to the mode in which this was expressed made his the surer instinct here.

By now Harman was calming down; his declarations of intent were losing their force. In a further ten minutes he was calm, smiling, eating his supper.

I asked Mr F to watch for opportunity to explore further Harman's thoughts and I recorded this impression immediately after our conversation.

In the discussion, the headteacher was asked about the school's links with Harman's home. He said that Harman's mother never visited the school, and home visits were difficult, not only because of her lack of English. One of the teenage daughters was sometimes there to be interpreter. But Harman's mother seemed apathetic and fatalistic, perhaps worn down by the number of her children and the brutality of her husband. It really seemed as if the school environment was Harman's only hope. But the trouble was that Harman alienated everyone there by his mindless refusals to everything; all he seemed to want to do was provoke trouble. Not unnaturally, this in turn evoked the sort of response that Mr F described ('his immediate thoughts were...'). It is also possible that the polarity of Mr F's feelings, his oscillation between 'saintly indifference' and physical force, could have something to do with Harman's own projected feelings; Harman had after all been at the receiving end of apathetic fatalism from his mother and brutality from his father.

The headteacher said that he himself had felt put on the spot when Mr F asked him what Harman's strange remarks meant. It was difficult, as headteacher, not to have an answer. It was also difficult at times not to take over, but to limit himself to encouraging the care worker, Mr F, to carry on.

One of the group suggested this was rather like a good father's role might be in supporting the mother with the children, and that this was something Harman had never experienced at home. Another said that Harman's 'contrary nature' seemed to involve denying even to himself what his real needs and wishes were – to be brought into the warmth, to be tucked up in bed, to have a bedtime story read to him – which all sounded like a longing for mothering, only this longing had to be smothered at birth, as it were.

The headteacher said those were needs that the care staff understood, and on the whole they were good at meeting them. The problem here was that Mr F was afraid he was dealing with a mad boy when Harman talked about the flooding, and the flooding with mad. Mr F was not sure that he could cope with that sort of problem. The headteacher also felt at a loss.

But perhaps that reflected Harman's own experience, of being overwhelmed not only by his own unmet needs as a baby and child, but also by the chaos, and brutality, of the life going on around him in his home. It seemed a momentous task that the residential school should in any way try and help him make sense of his life. On the other hand, it seemed that Harman had been able to respond very quickly to Mr F's proffered help: he clung tightly to his hand, he did try and talk with him, and he showed relief at the calm ending. It does seem that the head was acting like a father in helping Mr F as a father might help a mother in the containment of young children. The family observations in Chapter 11 ('The growing family and father's role') make an interesting comparison. Harman, although we cannot be sure, instead of receiving containment as a child, may have been used as a receptacle for the 'projective identification' of parental problems; he was in this instance having some of his basic infantile anxieties acknowledged by Mr F. It seemed to be possible in this institution to incorporate a family frame of mind into the caring arrangements for these needy youngsters.

THE ROLE OF KEY WORKER (A PROBATION HOSTEL WORKER AND DONALD)

We now turn to a probation hostel, where most of the residents stayed on a short-term basis (up to six months), while on bail or on parole or on probation with a condition of residence. The staff had the task of working with these often disturbed, suicidal or violent people, and of trying to help them find accommodation and work when they left. The staff had instituted a key worker scheme, to try to help the people in their care form a relationship with one person who would be there not only to help with practical problems but also to listen and be available at a deeper level.

Two of the difficulties have already been mentioned: that the residents were often disturbed, and that they were not there for very long. Another problem was the shift system for staff, so that they were not on duty at the same times each week. In addition there would sometimes be only one member of staff on duty, so that any interview could be interrupted by phone calls, visitors, or requests for help from other residents. Further, there were weekly meetings for all residents and all staff, and a separate meeting for staff, at which the key worker was expected to share information and impressions from his individual sessions with a resident. Each member of staff would be a key worker to about five residents, who would therefore have to share the staff member's time, attention, and interest. The residents were also free to relate to other staff members, visiting tutors and others, and to talk to them about personal matters; and each had his own probation officer outside the residential setting. If a staff member felt that a resident was forming a relationship and needed more individual time, this would have to be at the expense of the other residents for whom he was the key worker. In this setting the staff had to decide whether they would agree to see a resident individually as often as the resident asked for it, or whether they would limit sessions to the minimum of once a week.

The problems of boundaries, confidentiality, and continuity seem to stand out here even more than with Ivan (discussed in Chapter 3). Here, however, apart from the probation officer, all the staff shared a similar task, and that of the probation officer was not all that dissimilar. It was clear that the staff were creating a helpful environment in spite of the difficulties. The problems of their setting were frequently under discussion in their staff meetings, and they seemed able to remain open and receptive to the problems of their clients. The flexibility of the regime at this hostel is a contrast to some of the rigid defensive systems that have evolved elsewhere.

The seminar member described her work with one of the young adults, whose key worker she was. He had had frequent short prison sentences and the hostel staff were now trying to work towards helping him get settled, and find suitable accommodation. He was threatening to commit another offence in order to be sure to receive a prison sentence.

Donald began to talk to the worker about himself. He had had a stable home for the first eleven years of his life, while he was living with an elderly foster-mother. His own mother and a new stepfather then claimed him and he then had a very unsettled life passing the years till adulthood in and out of care and in recent years in and out of prison. During this time his foster-mother died. He said he still felt as if she were alive and talked to her frequently when on his own. But he also blamed her for deserting him (though it had not been her wish for him to be removed). The key worker asked if he had been to the funeral or to her grave; he had not done either. When he spoke about prison, he made it sound like a positive place, providing care and support for him. The key worker suggested that Donald felt returning to prison was like returning to his foster-mother's care, and he seemed struck by this. Over the number of sessions he had with the key worker he put into words a great deal of bitterness, and told the worker more than once that he intended to leave and commit another crime so as to get put into prison again. He did actually leave but returned voluntarily after a few days and seemed more ready to think about realistic plans for somewhere to live after his discharge from the hostel. He asked for help in tracing and visiting the grave of his foster-mother.

The framework provided by the hostel, and the work of his key worker, helped him struggle towards some sort of life outside prison. He may have been helped in at least taking some steps towards recognizing the depth of his feelings for his foster-mother and not seeking a somewhat shallow replica of her care in prison; this may have helped him to make a move to living more realistically in the present. In such an instance it would also be useful to think with Donald about his possible feelings of being deserted by the worker and hostel who only provided a 'short sentence' of care. There is some similarity here to feelings about 'breaking-up' at the end of a term which we discussed at the beginning of the chapter; we need to remember how important a break or ending in the contact with the institution itself may be for those in an institutional setting, and particularly a residential one.

The difficulties in these and similar examples are formidable, and need to be carefully thought out before offering individual work to a client. But it is still possible to give real help along the lines we are advocating, in this sort of a context.

THE CONTAINING FUNCTION OF THE INSTITUTION (THE SCHOOL AND LIZ)

Some schools employ a specialist teacher to work individually with disturbed children (for example Colin in Chapter 7 and Alan in Chapter 9). Others may have the services of a child psychotherapist for at least part of the week. Such a specialist teacher or therapist may be able to provide an additional space to that provided by the school itself within which an attempt can be made to contain and understand a child's disturbed or violent feelings. The relationship of the specialist to other staff and the boundary between them will always need to be considered, as the following example shows.

Liz, a tomboyish girl of thirteen, attended a residential school. She had lived abroad with her grandmother for nearly the first five years of her life, but was now living with her parents and six other siblings and half siblings, some older and some younger. She sometimes talked in a calm and reasonable manner. At other times she spoke, as we shall see, as if she were representing an object such as a toy car. Most disconcerting to the staff were occasions when she related in a manner which included laughter, loud belching and inappropriate physical contact; they found her unreachable at such times. This school was in an isolated rural area, and some of the children, including Liz, had recently returned from a half-term visit home.

Liz was having an individual period of time with Mrs R who took a special interest in children with exceptional difficulties, but also acted as a classroom teacher without a firmly demarcated boundary between her functioning in these different roles. Liz had started talking to Mrs R quite reasonably about the building structure she was making and then said her 'crazecar', referring to a toy she held in her hand, was crying about coming back to school. This was said in quite a sad way, but when Mrs R talked to her about this, the initially rational conversation was broken up by Liz making car noises, belching and trying to grab at and stroke Mrs R. Mrs R gently disengaged herself and asked Liz what she would be saying if she were talking instead of belching, and whether this belching was linked to possible anger when her building construction had collapsed. Liz said that 'crazecar' did not like Mrs R. She then said that this was 'pretend' and deliberately seemed to belch more. She muttered about being revolting, leading Mrs R to feel Liz was talking about herself, but when Mrs R said this Liz said it was Mrs R who was revolting.

Liz then worked on the building structure for a while and stopped belching. The end of their time together was approaching and Mrs R began to prepare Liz for the arrival of a group of children, pointing out she would need to adjust her behaviour to the group situation. In fact when the other children arrived Liz threw a jigsaw and almost the whole box of constructional bricks across the room. Other children then threw these around and chaos ensued. Eventually order was restored, the bricks and jigsaw picked up, and the children settled. After spinning around the room for a while, bumping into people and laughing, Liz eventually withdrew to a corner, sat at a table and read for the rest of the period.

In discussion we heard more about Liz – her family background, symptoms and experiences, and also about the reasonable intellectual progress she was making. But what we want to concentrate on here is that which is relevant to institutional functioning. We were told that Liz would often spin round, sometimes with considerable force, and bump into staff. In the school grounds, on seeing staff, she might divert from more ordinary behaviour to such spinning. Her behaviour often managed to make the staff members feel disgusted or incompetent. The frequent spinning, often from staff member to staff member, made it difficult for the staff to feel they knew what was happening, and the headteacher, when in contact with Liz, found it difficult at times to believe that she was really the head in charge of the school!

The headteacher had some hope of arranging therapy in a somewhat distant clinic for Liz, but some confusion had arisen between home, school and clinic about this. We are not describing Liz as mad but it seems, drawing on her naming of the 'crazecar' through which she sometimes spoke, that she could at times feel beset by feelings of 'craziness', and extruded by projective identification such feelings and confusion into the school. One can see from her various spins 'into' the staff and by the throwing of the bricks and broken jigsaw into the other children, how broken up and confused this communication was, and how the feelings of confusion actually got into the headteacher, the staff and children. One could say that at that time the school had become the receptacle for Liz's confusion; the staff needed to think about the effect Liz's projected feelings had on the institution's ability to carry out its function.

How could the school work with such a situation? The head saw helping children to be aware that they are unhappy and assisting them to seek appropriate intervention as part of the task of the school. However, a child such as Liz who has projected much of her thinking potential by spinning it into others, is in a weak position to assess her own feelings. If it could be provided, a relationship with a specialist teacher or therapist, more closely bounded in time and place, might help in that Liz's projections could be more closely held and thought about by one person. Without such help, a child's projections, which have the effect of fragmenting the staff's capacity to think, could lead to the school's ability to help that child and others becoming impaired. It is of course the sensitive approach of a school in its therapeutic endeavour to relate to the needs of disturbed children that made it so vulnerable! This approach can be contrasted with one which might attempt to enforce standards of behaviour at the expense of providing space for thinking about anxieties and difficulties.

Bion's concept of the container is relevant here too (Bion, 1962a). One can think of the school as a potential container: the confusions of Liz, the anxieties of the other children, the staff's anxieties with regard to the demands of parents and society are what require to be contained. It seems necessary for the school staff to be constantly aware of the potential damage to their thinking and containing function, as otherwise the school could indeed become an ineffective 'dump'. It needs to be recognized and accepted that different staff may be labouring from time to time under projected burdens.

THE WORK GROUP AND THE TASK

We see the staff as a potential work group, any such group aiming to carry out work-group activity: that is, mental functioning designed to further the task of the institution. In that way it has some similarity to the thinking functioning of an individual. Bion (1961) introduces and expands this concept, with particular stress on more primitive underlying 'basic-assumption' group activity which is liable to permeate or take over from a task-oriented work group. Where basic-assumption activity is predominant, underlying primitive assumptions can hold sway, such as a belief that dependence on a powerful leader is needed or that the dominant issue is the need to fight or take flight. Bion sees such basic-assumption phenomena as having the characteristics of defensive reactions to primitive anxiety. In a school under the dominance of such states of mind there would be no containment of anxiety.

In any institution which has a large input of anxiety, which is, as we have seen, likely to be the case with most of the therapeutic, educational and care-orientated institutions relevant to this book, there must be a strain on the work-group functioning of the staff and its capacity to stay working with pain in a containing manner. On the one hand the work-group activity may be in jeopardy on account of projections into it; in working with Liz for example, the head and the staff found it difficult to think. On the other hand, the work group may be undermined by 'basic-assumption' activity or caught up in the institutional tendency to build structured defences against anxiety, such as those described by Jaques (1955) and Menzies (1988).

As such problems seem unavoidable in institutions with tasks relating to the care of those with emotional problems, a staff commitment of a high order, including a willingness to examine projections between staff and clients, is necessary for effective work in this area. The institutional task itself needs to be clear and staff to be carefully selected. The understandable difficulties that workers may at times have in containing the projections of their clients need to be monitored, thought about, and carefully distinguished from the consequences of the recruitment of insufficiently skilled, unsuitable or even abusive staff.

The countertransference of the staff towards their clients and even to each other may be a relevant part of the work of such institutions. We are not thinking of a certain kind of sensitivity group, which could overstep personal boundaries and be unproductive to work-group activity. What we mean is rather that staff members need to think about the feelings that arise within them in the course of their work, and about the source of these feelings, and whether they are relevant to the work-group task within the institution. Feelings that are for example projected into the staff by their clients need to be thought about as part of the fabric of institutional dynamics.

Some staff find they can manage such work themselves. Others find it more difficult, perhaps due to the complexity of emotions entering the institution, and hence seek the services of a consultant to help them with their thinking. Some institutions, such as schools taking in pupils with emotional difficulties, use the services of a staff child psychotherapist in such a way. In others a staff member or members may take responsibility, possibly on a basis of rotation, for examining the institutional processes, or it may be possible for a professional from outside the institution to be brought in to help. However carried out, we think that such an attempt to think about and review what is happening can enhance the work of the institution, and bears some analogy to the use of a discussion group for thinking about work with individual clients.

Part 3

The Therapeutic Relationship

Chapter 7

The Relationship Between Worker and Client as a Point of Growth

The examples in this chapter have been chosen because they can be used to think about the possibility of change. In one instance a child had only just started receiving help; in the other examples, therapy had been carried on for eight months or a year. They offer different examples of what was being effected by the relationship between the worker and the child.

FINDING SPACE FOR ENVIOUS FEELINGS (A CLINICAL PSYCHOLOGIST AND BETTY)

The first example is from a young girl's fourth meeting with a clinical psychologist. We include it because this illustrates Betty's underlying difficulty which seemed to be an envious spoiling quality in her that soured every relationship. Once this was brought into the session it became possible to think of it as something with which she might want help. The session also illustrates detailed points of the therapeutic interaction. Betty, aged twelve, had a history of poor school performance; there were complaints of immaturity, attention-seeking and constant soiling and wetting. Social skills training and a practical approach to the problems, which included regular checking to see if she had soiled, had not succeeded. She lived with her parents and two older brothers and had recently started twice-weekly therapy with a clinical psychologist, Mrs Y.

In the session in question, on entering the therapy, Betty said 'sand' and the worker found herself moving an adult-sized chair over to the sand pit. Betty said no, she would use the 'baby chairs' today.

It is worth noticing the kind of communication made to the worker, who told the seminar that she felt it called up an almost automatic action in her. This indicates the likelihood that the worker was in receipt of a 'projective identification', a part of the patient omnipotently entering the worker's mind to make the worker at that moment enact something on the lines of being a kind of automatic 'servant mummy'. It seems important, however, for us to notice not only the controlling aspect of Betty, but also a 'baby part' that, despite its imperious clothing, seemed to want some contact with the worker.

Betty went on to offer Mrs Y a cup of coffee, filled the mugs with a water/sand mixture, saying as she handed a cup of coffee to the worker that it was not coffee but oxtail soup. This they pretended to drink.

In the discussion, members agreed that the oxtail drink substituted for the coffee did not sound very nice. The combination of the colour of oxtail soup (brown) and the word 'tail' which commonly means 'bottom' was too suggestive of Betty's symptom of soiling.

Betty decided to build a sandcastle, filling a bucket with wet, rather soggy sand, upturning it and sticking in some spoons as flags. She then placed a guard on top, followed by a soldier coming up stealthily with a gun. She described a shoot-out, ending with the dead soldier falling down the outer wall. She removed the flags, leaving the guard on top, and poked holes into the castle with her fingers. When asked, she said they were mouseholes, and proceeded to cover them up, removing the guard at the same time. She destroyed the castle by cutting into it with her hand, a piece at a time.

Next she was going to build a better castle which would 'work first time'. Having remade the sandcastle she picked up the guard, saying he had a muddy face. She placed him on top of the castle and said a 'woman came and cleaned his face'. She did not have a woman and used a crayon instead. 'Now he can see.' Once again the soldier crept up behind the guard, who turned suddenly, shooting the soldier who died and was thrown into a cup. Betty took the guard from the top of the castle and said she was going to 'finish off' this one too, but differently. She thumped her hand on to the top of the castle, the sand flying everywhere.

She upturned the bucket, placing some sand on top, shaping it into a smooth, circular mound. This time she was making a lighthouse, to light up two shops (upturned mugs). She stuck spoons and two crayons into the mound; these were placed horizontally and at right angles to each other. Betty spent a short time viewing her work. She then pulled out the spoons and crayons and raised the sand mound on top by adding some more sand. She squashed this with her hands and then rubbed her forearms in the sand. She looked at the worker, and asked her what this felt like.

How can one start to relate to this material therapeutically? Perhaps an appropriate answer, here as elsewhere, is that we need to recognize the truth that we have no answers. We can start, as our seminar group did, to enquire about how the worker felt. Mrs Y told us that she felt greatly interested, but also felt excluded from the lighthouse play.

The lighthouse was surely a useful building, serving a valuable function. Yet it, and the castles, were subjected to repeated attacks – some stealthy (the creeping soldier and the burrowing mice) and some overt (she cut, thumped or squashed each one finally with her hands). It looked as if there was a part of her that insidiously undermined and attacked other people's achievements and goodness; at any rate the worker was left with a feeling of mess and destruction.

Grasping two handfuls of sand, Betty moved her hands towards Mrs Y saying 'What do you think of this, then?' The worker told Betty she thought she was creating a lot of mess and perhaps this had something to do with the way she was feeling. Betty nodded, but seemed more interested in squeezing the sand between her fingers. She picked up more sand and said that it was 'dirty sand' but that it did not have to be. It could be nice and dry but she had put water on it so that it was dirty and wet. She looked at her hands and observed that they too were 'dirty'. (This was said with an air of pleasure.) The worker commented that she appeared to like the mess. Betty said 'Yes, it is soft', and, squeezing it between her fingers, gave the therapist a handful, inviting her to feel how soft it was. Mrs Y observed that the sand was soft and dirty at the same time and that it was both nice and nasty. Betty said she wanted to put some of the mess on her face, and also some on the worker's, so that they were both the same.

The worker now felt she had understood something, and talked to Betty about the softness, dirtyness, niceness and nastiness of the sand and Betty's pleasure in the mess. It seemed clearer now that within Betty's inner world there was a baby Betty who wished that her baby 'oxtail' bottom products should be seen as having the same value as the nourishment her mother could provide; and who envied her therapist's 'lighthouse' mind that could think and throw light on things. If she felt herself to be inferior, the baby might feel 'shot down' and make envious stealthy mouselike attacks. Betty wanted the worker and herself to be 'the same'; but for this to be so, the worker too must have some of the mess. It would have been useful to take this up with her.

These phantasy feelings depicted in play have clearly become part of the session and hence of the therapeutic process. Even the woman cleaning the guard's face seems to have some direct replica, albeit the other way round, in that the worker was to have a dirty face. Betty wished to be the same as the worker and hence exploring this relationship carries with it the possibility of change. Mrs. Y's feelings of being excluded from the lighthouse play may also be relevant, and we are now in a better position to make use of them in our thinking. They may represent a version of Betty's own envious feelings of not being part of, or the same as, the mummy who has the capacity to 'throw light' on things; envious feelings which Betty projected into the worker. The subsequent destruction of the lighthouse may be relevant here too as an attack on difference.

In the seminar, members thought Betty was preoccupied as to whether Mrs Y could 'contain' the mess; this does seem to involve thinking about what seems to be Betty's unbearable pain of difference and her envious feelings towards the worker's potential ability to throw light on her pain. It seemed particularly important for the worker to pay attention to how she was being used by Betty. It also seems important to note that, although much of the play and behaviour represented attack, it was conveyed to the worker, particularly in this part of the session, as a communication asking for thought and understanding.

Betty went off to spread some sand on her face and reached out to put a tiny mark on the worker's face. The latter wondered if Betty felt she had created a mess and that some of this mess had got on to her too. Betty commented that Mrs Y looked and that she herself looked horrid, and that once she had eaten sand: it tasted horrible. The therapist repeated the latter part of the statement in a questioning tone and added that she felt the 'mess' was inside as well as outside. Betty replied that she was always dirty and rubbed some more sand into her face, saying that it would feel rough if you rubbed it in with a scrubbing brush. Leaving the sand on her face, she turned the bucket over and picked up a handful of sand. She dropped this sand from a height into the bucket. 'Now I'm going to drop the sand from a greater height.' She repeated this action a few times, each time increasing the height, and finally said, 'A mess being dropped from a great height and it's going everywhere.' Betty did seem to be struggling with the difference she perceived between the worker and herself and with the painful realization that her 'oxtail' dirty bottom food did indeed taste horrible; it hurt, however, for this to be 'rubbed in'; she seemed to resort to a 'solution' of mess going everywhere, with some implication of involving Mrs Y in the mess.

After the mess 'going everywhere' Betty's demeanour in the session seemed to change. She said she had to clean up, right away; that's what had to be done after a mess had been made. The worker reiterated what Betty had said. She then went on to remind her of the previous week's session when they had talked about how Betty dealt with 'nasty' or 'bad' feelings by getting rid of them or avoiding them as quickly as possible, and wondered whether this mess could be 'thought about' or was just going to be 'cleared away'. But Betty was already piling the contents of the sandtray into the sink – 'everything must be washed for Thursday,' (the day of her next session) she said, and after that they were to clean themselves up. The worker repeated her comment about removing confused or unpleasant feelings as quickly as possible, but although Betty stopped and turned to face the worker for a few seconds and looked as if about to speak, she returned to her rather frantic cleaning activity. By this time the session was almost at an end. Betty said that although the worker was now clean, she herself was still messy and wanted to leave early with the implication of getting to the local café before the end of the session time. Mrs Y pointed out how she seemed to be in a hurry to leave, although she generally tried to prolong the session, and thought they should stay together until the end, as usual. Betty replied she wanted to get away from the mess; she felt dirty and not clean and wanted to go. By now it was in fact the end of the session.

The thinking in the seminar was that Betty, following on the 'mess being dropped from a great height and it's going everywhere' felt it was urgent to clean up the room, representing a 'messed' aspect of the worker, before next time. It seems that by making the mess go everywhere she felt she had damaged the cleaning, containing mind of the worker and so did not have confidence in the latter's ability to think about the mess or to help her to feel clean. Thus, although Mrs Y was working 'containingly' and thinking about the material, to Betty she became a damaged object, and it could have been useful to talk to Betty about her feeling that, in this instance, it was the worker who was unable to think about the mess. Betty, in her attempt to make the worker the same as her, seemingly felt that she had, like Macbeth, made fair foul and was desperately wanting to feel something like 'a little water clears us of this deed' so that by external cleaning the feelings of inner mess would be removed. However, her frantic Lady Macbeth kind of cleaning activity seemed in her mind only to leave the worker/room nominally but untrustworthily clean and she sought to flee to a cleaner, less contaminated place.

In looking at this session we see again the importance of the setting in the therapeutic process in action: how the room is used to represent meaning, the importance of the regularity of her session times to the patient, and how the worker's use of the 'time boundary' has a holding function in the work. We can also see how a more infantile part of the patient than her chronological age comes into the session, and how infantile feelings can be re-experienced in the 'here and now' transference with the worker, thus providing an opportunity for change. Finally, we are able again to examine the use of the concept of containment in action, in this instance to see how the worker can be felt to represent a damaged container in the transference.

BEARING HATE, RIVALRY AND JEALOUSY (A PSYCHIATRIST AND RUPERT)

We now move on to describe work carried out within longer-term relationships, starting with a psychiatrist's discussion of her work in a child guidance clinic in an inner city area.

She had been working with disturbed children on an individual basis for some while before joining the group. Most of the children had had a deprived and disorganized background and were in care. She had told the group that her feeling of not being able to give the children enough to make up for past losses had led to her giving them presents when she left, hoping that this would preserve something of her work for the children and lessen their feelings about the departure of yet another figure in their lives. Her work with the little boy, Rupert, threw light for her on how her own relationship with Rupert could be not only the focus of many feelings in him of jealousy, anger, despair and loss, but also the point of growth for him to develop strength to accept and live with these feelings and to recognize and cherish what goodness there was available for him.

Rupert, the youngest of six children, had been admitted into care when he was three, after his parents were convicted of indecent assault on his older sisters. Rupert's first foster-home placement broke down after seven months because of his behaviour problems. Later he was placed in a new foster-home. He was six when he was referred to a child guidance clinic. His conversation was inconsequential. He had started lying and stealing and it seemed as if he could not make a relationship with anyone. The possibility of moving from his foster-home was also being mooted.

In his first session, after he had explored the toys that were put there for him, Rupert announced he would do some pictures so that Dr M 'could put them up on her board instead of the ones that were there'. He agreed when she suggested he was wondering about the other children who come to see her and play in this room. She put into words his jealousy of them, and acknowledged that having their pictures there was difficult for him. In fact, as this was a shared room, she was not free to remove the other pictures before his session. She added his pictures to the ones already there.

At the beginning of the next session (they met once a week), he looked to check that his picture was still up on the board. He crawled under some chairs and explored this enclosed space, feeling the chair legs and knocking his head against the bottom of the seat. He said it felt like a house and got some doll's furniture and doll figures to put in it.

He put a doll's dress on his finger and said it was a mouse, to frighten this doll family.

Dr M: What would the family do?

Rupert: They will kill it with a knife.

Dr M: They feel very angry with the mouse for coming into their house.

Rupert said *he* was a mouse and crawled under the chairs and pretended to sleep. He said the family were sleeping as well.

Then he asked Dr M to hide the dolls. The mouse was then going to steal the furniture because the people had hidden from him. He got quite agitated as he took the furniture away and put it under a chair at the far end of the room and said, 'Now they'll be sad.' The doll family were then put beside the rubbish bin. Dr M commented the

(Rupert) mouse felt both angry and sad and he wanted the people to feel like that too.

He made himself a garden for his house but put brown Plasticine all over the plants and said it was dirt that was poisoning them and making them die. Dr M said perhaps he was showing her that he sometimes felt dirty and bad inside and that could hurt the good bits. She said if he wanted to show her about what he felt to be dirty poisonous bits, it would not hurt their time together; she would still carry on.

Report then telephoned a garden man to help in his garden. The man was out. Rupert said, 'He doesn't do what I ask. He doesn't come when I want him to.' Again, he spoke with urgency and looked anxiously at Dr M. The (toy) phone rang; it was the police wanting to speak to Dr M. She suggested Rupert might think the police go around looking for bad things and Rupert might feel so bad sometimes that he thought the police would call for him. Rupert nodded. Dr M said she would try to understand these 'bad' parts and help him with it, and added that there were two minutes left to clear up in. The (toy) phone went again and Rupert said into it quite forcibly, 'You must be my friend and don't aggravate me.'

A few weeks later it was the week before Christmas. Rupert ran ahead into the room and checked to see if a spoon was still in his drawer as he had left it. He looked inside the buckets and asked Dr M if she could remember what he had been doing with them yesterday – 'I mean last week,' Dr M remarked that he remembered her room when he was not in it and that he was asking her if she also remembered him. He nodded and asked who had put a brick in one of the buckets. Dr M said he wanted to know about the other children who used the room (the buckets were for anyone to use but she had given Rupert a drawer of small toys kept just for him). Rupert started running water into a bucket.

He looked to check that his picture of a house was still up on the board and said it was a flat where people were unhappy. He asked who had done the other pictures on the board and said he would replace one of them with a new one of his own. As before, Dr M did not let him remove the other pictures.

He said he had made a card for the social worker who brought him. Then he went back to the tap and said it was important to fill the large bucket right up to the top. In fact the water was now flowing over the edge on to the table and down to the floor. Rupert placed paper towels on top of it. Dr M said she had a feeling of tears and unhappiness falling on to the floor. Rupert said yes, and added that the paper towels were like a baby's nappy.

At each stage in this session, Rupert urged Dr M to move the chair nearer so that she could see more closely what he was doing. He returned to looking at the pictures and began to rearrange them on the board, banging the drawing-pins in hard with one of the spades. He was clearly getting as near as he could to attacking the other children's pictures. Dr M made sure that he did not in fact damage any of them, and tried to relate what he was doing to what he must be feeling about the other children she saw. When it was nearly time, he asked Dr M to draw him a picture. He asked her to write his name on the back. He did not look at all at what she had drawn but was very happy, saying 'You have given this to me.' He cleared up the water on the floor carefully and left.

The next week (after Christmas) he decided to change the pictures around again and said again he wanted the board to have only his pictures on it. Most of the drawing-pins had been bent by his previous efforts so he decided just to put up the apple picture from his very first session. He made the apple bigger, saying the farmer had given it to him because no one else cared about it. He wrote on it 'To Dr M, from Rupert,' He then wrote 'Rupert', 'Rupert', 'Rupert' many times on a piece of paper and put it in his drawer, telling Dr M that that would make her remember him when he was not there.

He put up the picture of what he called the 'bad flats' on the board again and said again this was where the children were unhappy. He started hitting the flats with a spade and hitting the tree saying, 'No one cares for them so I might as well knock them down.' When Dr M said he seemed very angry about these flats, he told her yes, the children were making too much noise.

When it was nearly time, he drew a new picture, wrote Dr M's name on it, and gave it to her and said 'We'll look at it together next time.' He put the hammer into a drawer 'so Dr M could hit at the flats when he was not there, if the children were too noisy'. On his way out he asked Dr M to write something for him during the week and put it in his drawer.

As his sessions continued, it became a routine that he wanted the light switched off and the door shut as they left. His drawer became very important to him. He would wrap up a spoon or a box of crayons in paper and put them in the drawer at the end of a session and check next time: 'No one's found it.' Before the next holiday he wanted to take the wrapped parcel away with him 'in case some robbers come'. He often called Dr M closer 'to watch carefully what he was doing' and made her a 'thinking hat' out of paper.

She had to experience a lot of painful material with him, especially just before or after a holiday break. She was told to telephone him (with the toy phones) but each time he banged his phone down saying, 'Wrong number' or left his phone off the hook. He hid under a coat, and fell out of 'bed'. He told Dr M to throw things at him. He went to hide and told her 'You say you're sad because I've gone.' And then 'I'm phoning another boy to come. But you can come tomorrow.'

It looked as if the mouse who crept into the doll's home was Rupert himself, an unwelcome intruder everywhere. The doll family were going to kill him with a knife. When the doll family hid from the mouse he stole the family's furniture in revenge.

Rupert himself was trapped in a vicious circle where deprivation led to angry attacks and bad behaviour on his part; this in turn led to further rejection of him by others.

The mouse's wish to belong somewhere was paralleled by Rupert's relationship with Dr M. He showed Dr M how much he wanted to 'belong' in the room of her mind. He wanted his picture to be up on the board and he checked to see if she remembered him and would continue seeing him. He also made it plain that he wanted to be the only one, the only child she saw; the violence of his jealousy of the other children seen by her in the room was a recurring theme. But in this relationship he was not punished and sent away as he feared (the police wanted to speak to Dr M). Dr M certainly prevented his acting out his jealousy by spoiling the other childrens' pictures. But she also put into words his flooding mess of tears, jealous hatred, anger, loneliness and despair. Rupert could begin to feel that he was understood and contained.

It was quite clear to Rupert that Dr M's capacity to think about him, remember him and hold on to him in her mind was all important, and the present that he wanted from her was to be given this ability to hold on to goodness within himself (and not say 'No one cares for it so I might as well knock it down.'). One hour a week is not very much time in a child's life; nevertheless it is moving to see how Rupert valued and treasured this time and used it to grow. The pressure on his foster-family grew less as Rupert explored the overflowing bucket in the session, instead of urinating over the wallpaper at home. After eight months' therapy, there was no longer talk of this foster-placement breaking down.

MOVING FORWARD FROM MINDLESS BEHAVIOUR (A SPECIALIST TEACHER AND COLIN)

We read in Chapter 1 that the staff of Len's school asked for help with him because of his severe withdrawal and failure to learn. A very different problem, that of a noisy, restless child disrupting the class and attacking other children or the teacher, led to the referral of Colin, then in his last year of primary school.

The session is taken from a slightly later stage in his therapy when he had already made a firm relationship with his worker, so this gives us an opportunity to think about the nature of the relationship. The material also reflects some of the problems inherent in carrying out this type of work in a school setting.

Colin was referred to a specialist teacher in his primary school when he was nine. He was violent towards other children, often dangerous. He was rude to the teachers, and impervious to any form of punishment. He shouted abuse through the school railings at anyone who happened to be passing by. He was often found stealing from other children, or stealing school equipment.

The specialist teacher, Mrs V, learned that Colin had had a very disturbed start in life. His parents quarrelled violently and his father left home shortly after his birth; within a few months his mother became pregnant by another man. Colin's behaviour had always been bad at home; he stole things at home as well.

Mrs V was asked to see Colin on his own for four periods a week, to see if she could make contact with him and try and understand with him the driving force behind his behaviour. The first months were spent trying to keep him within the playroom and trying to find some way of making any sense out of his restless, mindless activity. Colin began to show signs of looking forward to the sessions. A large wendy house in the playroom became the centre and focus of his sessions: he was at his most violent when in it, but it was also when he was in the wendy house that he began to be able to talk about his bad behaviour.

The sessions were then disrupted by industrial action, by the half term break, and by Mrs V's absence in Bristol for a day. Colin's behaviour outside the sessions, which had improved considerably, now relapsed. Mrs. V's account of the sessions that follow show how, once the therapeutic setting is re-established, Colin is able to explore with Mrs. V something of his inner world, and something of the forces that prompted his behaviour.

As I entered the classroom Colin turned and pulled a face and giggled. His class teacher looked at me with a look which spoke volumes about the morning she had had. Colin put on his coat and walked into the hall, whereupon he produced a plastic toy which fires off a spinning helicopter-like thing when a string is pulled. Colin pulled the string, the thing whirled off and Colin whirled off after it.

I stated quite firmly 'Colin must not play with that in the hall'. 'Yes miss', he replied, and giggled further. He came up to me, then whirled away again, at which point I took hold of his arm and said that he must come with me. There was a teacher sitting on the dais doing some art work; she gave me a sympathetic look as I guided Colin out of the hall.

On passing his sister's classroom he tried to pull faces through the glass at her and at other children. I said, 'No' quite firmly and marched him away. I then said that it was better if I held his hand, and he said, 'Yes'. I took his hand and out we went into the playground. He asked if he might twirl the toy now we were outside. I said yes, he could just once and then he must put it in his pocket because we had to cross the road.

I walked across the yard as he fired off the toy and as he picked it up I held out my hand and he ran up and put his hand in mine. Colin said, 'What did you do in Bristol yesterday?' I said that I had been to see someone. He said that he had been there and I mentioned I remembered he had told me he had an aunt there. I felt that even though he appeared to be 'flying away from things' he was making a point about my absence.

On reaching the other building Colin ran across to the front door and stopped inside and waited for me. Inside, the headteacher said to Colin that he wanted to see him and did I know he had been naughty, and something about a watch – perhaps Colin's class teacher had told me? I nodded and tried to steer Colin away to my room as I felt that it was bad enough for Colin to know that I must hear a lot of things, without someone making a point of telling me in front of him.

When we got into the playroom he seemed at a loss and wandered about a little and then said, 'Sir wanted to see me because I strangled a boy.'

I said, 'You were fighting?' and he said, 'Yes.'

He went into the wendy house and began banging about. I looked through the little window and he said, 'I smashed a watch. You know, miss (his teacher) told you.'

I said, 'You don't like people telling me things?'

'No,' he said.

'Was it an accident?' I said.

'No, Mick told me to do it.'

'So you think it was his fault?'

'Yes,' – pause – 'No.'

In the main room, he got out the tape recorder and played a tape. Then he went into the wendy house again and said 'Come in when I call.' When he called he sounded rather friendly and welcoming, but when I got into the wendy house I saw with a sense of shock that he had rolled back his eyelids. He stood like that giggling and I said, 'You're trying to frighten me, you like frightening me.'

He said, 'Yes' and came back into the larger room. He began to play the tape again and speeded it up, giggling at the sound of it.

'My mum smacks me when I giggle and then I can't stop... something makes me do it, I have been like it all year.'

'You want it to stop?'

'Yes... my friend has gone away. Not Jerry, another one.'

'And you miss him?' For a moment he seemed sad.

He leaned on the cupboard and it opened. He put on a coat that was there. He picked up a spray can which I took off him. He sat down.

I said, 'You don't seem able to stay still for long.'

'It's silly,' he said.

I asked what it felt like, and he said, 'Silly.'

'And you don't feel you can stop it?'

'No.'

He went to his box, but then took out an old calculator from the cupboard. It was jammed. Colin said he was going to drop it to unstick it but he wasn't going to break it. Then he threw it down and kicked it against the table. I said, 'Perhaps you do feel like breaking this?' He asked if I would tell sir. I said that what happened in the room with me was between us and that I did not tell others. He seemed to accept this. I said we would have to go soon. He asked if he could twirl his toy, but then having twirled it, he could not find the top, and became distressed. I helped him look and when it was found I asked him to put it back in his pocket. He did, and took my hand as we walked back to his class.

Colin was sitting quietly in his classroom when his next session was due to begin, watching some other children play with puppets. He was reluctant to leave but took my hand and we slowly walked out.

He was very subdued and said, 'I wanted to do the puppets.'

I said, 'I'm sorry you had to miss them, and you must feel cross with me.'

Once inside the playroom he said, 'I want to go in ten minutes.' I acknowledged this but said he would have to stay until two o'clock.

'I don't want to, I'm going to miss my puppets.' I said I was sorry about the puppets. He told me his puppet was an owl.

He then went into the wendy house and began to clatter on the typewriter, banging on it heavily. I looked through at him and eventually went in. He looked round and said 'Yes?' as if he were the teacher and I were the intruding child. I said I wanted to see.

He began to dismantle an old duplicating machine, saying 'I'm going to take this motor', in a way that implied 'If I can't have my puppets I'll have this.'

I said, 'If you can't have what you want you'll have something else?' He did not answer but carried on pushing the plastic bag part of the machine, which spewed out the rather foul-looking remains of old printing fluid on to the floor. I said that he wanted to mess up my things perhaps because I had spoiled his. He denied this and then went to fill the bag with water from the tap, through the tube extension of the bag. Then he squirted water out through the tube into a cup.

He filled the bag again and went to water the plants. This he did very solemnly and carefully, going back for more water when needed. When all the plants were watered he said, 'There's a doll that drinks here.' He picked a cloth doll and first gently gave it the water. He asked where the scissors were, and I gave him some. 'I have to cut a mouth,' he said. He did this and then stuck the tube in and said, 'She is only a baby.' I asked if the tube hurt her and he said it didn't, but it looked like a hospital drip to me. Colin went to get another doll and made a hole in her mouth. He pushed the tube in and said she was drinking.

It looked horribly forced to me. The water began spurting out of the doll's head on to the floor. He seemed surprised and then showed me a hole where it had come through. He left the doll on the floor.

He filled a little pistol with water and squirted it into the sink. He filled it again just as I was telling him it was time to go. He said that he wanted to water a little tree outside and I said that he could on the way. We went outside and he squirted the gun at the tree and asked if I would get more water. I returned with the water but could not see him. I called and then began to water the tree.

'I thought I was going to water it,' said a voice from a bush. 'Yes, you can,' I said, He smiled, watered the tree, and then set off to the gate. He waited at the gate for me to take his hand.

In the discussion that followed, several members of the group who worked in schools in a similar way said that other teachers naturally enough tended to report to them any misbehaviour of the children they saw individually, as if it were their sole responsibility, sometimes almost their fault. This laid on them a burden of carrying guilt, and of needing to achieve results. They often felt isolated in what they were trying to do, as colleagues would imply that it was easy for them, seeing only one child at a time, whereas they had a whole class to contend with. If a child's behaviour improved, but then relapsed under the impact of a long holiday break or other interruption, as with Colin, it was difficult to help colleagues see any connection between the two: the relapse was often taken as a sign that the whole method was no use.

It was also difficult to convey to them the significance of their relationship with the child and why, for instance, it was better not to discuss a child with the specialist teacher, in front of the child himself. Some workers found it was difficult to explain why their sessions needed to be at the same time of day, and why it was better not to encourage the child to be twenty minutes late for his session while he completed a class project.

Mrs V had been working in this specialist role in her school for some time, and was fortunate in the support and encouragement she got from her colleagues; and she had also been working with some of the children long enough for the benefits to have become apparent to the school community. All the same, it was apparent that she was subject to some of these pressures, and that Colin also found it hard to accept that his relationship with Mrs V should be invaded by a third person, whether this was the headteacher or his class teacher.

He seemed to link himself concretely with the spinning helicopter that went whirling off at random. This was his response to the series of breaks in his sessions; he no longer felt 'gathered in', securely held. He did not appear to feel angry, or sad, about the missed sessions; instead the mindless whirling and silly giggles seemed to be his way of getting rid of any feelings. All that was left was his extremely irritating, 'naughty' behaviour. Once they got into the privacy of the playroom, and specifically into the smaller enclosed space of the little wendy house, he began to tell her something about his acts (not his feelings). He was unable to make any link between his murderous attack on another boy and his smashing another boy's watch with his anger, hurt and jealousy at not seeing her, and wondering who she was with instead.

Mrs V described for the group what was happening when Colin was in the wendy house playing the tape. She felt excluded and unwanted, and wondered what was going on in there. When he called her, it sounded like a welcoming invitation, so she went in with a feeling of pleasurable anticipation, only to feel an appalling shock at being confronted by this eyeless monster. Colin conveyed to her something about a hoped-for friendly reunion between two people that goes appallingly wrong; instead of a hoped-for friendly welcome, there is a sightless horror.

And in the next session, instead of an affectionate feeding, the baby dolls have holes cut into them and are force-fed. The relationship at this point has similarities with a mother-baby relationship which has gone badly wrong. Colin would have a chance to explore and perhaps amend it with Mrs. V but only if she can be attuned to the feelings he arouses in her, and can hold on to them and think about them with him long enough for them to become tolerable.

Watering the plants and feeding the dolls gives way eventually to firing a water pistol; his murderous feelings about other children are now brought into the session, where they can be acknowledged and thought about, especially in relation to the ending of his session and the next child that takes his place. His naughty behaviour outside in the school now begins to have some meaning, and looks like an acting-out of the unbearable feelings aroused in him by the repeated cancellation of his sessions, and the suspicion that other 'children' were enjoying her company elsewhere.

The play of cutting into the dolls and forcibly feeding them is a symbolic representation of his conflicting, violent feelings portrayed within the session, and available for understanding there, as opposed to a mindless whirling and giggling evacuation. So the long months of work with Mrs V are helping him move towards being able to contain, think about, and control violent emotions. When the experience is too extreme for him, he 'speeds up the tape and giggles', a way of evading thought, and mental pain, that will be discussed further in Chapter 13.

RECAPTURING THE ABILITY TO LOVE (A PSYCHIATRIST AND SAM)

Sam was nine when his social worker referred him. His father had left when Sam was nine months old; there were then two different stepfathers, each of whom was said to have bruised and beaten Sam (his mother had also caused him injuries). Sam's mother moved frequently so he had been to a number of schools in his first eighteen months of school life. When Sam was six he and his two younger stepsisters were taken into care because of repeated non-accidental injuries. Sam's symptoms included difficult behaviour, vomiting, wetting and soiling. Attempts were made to foster him but two foster-home placements broke down because he was upsetting the other children. When he was referred to the child psychiatric department he had been in a children's home for two years. His mother's visits were infrequent and unreliable and had finally ceased. In the children's home he was disruptive and over-active; other problems were bed wetting, temper tantrums and stealing.

It was arranged that he should see Dr N for weekly individual play therapy. The social worker and the care staff of the children's home asked for time with Dr N to think about the best ways of handling Sam's difficult behaviour, and fairly frequent meetings were held at first, but kept separate from her work with Sam.

His first sessions were spent arranging a battle between toy soldiers, in which he and Dr N were on opposite sides, and he killed most of the soldiers. In the next weeks the battles became very confusing as from moment to moment Sam would switch from being a baddie to a goodie, or be a baddie pretending to be a goodie, or a goodie disguised as a baddie; Dr N was told she was on his side, but a moment later was an enemy. It seemed that Sam could not manage to draw any firm distinction between good and bad or love and hate; the goodies and baddies kept getting muddled up. The ability to achieve a split between idealized and feared seems to be a necessary early step towards mental growth. Here, Dr N had the impression that Sam was not able to make any use of her help in these first weeks. Even if she was told she was on Sam's side, she still ended up being shot by him. Each battle ended with everything being destroyed, and the common feature to each session was the feeling of emptiness and desolation with which Dr N was left.

Most of Dr N's questions or comments were ignored, or met by a belittling reply. Sam soon took on a very controlling role as the General, while Dr N was just a soldier. Sometimes Sam was the teacher while Dr N was the child, but the roles were basically the same: she was ordered to fetch and carry for him; she was mocked and punished for being so stupid. It became very difficult for Dr N to think in these sessions because Sam was so controlling. When she tried to suggest what he might be feeling she was met with sarcastic replies: 'Really?' or (perhaps revealingly) 'You kill me.'

Sam seemed to be making Dr N feel she was forever the victim, who was attacked and betrayed and who never knew from moment to moment whom she could trust. In the games she was helpless and vulnerable and therefore this meant she deserved to be mocked and belittled. It gradually became clear that Sam was needing her to 'carry' his own unbearable experience. She had to feel the pain, to tolerate and try to digest it as he had been unable to do.

Gradually one or two clues emerged that he did in fact value these sessions and treasured his time with her. Stories about having to fight off robbers who were trying to steal his jewellery or his gold gave way to more explicit anxiety about guarding his box (a small collection of toys and drawing materials that Dr N kept for him to use in his sessions). He asked how his box could be kept safe when he was not there. Another time he asked why it had not got his name on it. He wrote a label for it with his name followed by 'please do not touch'. In a later session he complained that his box was the wrong way round on the shelf and his name could not be seen. The box obviously carried a lot of his feelings about Dr N; her importance to him and his need to feel she remembered him and thought about him. It was also a focus for the shakiness of his trust in her, and for his suspicions about the other children she saw.

He became very fond of a soft furry toy dog, and began to let Dr N see a glimpse of a gentle side of his nature, stroking her hand with a soft puppet: 'This is Boo Boo, he has come to help you.' After some months of therapy he made a house for himself with furniture and sat in it carefully dressing some dolls. He made a nappy and put it on the baby doll. But then he told Dr N 'We must kill the babies ourselves before the others shoot them,' and again later he dressed himself in a baby's gown and sat on the top of the toy pushchair, asking Dr N to push him backwards and forwards. He sat still and silent while she did so and while she spoke about his baby feelings. Then he made a trumpeting sound and said 'When I hear the war cry I must turn into a soldier again.'

His distracted, over-active, aggressive behaviour in the children's home had disappeared, and he no longer had temper tantrums. The staff found he could turn to them for help when something went wrong. He was still wetting, however, and still taking other children's possessions and there was obviously not going to be any quick solution to Sam's problems.

The care and concern of his social worker and the staff of the children's home were obviously essential to Sam, and the improvement in his behaviour in the children's home and at school was an encouragement.

The work with Dr N was helping him recapture the ability to love, to recognize and try to hold on to anything good in his relationships with other people, and to value any good qualities of his own. The question remained how far he was going to be able to strengthen this capacity in the face of his distrust of her, his envy and suspicion of the other children she saw, and also in the face of his real difficulties in the outer world. With Dr N's help he had, it seemed, developed a greater capacity to separate good and bad, projecting his 'bad' feelings outwards, and thus creating space within himself for the softer baby feelings to develop at least partially. Such 'splitting' (which we discuss further in Chapter 14) is a necessary developmental step prior to integration and illustrates the therapeutic relationship as a point of growth.

Chapter 8

Working with Negative Feelings and Behaviour

BEING MET WITH HOSTILITY

Offering time to someone, listening and trying to understand, but being met with sullenness, silence or angry attacks, is a daunting experience. Many of the children and young people described in this book fall into that pattern. It cannot have been easy for the worker concerned to bear the sarcasm and contempt shown by Ahmed (Chapter 2) or the belittling, disruptive and unresponsive behaviour of Harman (Chapter 6), Colin and Sam (Chapter 7) or Graham (Chapter 9). These were not isolated moments in an otherwise positive relationship: they were the unrelenting pattern over many weeks or months.

For some of the children, play itself was impossible. They could not play in a symbolic way to work through their anxieties. Many of them would have been categorized as having 'behaviour disorder' and until fairly recently they would perhaps have been considered unsuitable for individual therapeutic work. Nevertheless, they form a considerable proportion of children and young people referred for help to one or other of the professions whose work is described in this book.

As we have seen in Chapter 1 ('The client's initial perceptions of the worker and the setting'), a child or client may come to his first (and later) sessions with fear, anger or mistrust which have nothing to do with the personality or physical appearance of the therapist. Nevertheless it is hard not to feel a personal sense of rejection. It can be difficult to believe in the positive value of our work, when confronted repeatedly with hostility.

A SILENT CHILD (AN OCCUPATIONAL THERAPIST AND ANDREW)

Miss B brought some sessions for discussion in the first term of the course that gave us a chance to think about how to work with silent or negativistic children. She gave the group some background details about her patient, a 10-year-old boy called Andrew. He had been referred by the paediatrician. Andrew's symptoms included repeated soiling at home and at school, and also apparently in his sleep. He was described as sullen, disobedient and unresponsive. His mother narrated the appalling circumstances of his first five years. When he was born, there were three other little children under five. Andrew's father was an alcoholic and used most of the money coming into the family on drink. The electricity remained cut off for a year because of unpaid bills. Sam's mother left home for a year at this time and she left his father several more times in the first four years of Andrew's life, taking the children with her, before the final split. Another child was born before she left.

Miss B had started seeing Andrew for individual once-weekly sessions three months earlier. He was almost completely silent and immobile, and it was obvious that the degree of his silence and inactivity was more than just a child's caution or anxiety in response to a strange environment. Even after a number of sessions he was still unable to talk or play. She saw him twice, then he missed a week because he had gone out to play and no one had gone to fetch him.

The session we now present followed on this missed session and was the third time she had seen him. After this Miss B was due to start a seven-week holiday break, about which she had told Andrew when they first met.

Andrew had so far been seen in a different room each time, because of building work. Miss B's account follows.

I brought farm toys, wax crayons, crayons and paints into the room. Andrew came in with me. I asked if he had enjoyed his school holiday so far; he said yes. I asked when he went back to school; he shrugged. I said I was sorry not to have seen him the week before. He sat down but still looked awkward, clenching his fists and occasionally looking up at me. I asked if he was confused about coming to see me; he eventually shrugged. I said that by spending fifty minutes together I could get to know him better and perhaps understand and help him understand things that were difficult for him. Andrew made no response and remained silent both to my suggestions about his feelings and to my attempts to help him tell me anything about home, school or holiday.

After about twenty minutes I asked if he would like to do a painting; he shrugged. I said I would fetch water to mix the paints. He was sitting by the paints when I returned. I began mixing paints and water; he watched me closely. I asked him again if he wanted to paint, but he did not move. A little later I placed a pot of paint near to him; he mixed it carefully and asked me if it was OK. I said it looked fine and asked him to try it out on the paper. He did this and then mixed another colour and tested it. When all the paints were mixed he sat and waited. I offered him paper and then began to draw on my paper. Andrew suddenly picked up his pencil and started. He became absorbed in drawing and painting a picture which he said was of himself and his younger sister Louise on the beach on holiday. When he had finished, I chatted a little about his family; he answered my questions and named them. I asked if he wanted to draw anything else but he did not reply. We waited until the end of the session which was about ten minutes and Andrew then washed the paint brushes and helped me to clear up.

Miss B did not refer to her seven-week holiday break, which was to follow this session. When Andrew left the room, his mother was there with a large bag of shopping;

Andrew ran up to her eagerly and offered to help carry it for her. The following session was the second one after the seven-week holiday break. The first one had had to be held in yet another temporary room; from this one on, they had an established permanent room.

Andrew and I used the new playroom; Andrew immediately sat down on the chair, leaning right back, so as to sit comfortably. But he looked tense, looking around the room and occasionally at me, shuffling his feet and playing with his hands. He often frowned and clenched and unclenched his fists. I asked him how he was and he said OK. I said it was a newly decorated room, and as with the other rooms he could use the time and everything in the room as he wished.

We continued in silence for about half an hour. Andrew continued to look at me occasionally. I always met his gaze, and sometimes he gave me a half smile. Most of the time he looked at his hands and played games with them or cleaned his nails, sometimes he sat on his hands. He asked if he could go to the toilet. I said, did he know where it was? He said yes; I said of course he could go.

When Andrew returned he pushed the door to but did not close it properly. I said perhaps he did not want the door properly closed; he shrugged. We continued sitting. I commented that Andrew was looking at his hands a lot and using them for little games. He pulled a thread from his tracksuit trousers and spent some time twisting it around his fingers, pulling it tight and snapping it; he then rolled it on his thigh. He asked again if he could go to the toilet; I asked if he was asking because he needed to go to the toilet, or was it difficult for him to sit with me. He said he did want to go to the toilet.

When he returned Andrew left the door slightly open, and sat down again. He put his hands inside the muff on his tracksuit top, and played games with his fingers through the cloth, particularly thrusting forward his fingers; he seemed to be watching what his hands were doing. I said he wanted to see what his hands were doing, but did not want me to see. A little later he let his finger tips show at the end of the muff, then quickly hid them. I smiled; he was watching for my reaction and smiled back playfully. He repeated this, then continued to play with his hands hidden.

I warned Andrew we had only five minutes left; he pursed his lips and took his hands out of the muff and reverted to clenching and unclenching them. When I said it was time to finish Andrew hesitated before getting up and leaving the room with me.

Miss B said she was finding it difficult to know what to do with Andrew. She thought he seemed quite anxious, by the way he twisted his hands and so forth, so she had tried to encourage him to paint. He asked if his mixing of the paint was OK; she said it looked fine 'because she wanted to help him over his anxiety so he could get on with the painting'. One member suggested she could instead put his question back to him: 'What do *you* think, do you think it's OK?'

The leader suggested the group could explore together what Andrew's anxieties might be. Many ideas were offered. He had been referred for soiling day and night, and had been physically investigated in the paediatric department of the same hospital where he now saw Miss B. Perhaps he had had anal examinations which he may have experienced as intrusive. He might be anxious about something physical being done to him now. Also, he might be afraid that Miss B would be angry with him if he 'made a mess' with the paints. Miss B said at the end she thought she could have talked about some of this with Andrew rather than try and reassure him by saying his mixing of the paint 'looked fine'.

Miss B referred again to Andrew's 'difficult silence' and shrugs. A member said this was just Andrew's sullenness and negativism, implying there was nothing here worth further investigation. Another felt that the difficult silence was what Andrew brought to the therapist and suggested that his later play with his fingers sounded like a baby's game of 'peek-a-boo'. She felt Andrew was needing to be a baby here in the therapy and that this might be one reason for his not using words. She wished he could ask for a cuddle and a hug; but she supposed he couldn't be lovable just yet. Someone said that when Andrew ran to help mother after the session wasn't that a slap in the face for Miss B, the worker? Someone else said on the contrary, the lovableness *should* have gone to his mother, and the difficult behaviour to the worker. Miss B said here that in fact the social worker reported that Andrew's soiling had stopped at school (though not at home yet) and that mother was finding him much easier to cope with.

The group was still as a loss over what Miss B could do about Andrew's silence. The leader asked at this point whether Miss B had referred at all to the missed sessions, the seven weeks' holiday, or the three changes of room? Miss B said her long holiday and the room changes had certainly come up over and over again with the other children she worked with. But she had never mentioned them to Andrew because she didn't think the sessions meant anything to him. He always seemed so uninterested and uninvolved. Similarly she had not thought there was any point in giving him a small box for himself, since he never showed any interest in the toys; and the picture he had done of himself and his sister on the beach was lost in the room change-overs.

The leader suggested Miss B was having to carry the whole burden for Andrew, that he left it to her to give any meaning to the missed session, the holiday break, the repeated changes of room. In fact he seemed to be inviting her to attribute no value to their work together, and she had been rather despairingly agreeing with this (by feeling the room changes, missed times, lost picture, did not matter). The leader made brief reference to soiling being a way of getting rid of something concretely, instead of letting it be held on to and thought about. A health visitor in the seminar asked if this could link with the chaotic early years of Andrew's life which Miss B had outlined to the group. His mother had had to struggle to look after four small children with very little money and no support from her alcoholic husband; sometimes she was homeless. It is easy to imagine that in these circumstances she might not have had much time or energy for Andrew; there might not have been much space for him in her mind. In this context it is obviously especially unfortunate for this boy that there had had to be so many changes of room and missed sessions.

Miss B had felt she did not want to try and look for lovableness, or coax him out of his difficult silence; that it was indeed the silence itself that Andrew was bringing her. But it seemed as if he could not give any content to it. Here we might think about a baby who is apathetic or withdrawn and does not even protest. A vicious circle gets set up: people give this baby less attention because it is demanding nothing. Similarly Miss B did not talk with Andrew about her seven weeks' holiday, or about his feelings over the rooms (though she had seen the need to with other children she worked with) because 'she didn't think the sessions meant anything to him; he always seemed so uninterested and uninvolved'. (Nevertheless he did seem able to pick up something from her gentle attentiveness; some joy and cheerfulness was released for mother at the end of the first session; and his game with his finger tips in the second session gave Miss B a second's glimpse of a positive interaction.)

Throughout this book, and particularly in Chapter 10, we describe how a baby can communicate feeling states to his mother and how a mother receives the chaotic sense impressions of the baby, ordering them and giving them meaning. These major insights developed by Bion (1962a, b) from the work of Klein (1946) have made it possible to attempt working with silent, and negative, children in a similar way. Recognition of negative feelings leads to a feeling of being understood and to a lessening of anxiety; this in turn forms the basis of the truly positive feelings a child or client develops.

And if the negative feelings are brought into the sessions and accepted there, this can help a child to bring about a helpful split between good and bad, positive and negative, love and hate. So it did in fact seem very encouraging that Andrew could turn with love towards his mother at the end of the first session we discussed. If the negative feelings are acknowledged in the sessions and not evaded or denied, then loving feelings are freed to make the most of what the home environment can offer. And perhaps the negative feelings themselves can get slowly modified in time (as we shall see with Graham in Chapter 9). A child or client can gradually see how much his own mistrust or cynicism had added to a bad experience. (Sam's mistrust of Dr N with regard to the other children which we discussed in Chapter 7 is an example.)

A CONTROLLING CHILD (A PSYCHIATRIST AND ANNABEL)

Dr C brought to the seminar two sessions with Annabel, a 9-year-old girl he had been seeing once weekly for some months. Annabel lived in a comfortable middle-class home; she was the only child of rather elderly parents, who were both successful in their different spheres of life, and had fairly rigid ideas about the upbringing of Annabel. Her mother found her manipulative, 'hard', unloving and difficult to control.

The room in which she was usually seen had been extensively altered and made into two smaller ones and no other was available. In the first session brought to the seminar, Annabel had refused to come into the therapy room at all. She elected to spend the session in the waiting/reception area where the secretary worked, within sight and sound of anyone who happened to come in. Most of the time Dr C could not see what she was doing, and when Annabel spoke it was mainly to the receptionist, to the exclusion of Dr C. It was also plain that the receptionist, and anyone else coming in and out of the waiting area, would be able to hear everything Dr C said to Annabel. In the second session Dr C invited her to choose between playrooms. Annabel asked Dr C why she came, and he replied, 'To help us think about your relationship to your mum.' The last half of this session was also spent outside the therapy room, mainly on a rocking-horse in the corridor.

In the discussion afterwards, Dr C asked whether being outside the therapy room really mattered. He felt he should not impose rules on Annabel. He thought perhaps she needed to rebel, as her parents were rather rigid. He also thought it was helping her express her feelings about the non-availability of her usual room. Someone else agreed, saying surely he could only go along with what Annabel did, as his function was to 'mirror'.

Another member questioned whether it could still be called therapy if in fact

Annabel was simply sitting in the waiting room chatting to the receptionist? Others asked if it was wrong to have rules, such as staying inside the room, if the reason for them was explained to the patient. This led to a discussion of what indeed might be the reason. Would it just be for the therapist's peace of mind and to save loss of face in front of colleagues? Or would it be empty rigidity for its own sake? Someone said that Dr C could not in any case avoid the disruption to the playroom by the workmen. The leader suggested that Dr C did carry responsibility for the boundaries of the therapy. He needed to make it plain to Annabel that he was offering a firm commitment with a regular time and a regular place for their work together as far as it was in his power to do so. Offering and safeguarding this framework would be an indication of the worker's willingness to struggle to retain and think about the patient's material. In the second session Dr C again abdicated responsibility for the setting by inviting Annabel to have a choice of room, and this seemed to give rise to feelings of insecurity in her; she asked why she was coming, and then spent the last half of this session outside too.

Dr C's reply to her question, that it was to think about her relationship to her mother, also led to discussion. The group spent some time speculating about her relationship with her parents. The leader pointed out that it could only be speculation since it could not be observed directly by Dr C. But Annabel's relation to Dr C himself *could* be observed. She was making him feel excluded while she had a cosy chat with the receptionist, and this negative behaviour was occurring in the present. Dr C said he found it impossible to talk about it in front of the receptionist, another reason for the privacy of the therapy room.

Someone asked whether he should physically enforce the boundary; should he carry Annabel back into the room, or should he lock the door once she was inside it? Similar dilemmas faced the worker whose sessions with Nicholas are described later in this chapter.

Here, it is worth noting that while workers tolerate a good deal of behaviour that would not be tolerated in other contexts (as for example with Nicholas below) we feel that a worker should make it plain that he or she will not collude in a child's wrecking the session by effectively making it impossible for it to be held; and the worker would need to make it clear that the session took place in a designated room.

Dr C told the group that Annabel was very controlling when they were in the therapy room, adopting the role of a strict teacher, saying to Dr C things like, 'You've wasted that paper' and 'Stop that silly noise!' She set him a maths test and marked his work 'not very good'. Dr C realized he was feeling bored, his comments were ignored and he felt belittled. Annabel told him that she had 'lost' a maths test because of day-dreaming. Dr C asked her what her dreams were about; 'nothing much' was the answer. Some members of the seminar felt the day-dreams would have been valuable material. On the other hand, the day-dreams were Annabel's way of escaping from struggling with something she could not manage, and there was a risk that if Dr C pursued these day-dreams, it could also be because they seemed an easier, pleasanter alternative to tackling the more difficult theme. Dr C was finding it difficult to see any meaning in the irritating maths sequence, which repeated something Annabel had done with him over and over again in earlier sessions.

One of the problems with repetitive behaviour in therapy is that the worker is likely to feel that she had explored it so often, there is nothing new to say about it; it then becomes very difficult to remain open to each session as a new experience. The temptation is for the worker to shut herself off from the emotional experience of the session. Sam, who was described in Chapter 7, also played at schools or soldiers over and over again and was always the domineering authority.

Some children, particularly of junior school age, often spend a lot of time playing repetitive 'school' games and behaving in a very controlling way towards the therapist. Workers sometimes feel that this is wasting time and that they should encourage the child to do something more imaginative and produce 'valuable material' – perhaps like Dr C asking Annabel what her dreams were about. But was there anything in the way she used the relationship with Dr C itself that could be thought about? Annabel may have had quite strong feelings when she found her usual room had been altered and effectively no longer existed. She did not make any direct reference to her feelings about it; but she behaved in a way that made Dr C feel excluded. She was also making him feel baffled and foolish in the maths tests. If Annabel was making him experience uncomfortable feelings, could this not also be valuable material? We have seen in Chapters 1 and 2 that the therapist's mind can act as a container for holding feelings emanating from the patient and so provides a basis for experiencing and thinking about emotions that the child in this instance may not be able to do herself.

ACTIVE AGGRESSION IN THE SESSIONS (A SOCIAL WORKER AND NICHOLAS, A MENTALLY HANDICAPPED ADOLESCENT)

The next illustration follows a therapeutic relationship with a disturbed, aggressive adolescent over a number of months. We hope it will be possible in this way to see how his disturbed behaviour begins to acquire meaning.

Mrs D, a social worker with responsibility for the mentally handicapped, was asked if she could offer any help to Nicholas. He was fourteen, living in a hostel and attending a special school. He had been brought up by his widowed mother, who also had the care of her own housebound mother. She lived in a town some distance from the hostel though she visited him fairly frequently. He also had regular contact with an uncle and aunt who lived locally. His speech had been normal until he was seven, when he had been sent to a boarding special school; since then he had been an elective mute. His behaviour was unpredictable; he seemed unable to make relationships, and was failing to learn. Mrs D recognized that he was severely disturbed, and no other source of help being available, she decided to see him for weekly individual sessions on a trial basis to see if he could gain any benefit.

A number of sessions were brought to the seminar for discussion over a period of time. Some of the understanding that emerged in these discussions is included in the narrative of the sessions to make this chaotic material more accessible. But some general discussion on his difficult behaviour is grouped together at the end.

In his first session he took the box of equipment Mrs D had got ready for him (pencils, felt pens, paper, Plasticine, a few cars, a soft ball, etc.) and threw each item one by one at her. Then he collected all the strewn objects into a plastic bag, and handed that to her. He continued, making little parcels of whatever he could find, and giving each one to her. Then he got inside a blanket on the couch, and very insistently wanted Mrs D to join him there. For each of the next four sessions, Nicholas began in the same way; he took everything out of the box and threw it at Mrs D. The second session after the Christmas break began differently, however: Nicholas threw the soft ball to Mrs D and indicated she should throw it back, and this became an interchange.

Every following session for many months began with this ball-throwing to each other. It was tempting to read into it some sort of comment on their relationship – a coming together and a going apart – a soft-ball therapist? One that got lost and had to be looked for – if it was thrown hard would it come back hard? If he was angry with her when she ended the session, would she take it out on him when they next met?

We discussed if one could think Nicholas was in this way working out something about his relationship with Mrs D. Freud described his grandchild's game of dangling a cotton-reel over the side of his cot and pulling it up again, in the context of working out something about his mother's absence (Freud, 1920).

But with Nicholas the ball game seemed more of a concrete experience, an event in itself, with no meaning to it in his mind, but just a pleasurable evacuation. He often burped or farted while throwing it, as if this ball-throwing was also passing over to her some concrete gases from inside him. When the ball rolled into a corner he stood with his back to her and threw it at her 'backwards' from his bottom, often with much laughter. When she spoke of his anger at her leaving him and turning her back on him, he again laughed noisily as if to get rid of an unpleasant experience. Sometimes he seemed to 'act the fool', deliberately making himself look like a caricature of a village idiot. Mrs D therefore had to give meaning to the ball game; in Nicholas's mind it was without meaning. The difference between a concrete evacuation and the ability to experience a feeling with meaning is discussed in Chapter 13. ('The capacity to tolerate mental pain').

The ball game was always followed by, or sometimes interspersed with, throwing everything from his box at Mrs D, sometimes quite violently. Often he threw his spit at her too, sometimes launched directly from his mouth, sometimes collected in a beaker; after a while water from the tap was added and thrown. He began trying to clutch her hair, then to pull it. Nicholas's actions were not symbolic representations of his feelings; they were concrete events designed to avoid mental states. When he bombarded Mrs D with everything indiscriminately from his box each session, this was concretely getting rid of the confusion and pain that he experienced; and that he was perhaps especially experiencing in relation to her comings and goings. She found the bombardments and hair pulling exhausting: it was impossible to think about what his feelings might be, as she was having to concentrate all her attention on struggling to defend herself. The physical pain and the mental paralysis were induced in her by him; the question was, how could she work on it and in what way could it be made meaningful for him? And was he bent on attacking and destroying her capacity to think, or would he ever allow himself to benefit from it? Mrs D had to clarify continually, both in her own mind and to Nicholas, what actions made her work not possible and therefore could not be tolerated; and in what way a prohibition (of his physical attack on her, for instance) was not the same as a punishment or a rejection.

The other theme that was present in his sessions from the start was his use of the couch in the room. He began by trying to insist Mrs D join him on it and lie down under the blanket closely together with him. Later he lay on his own, stroking the soft blanket and sometimes looking dreamily content. This seemed to be a concrete experience of a lovely relaxed feeling when he was close together with a gentle, warm mother.

He seemed to need or demand a concrete togetherness. In some sessions he tried pasting transparent sticky tape over her hand, or round her head, or sticking a little star on to his cheek, as if these could be ways of joining people. There was no doubt that for him, each and every session centred on her and on his relationship to her, though this seemed to exist in physical terms only. 'Now he set out in earnest to get my hair, and I got up from my chair the better to stop him grabbing it. He occupied my chair briefly but then came back to me. What started as a hair-pulling attempt became now also an attempt (1) to get me on to the couch, or (2) to get me sitting on his lap, or (3) to push me on to the table, or (4) to sit next to him on one of the small school chairs.'

All his sessions now became variations on the following themes: the ball game; throwing everything at Mrs D (Sometimes with spitting and hair-pulling); lying on the couch; and an issue over leaving.

From the second session onwards, he resisted leaving at the end of the session, wrapping himself in the blanket or clinging to the couch. Sometimes he tried to smuggle out something from the session with him – the soft ball, or a book. Later, he would dash out early and hide, so that Mrs D had to look for him; or he would dash out naked. The ending of each session became the most intense part of it, and it was plain that each ending was a very charged experience for him; but he dealt with, or evaded, or overturned, the emotions involved, by wild action of one sort or another, or by evoking action in Mrs D (dragging him out, chasing him across the playground, etc.)

Through all this, Mrs D, as best she could, was following the movement of the sessions and the sequence of events in each, and trying to put into words the meaning of the feelings Nicholas was arousing in her, or the thoughts she was having around his actions; indeed, sometimes trying to think at all herself rather than just act.

The last session before the summer half-term break provides an example:

Nicholas began his usual ball game, but he kept looking at the clock. Mrs D talked to him about their time together, her comings and goings, and reminded him that there would be no session the following week when it was half-term. Nicholas started spitting, often in apparent response to what she was saying. She talked about the spitting, and the possibility that for him it was a form of communication. Perhaps he felt she spat him out over half-term. He needed her to feel what it's like to be spat out, thrown out, not wanted, not needed. He deliberately rolled the ball under the table and left it there. He looked at the clock, then took a carton and threw the contents at Mrs D, mainly singly but sometimes in pairs or in handfuls, then the box lid, and finally the empty box. Mrs D spoke of his pain at being left; he could not express it in words but perhaps something of what she said felt right to him. He went to the sink and started to throw water at her. She followed him to the sink to control the taps. Soon, he sat in her chair and started to throw back at her all the things scattered round the chair.

Mrs D wondered aloud about Nicholas taking her place, whether he was showing her his view of what happened when he let out his feelings; they were thrown back at him. She talked about his difficulty in letting himself experience his own painful feelings. He fetched the white soap (which he at other times had used for gently soaping her hand, or his own) and threw it at her hard, then lay on the couch as if resting. His restless 'throwing at her' had gone. He got up after a while to wrap up the beaker in a parcel and laid it at her feet. He turned the light out and got ready to leave voluntarily.

In this session Nicholas can be seen responding to Mrs D's words, experiencing some relief and peace through them, and trying out a new way of dealing with the break (a gentle present of the beaker in a parcel).

In the first session after the summer holidays (the first long gap in their work), Nicholas tried repeatedly to get spit on to Mrs D, and struggled to get a towel off her which acted as a shield. In between the struggles he wanted to get on her lap and snuggle his head down on to her bosom. She talked to him about his bad/good feelings, and his problem of remembering her from one session to the next (and over the holiday) and keeping her in his mind. He made some gestures while he listened to this, putting his finger first to his nose, then his cheek, his temple, and finally his forehead. Perhaps he was trying out whether these 'thoughts' about her had a physical site which could be located? If so, at least there was some idea they were linked with his head. It did not seem that they had become *his* thoughts yet.

Mrs D always made a calendar to show him when the holidays would be; this had always been totally ignored. But before the next holiday break (Christmas) he took note of the calendar for the first time. He lay on the couch looking at it from time to time, and when the contents of the box were later thrown across the room, the calendar was spared. It seemed possible that he was, for a fragment of time at least, beginning to think about her coming and going, and about the break for which she was now preparing him.

After Christmas he brought two dolls into the session and played with them for a long while. At first the two dolls were in endless activity together, hitting each other or locked together, but never face to face, always upside down or upside down and back to front. Then one doll repeatedly pushed the other doll off the couch. Then he lay tucked up with one of the dolls on the couch. The last ten minutes of the session passed peacefully, he almost seemed asleep, and he left the room peacefully and at the right time (a rare event).

It would be wrong to think of this play with the dolls as symbolic, representing feelings; it had more the quality of a halfway state, an actual experience and thus of a 'symbolic equation' (Segal, 1973). But it represented a step forward from the concrete action of pulling Mrs D's hair.

Before the Christmas break Nicholas began saying a few isolated words, barely recognizable and not obviously vehicles for thought ('donkey', 'ee-aw', 'piggy'), though each one might have contained a thought encapsulated in it. (Mrs D felt sometimes she was being made into a donkey.) His teachers reported after this that he had begun speaking a bit in class.

In the discussion group, the question arose whether Nicholas was just being naughty. Someone asked if he did not need to be disciplined; could it be right to let him spit? If Mrs D were so permissive, it would surely just encourage him in such behaviour.

One member referred back to the sessions with Annabel, where it had been suggested that the worker should be firm about not condoning one type of behaviour (staying outside the therapy room and chatting to the secretary) whereas here much worse behaviour was tolerated. The leader suggested this highlighted the general guiding principle: that behaviour should only be restricted if it were rendering therapeutic work impossible. This would include substantially damaging the room's equipment, hurting the worker, interfering in some way with the therapeutic opportunities of other children, and any sort of self-injury. It is clear that in Mrs D's work with Nicholas it would have been collusive with anti-thinking processes if she had acquiesced in much of the sensuous contact that he sought. But as we saw in the description of the sessions, it can sometimes be a thin dividing line between safeguarding the therapy and becoming the policeman. Mrs D found that some of Nicholas's behaviour literally made it impossible for her to think, and this became one of the central issues of her work with him.

Nicholas had been born with a mental handicap, and we know nothing of his early experiences except that he was talking normally until his departure for boarding school when he was seven. From that point on, he seemed to have thrown away his capacity to talk and to think. He seemed to have given up trying to come to terms with his disability, or his feelings. Instead he reduced everything to a concrete act which appeared meaningless to people around him. Mrs D's work represented a chance for him to see how much could be salvaged.

Very little had been written about doing this sort of work with mentally handicapped children and adults until the welcome contribution of Sinason (1992). In Nicholas's case, he had thrown away the mental powers he was capable of, perhaps as a defence against the pain of feeling rejected and thrown away when he was sent to boarding school (so much of his sessions was on the theme of throwing away; leaving; being left). So he represented an enormously increased problem for anyone trying to work with him. Most of the time he was trying to make use of Mrs D on a physical level. Some of the material above suggests that it was beginning to become an emotional experience for him; perhaps he could even be beginning to think about their relationship. (The emotional basis of thinking is discussed in Chapter 13.)

IDEALIZATION AND NEGATIVE FEELINGS (AN OCCUPATIONAL THERAPIST AND MIGUEL)

The children described so far in this chapter were overtly hostile, silent or destructive, and their negative feelings were fairly explicit; but of course this is often not the case. We need also to consider the place of negative feelings in therapy as a more general issue. Is it possible for therapy to take place without any negative feelings coming into it at all? It might seem reasonable to offer a child a pleasant relationship and give him a happy experience he has not had before. One seminar member brought her work with Miguel for discussion, which gave the group a chance to think about these issues.

Miguel's mother was an immigrant who had turned to alcohol and theft when she found herself with a small baby, unsupported by husband or relatives. Miguel spent his first three years partly in care (at times when his mother was in prison) and partly at home, where his mother was sometimes drunk and neglectful. She married and another baby was born. Her husband was very supportive and Miguel's mother succeeded in her struggle to give up drinking. However, Miguel, then aged five, began wetting and soiling and running away from home.

Miguel was referred for weekly therapy, and the worker provided him with a drink of squash and a biscuit each time. When the Christmas holiday break drew near after two months of sessions, Miguel made the worker a card: on the front was a picture of a Christmas cake with icing. He wrote the worker's name above with hearts round it. On the back he drew a boat; he said it was a 'holiday ship' and added a small figure of a burglar climbing down the side. Miguel kept rubbing out details and the picture got more and more dirty and smudged. He then drew a separate picture of a witch and a moon.

In the discussion that followed the worker said she felt sad, as she thought the front and back of Miguel's card meant that all the goodness of their time together would get lost at home over Christmas. She felt he had had such a bad experience of mothering, she was hoping to offer him a better experience, but she felt it could not survive his bad situation at home. Another member asked if the work could really achieve anything if a child's situation undermined all the good that was being done. Someone else pointed out that it did sound as if Miguel's mother were managing better now. The question was asked whom the burglar represented: several people felt it did not necessarily represent his bad experiences at home, nor refer to his mother's conviction. One member said that her holiday breaks had seemed important and difficult to the children she worked with: could the holiday ship be linked with the worker's Christmas holiday, and the burglar be something to do with Miguel not wanting to feel left out?

The card with the cake and hearts sounded as if Miguel was clinging to an idealized relationship with the worker. Sometimes it is tempting for the worker to accept this comfortable role, where the child seems to be bringing her affection. But this idealization has to be distinguished carefully from gratitude for hard work done in the therapy. In Miguel's case it sounded as if less affectionate, envious and smudgy feelings were being split off and denied and relegated to the back of the card. And the burglar, as suggested, might have a link with Miguel's secret attacks on the worker and her holiday.

One worker said she was afraid to put into words anything negative with regard to herself in case the child decided not to come any more. Miguel's worker said she had wanted to establish a friendly relationship with him and help him see the sessions as a good experience by giving him the drink and the biscuit. However, as we saw in earlier chapters, a child comes to his first meeting with preconceptions about the worker and the setting and when he sees these are recognized and understood the first step has been taken towards forming a therapeutic relationship. The food and gifts can only get in the way and may even feel like a bribe.

If negative feelings occur in the session, we have seen in this chapter the importance of accepting them and trying to think about them. Sometimes a child may try to keep the relationship with the worker idealized and 'sugary sweet'; but if we collude with that, the negative feelings tend to get acted out at home or at school with greater force. If the worker finds herself laying the blame for everything at the parents' or foster-parents' door this surely suggests that the negative issues within the session, and especially the child's negative feelings towards the worker, are being evaded. If we can help a child with his destructiveness, cynicism and envy within the session, he is more able to make positive use of whatever good qualities his home environment may have.

On the other hand the worker is not there to be the recipient of every form of physical attack. If a child finds he can continue throwing toys at her or soaking her with water, he will feel that no boundaries are set anywhere to his destructive attacks and that there is nothing to stop his own bad impulses actually invading and spoiling everything. The particular difficulties in setting such boundaries with a child such as Nicholas who is unable to think about his own feelings are discussed above. Limits clearly need to be set, to preserve the room and the worker for the next session, and to enable the worker to continue in her therapeutic role in the present session. The danger is that a very disruptive child may cause a worker to step out of this role and become punitive, using more force than necessary to control rather than continuing to see it also as a communication.

Just as a worker can be seduced by an idealizing child, so too a negativistic child can tempt her to avoid thought. If the worker is impelled into action, this colludes with the child in avoiding mental pain. With children who repeatedly run out of the room or persistently attack communal possessions, the walls and furniture of the room, or the therapist's body and clothes, each worker probably needs to think out what seems to be the appropriate way of managing this, the aim always being to safeguard the work she is trying to do. She will need to think about what the child is trying to express, what she herself feels she can work with, and the maintenance of the setting for others, as well as for the child whose session it is.

The work we have described in this chapter is indeed difficult. We have seen the need for workers to bear belittlement. They also have to carry the pain of not knowing and not understanding, which may be very much to the fore with a silent child; the child may also be projecting feelings of uselessness into them. We have also seen how management issues with colleagues may be involved. Negative behaviour outside the room, or for example very noisy behaviour within it, can strain relationships with other staff and call for continual vigilance in the maintenance of the setting. We have seen how behaviour such as that of Annabel and Nicholas outside the session could be written off as merely naughty, with the worker perhaps being viewed as incompetent.

There may also be the struggle for the worker within the session not only to think but also to manage the negative behaviour and her own response to it. It may be necessary to restrain violent behaviour, but the forceful violent input into the worker may make it difficult not to overreact when personal boundaries of tolerance are under threat. To retain a containing approach may be a constant struggle, additional to the complexity of what is presented. In these circumstances a worker may well be in need of some help for herself. A thoughtful discussion group with colleagues could be of help and professional supervision could be most useful. If a worker attempts what really seems to be courageous, pioneering work such as Mrs D undertook with Nicholas, professional supervision does seem to be essential.

Chapter 9

Endings

We are not always able to continue work with a client for as long as we should wish; sometimes endings are forced on us because of circumstances we cannot alter. How can we help the client if the ending is premature?

In more favourable circumstances we need to think about how to assess when a patient or client is becoming ready to finish, and what sort of work needs to be done towards the finishing.

PROBLEMS OF A PREMATURE ENDING (A SPECIALIST TEACHER AND ALAN)

Sometimes it can be part of a career structure that staff stay in a post for a limited, prearranged length of time. In one hospital department, for example, registrars were originally placed there for six months, full time. When they were given the opportunity to work individually with children, it was quickly apparent that this was too frustratingly short a time both for the therapists and for the children they saw. It was possible to rearrange the placement so that they could work fewer days each week, but over a whole year. It still meant however that their work with a child had to be broken off when they left.

We discussed in a seminar group the problem of how to end with a child when the work has to finish, not because the child is ready, but because the worker is leaving. One seminar member said she had decided to end her sessions with a child abruptly and make a quick break when she left the department, because you couldn't do anything about it anyway. In the discussion that followed, another member of the group described the distress she had felt when she had had to leave her own child in hospital, and the nurses had whisked the child away 'because it would be easier for her like that'. Another said he could still remember how he had felt as an 8-year-old when his uncle took him to boarding school and walked away promising to 'come back very soon to fetch him'; he thought he had felt even more desolate because he had been given no chance to say goodbye. After thinking about the discussion, the original speaker decided to plan her ending with her patient over a number of sessions so that the child had time to experience the ending and express his feelings about it, and have them understood and acknowledged.

This can be extremely painful both for the worker and the client. We may have to face the possibility of not having helped, or of seeing our work thrown away under the impact of a premature finish. It seems important that we at least acknowledge and recognize the child's feelings.

Mrs O was faced with telling the children she saw individually, that she would be leaving in two months' time. She described the response from one child: 'I dreaded telling Alan that I was going to leave because he has such difficulty with endings. He finds the end of each session difficult and expresses this in a very graphic way by dropping dolls, throwing things in the bin, or falling on the floor.'

In the session she described to the group, he was talking about the future – 'in so many weeks ...' and 'up to Christmas ...', so she felt this was a reasonable time to tell him, and said 'I will be leaving after Christmas and someone else will be looking after you.' Alan asked 'Why?' and 'Do you have to go?' Then he began throwing toys out of a cardboard box whilst looking very sullen. Mrs O said that perhaps he was feeling thrown away like the toys. He climbed right inside the box and began to tear it in pieces while sitting inside it; he threw the pieces across the room. Mrs O said that endings and leavings sometimes feel like being torn apart. Alan burst out angrily 'You might as well forget it, there is no point in coming anymore, it's best just to forget.' Mrs O said she hoped he would still come because they had nice things as well to remember, but Alan said no. He told her he was not going to leave at the end of the session; then, that he would not be coming back. While Mrs O was trying to talk about her leaving, and how it made him feel, he began throwing things directly at her. She said she could see he was very cross with her, and that perhaps he wanted to hurt her because she had hurt him with the news of her leaving. Alan persisted with throwing things and the session had to be terminated early as a result; Mrs O said she herself was left feeling rather battered and torn apart.

A short time later, Mrs O was sitting in her room with another child when Alan and another boy she worked with began shouting and kicking at her door and generally making a fuss. Eventually they were taken away by another staff member; but at the end of the second child's session, when Mrs O went to open the door for him, the door burst open and Alan was the other side of it, pushing her and the child back into the room.

Mrs O was made to feel very persecuted by Alan; also she was aware of the attack on the other child, whose whole session, including its ending, had been spoilt by Alan. Mrs O and the other child were being made to carry the full burden of feelings for Alan: the resentment, disappointment, rage, and shock aroused in him by her news. Mrs O hoped to be able to help Alan with some of these feelings in the two months that remained. Alan, like most children in his situation, had probably experienced the abrupt termination of many other relationships, for example the breakdown of foster-home placements, sudden changes of school, or being taken into care.

Mrs O hoped that by giving him time, and by sharing the full violence of his feelings about ending, he might be able at the end of it to hang on to something positive from the relationship. Alan's reaction to the ending also illustrates some of the problems encountered in a setting where a number of children see the same therapist at different times. Any one child's feelings of jealousy are obviously heightened when he sees another child going off for an individual session with 'his' worker.

Mrs O had dreaded telling Alan because she had already seen that he had such difficulty with endings – the ending of each session, and presumably each ending before a holiday. This had been true of Nicholas (Chapter 8) as well, who either clung on to the room (the couch, or a chair) refusing to be prised away, or else dashed out early, sometimes naked. For many children, the first half of each session is dominated by their feelings of anger, bitterness or deprivation since the last session, and in the last half by their anticipation of the new ending to come; sometimes very little work seems to get done in the middle. But their inability to tolerate separation, or to hold on to any goodness when away from the worker, may itself be the central area where they need help.

When Mrs O told Alan she was leaving and mentioned the 'replacement' worker in the same breath, he may have felt she was deflecting his anger by swiftly offering a substitute for herself. The offer of a substitute was also a denial of the importance of their relationship. Similarly, when she said there were 'nice things to remember' from their time together, he may have felt she was trying to cajole him away from his anger. This could have further provoked his rage, and it would have been more helpful if Mrs O had stayed with his angry feelings instead of trying to mollify them. A child may be more able to be in touch with the idea of a new worker having real mental space for him, if the worker can be named.

Mrs O's decision to leave was not taken lightly, and in the group discussion it was apparent how much anxious thought she had given to the effect her leaving would have on her clients. In our professional work we cannot always avoid a disruption of this sort, however carefully we plan. In these circumstances it is never easy to ensure that our own feelings of responsibility and perhaps guilt do not interfere with our perception of the client's needs. The temptation may be to cover over the pain of the ending for ourselves as well as for the client.

In Chapter 13 ('The emotional basis of thinking') we describe how a mother helps the baby to have a capacity to hold on to the pain and loss of separation and eventually to encompass it in his mind. This is similar to the role of the worker, to give space for the child's feelings about ending a session (which could include warning him five minutes beforehand) and about holiday breaks. Mrs D made a calendar for Nicholas (Chapter 8) and after he had consistently disregarded it for some weeks, a session came where he lay touching it and seemed to be letting it exist in his mind for a moment. The ending of each session can be a preparation for the final ending. The importance of planning and preparing for an ending needs to be clarified with everyone involved in the therapeutic team, as we saw with Bob (Chapter 4) where the worker was faced with the possibility of his therapy being abruptly brought to an end. It was apparent from the description of his session that the relationship with the worker was meaningful to him, and he explicitly asked her about future sessions.

The question as to whether they could be felt to stay in each other's minds after the 'therapy shop' was closed seemed to be a crucial point for him. When he was reminded that the session was about to end, he enacted a hurly burly of 'going to the bathroom' which involved a mixture of being cleaned up, thrown down the toilet and crowded out, as if this was what endings made him feel. Bob's symptom of soiling had cleared up during his stay in hospital but it is not difficult to envisage it returning if his sessions came to an abrupt end. For Bob would see the ending as a desertion; he would feel dropped out of the therapist's mind.

We suggested that the worker needed to try and clarify with colleagues the timing of Bob's discharge. But if it had to remain uncertain, then this additional pain was something that had to be consistently and openly faced in the therapy by both worker and patient. In the session quoted, for example, the worker would need to allude to the uncertain future of the therapy when Bob mentioned his next session, when the train sank, the tiger fell off or when the shop closed down.

HELPING A MENTALLY HANDICAPPED YOUNG ADULT ACHIEVE INDEPENDENCE (A SOCIAL WORKER AND GRAHAM)

In the example that follows, Mrs L, a social worker, enabled her client to effect substantial changes in his life. She knew that she would be leaving the area some months later, and that a colleague would be available to give her client further support, so in one sense work with him would be continuing. But in another sense, Mrs L and her client had completed their work together and she was able to work with him also on the ending of their relationship.

Graham, a young adult, had been an in-patient of mental handicap hospitals for a number of years, in wards for disturbed young patients. He had a fairly severe speech defect which made it difficult to understand what he said. This may have contributed to an underestimate of his mental abilities (an IQ test when he was eighteen resulted in a score of 62). Although there have been changes in legislation and terminology since this account was written, the work remains valid.

He was illegitimate and abandoned by his mother at birth. He was received into long-term care, together with his older sister, and brought up with her in two successive children's homes. Because of stealing and delinquent behaviour, he was sent to an approved school. He continued to show problem behaviour and was certified under the Mental Health Act as subnormal and mentally ill, and admitted to a mental handicap hospital on a legal order. This of course meant, among other things, that he was permanently separated from his sister, his only known relative.

Graham himself bitterly resented the forced admission to hospital and showed his protest by constantly absconding; once 'outside' he broke into houses and stole goods. When charged with these offences, he threatened self-injury, and following a court appearance, he was committed (still in his teens) to a special hospital on an even more restrictive order of the Mental Health Act under a section which could not be dissolved without reference to the Home Secretary.

He remained in this special hospital for some years. He claimed later that he gained nothing from being there: no help with speech or educational skills or with work training. He was then returned to the original hospital. Graham himself thought the reason for the transfer was that his place was needed for a more disturbed patient – in other words that the transfer was not based on a recognition of his rights or needs. In these situations, admissions and discharges were sometimes arranged on an exchange basis, so his suspicion was not necessarily without a basis in fact. He was still subject to a restrictive section of the Mental Health Act. He pleaded for more freedom. The ward staff soon had few behavioural problems with him and he began to show some capacity for development. He developed good relationships with some of the ward staff and joined in activities with them, e.g. table tennis. He occasionally got into fights, but it was noticed that sometimes this was just because he was stepping in to side with a less able patient who was being victimized by another patient.

He was given a part-time portering job in the hospital, got on well with the other porters, and was reliable about keeping time. The consultant psychiatrist gained permission from the Home Office for him to go unescorted outside the hospital gates. Encouraged by ward staff, he developed a hobby which showed he had considerable ability and intelligence in some directions, and he pursued this with enthusiasm once outside the hospital.

The social worker (Mrs L, a member of the course) first became involved with him two years later, a month before the Home Office agreed to the consultant's recommendation that the Mental Health Act section be discontinued in his case. Mrs L then worked with him over a three-year period to help him to be discharged from the hospital and make a life for himself outside.

After three months he was moved from the acute male ward to one of the hospital's outlying hostel units. A few months later, he was given a place in a social services rehabilitation hostel for mentally handicapped people. He stayed there for just over a year and then moved to his own single-person flat. He kept his part-time job as porter at his old hospital and now managed on his own, living as a normal 'free' member of society for the first time in his life. He continued seeing Mrs L regularly once a week. He had been in his own flat for eighteen months and managing well. Mrs L moved to another job.

It was apparent, listening to Mrs L's account, that Graham used the contact offered by the ward staff, the female care worker at the rehabilitation hostel and herself positively to help himself achieve independence. It is worth therefore giving her account in some detail to see in what way Graham was able to use the relationship with her.

Graham's main daily contacts for years since his teens had been male patients and male staff. At first his approach to me was sceptical and monosyllabic. He relaxed a bit during his time at the hostel as he saw the female care worker and I were really trying to move things the way he wanted them to go. Discharge to his flat, although wanted, was an anxious time for him and unfortunately coincided with a DHSS strike, which led to endless problems with his money. I had to go with him to the emergency payment section (remember Graham had a severe speech defect so could not easily make himself understood), on more than one occasion; then his Giro and disability pension book went astray in the post and I had to go with him again to make a statement about not having received them.

A lot of anxiety spilled on to me in this early phase in the form of anger, and he had times when he would come and see me and go on at length at me, treating any comment or suggestion from me with derision, saying things like 'I know that, woman!' He was guarded and scornful and always seemed inaccessible to suggestions, and yet it seemed that by just staying with him, sometimes literally sitting with him for fifteen minutes while he fumed in exasperation, he would slowly become more constructive. When feeling under pressure, he would for instance refuse to stay in to receive a visit from the supplementary benefits officer, would threaten to give the flat up, would threaten to behave in other ways to damage his interests, but then eventually would manage not to.

It was clear to Mrs L that Graham's belittling and dismissive behaviour was a necessary part of the process. These kinds of feelings needed to be expressed to the worker and understood before Graham would develop more strengths.

> In the earlier stages of our three-year relationship, he needed a lot of help with practical things: formal letters about his flat/money, liaison with social security and general help and teaching about procedures as to how to tackle various sorts of problems.
> In the last six months he used his regular weekly interview to talk about attitudes to authority – 'they don't care' – and his past life in approved schools, and in high-security hospitals. He started to look at his worries about things he could not do and lacked confidence over, and at things he could do.

Previously he had not been at all used to discussing feelings. Also he had lacked confidence in his ability to make himself understood.

> He now keeps his flat tolerably in order. He does his own washing, manages his own money and bills, looks after his own shopping, food and self-care. He decided he wanted help with his speech defect and at his own request attends for weekly speech therapy. [Mrs L, through getting to know him, was finding she could understand his speech more easily.] He has joined a club at a local church centre where he has some help with literacy skills and also a social group. He has kept in touch with some friends among the staff and patients at his hospital. He was able to tell me how much he now finds he suffers from loneliness.

A gentle caring side of him had always been there, but unrecognized. He talked about an incident in his late teens when he had refused to exploit animals. He told the social worker how he had stood up for some patients in a ward dispute.

> The termination of our work was discussed by me with him well in advance, and seemed to be a positive tool for focusing some discussion about his feelings.
> One example concerned his frustration over a rented TV. The firm continually let him down by not collecting it when they said they would. This seemed to symbolize being messed about by authorities. His anger suddenly spilled over on to me in a lot of questions. 'Why do I have to see a social worker? What is in my file? I want to see it! Why do I have to talk about myself and you don't talk about yourself?' He was able at this point to respond positively to a linking of his feeling about being messed about by the TV company with the feeling of being at the mercy of me/the hospital.
> This kind of discussion was repeated on another occasion in connection with his unexpectedly high electricity bill. He was convinced he was being cheated by the electricity board and said, 'They always do what's best for *them*!' He related this to his transfer back to the mental handicap hospital from the special (secure) hospital. He felt he had only got out of the latter because it suited the authorities, not because they were considering his needs. But again, he was able to accept the link I made between feeling cheated by the electricity board and feeling exploited by other authorities, including myself and the social work department, which he could feel was letting him down also in my leaving. His irritation at authorities always acting as if they were in the right seemed mollified at the end of the interview.

He had previously seen people in authority as rigid, without chinks in their armour, always having to present themselves as being in the right. Towards the end of this interview, after discussion of the electricity board and the hospital, he noticed that Mrs L had a split in her shoe and said so, whereas his were smartly polished. He took pleasure in pointing this out to the worker and he and Mrs L laughed about it. This incident seemed at the end of the interview to mollify his feelings about 'authorities' a bit – he had withdrawn some of his projections.

By the time of the termination, he expressed some thanks for help received. We were able to wish one another well. He was also able to accept the offer of another social worker.

It seemed that giving him regular time helped him to develop himself in various ways; he was able to learn and gain confidence from this both practically and in expressing himself.

My work seemed to have an important 'containing' function, gathering up his anxieties and angry feelings and helping him to temper them and get them under his control. I recognized with him the events which had in reality been harsh for him and tried to show him that other experiences could be better. Projections arose but could be withdrawn and modified a bit as his strengths increased.

It was clear that Mrs L first of all accepted Graham as he was: belittling, surly and rejecting. She held on to the relationship through many difficult months. She recognized where appropriate the harsh reality he had experienced and that he had just cause for grievance, but she also helped him recognize that other situations could nevertheless be different and that it might be possible to make a positive relationship with her in a more conscious way, and link it with Graham's feelings about life and what life had done to him. She said she might not have understood and used those incidents in that way before her experience in the seminars. She helped him see that the anger, resentment and bitterness he was displacing on to the television firm and the electricity board belonged to his relationship with her and the hospital and his feelings about her leaving; this was part of the work she did with him to help him through the painful experience of saying goodbye.

When he found he was being understood, this seemed to make him want to improve his speech, and he found it was worth working on his difficulties. He began to use speech as a means of exploring his feelings. He found it quite hard to expose himself to the 'not-knowing': but the experience of being listened to, and having his feelings understood, increased his wish to communicate.

Perhaps his mental suffering had increased (he was feeling loneliness for the first time); but his capacity to do something about it, and take responsibility for improving the quality of his life, had also increased immeasurably.

DIFFERING RESPONSES TO ENDING (A COUNSELLOR AND GLORIA)

Even when a worker is able to choose the time for ending a session and to base it on her assessment that the client is ready to finish, it is important to leave enough time for the impact of the ending to be felt. We shall see, in the section on observing a baby

(Chapter 10), how weaning arouses strong anxieties which are linked in the inner world with the death of the loved object. (The concept of a loved, or good, object in the inner world is discussed more fully in Chapter 14). We shall see how Dean struggled with anxieties about not being lovable enough or good enough. There were also moments when he seemed to experience the weaning breast as one that was cruelly attacking and depriving him.

These persecutory and depressive anxieties are stirred by the ending of any close relationship. Ending sessions with a worker can give the client a chance to work through some of these feelings instead of getting rid of them or otherwise evading them. If they can be worked through, it can lead to an inner enrichment; something of the good relationship can be internalized, and can lead to inner strength.

Persecutory anxieties were aroused in Mrs Adams (Chapter 4) when the health visitor had tentatively suggested visiting less regularly. The idea of a reduction in contact, with an inbuilt notion of ending sometime, may have felt to her as an attack coming from the health visitor. The health visitor found that all her work with Vincent's mother seemed suddenly to be wasted. Mrs Adams did not want to let her into the house at the next visit, and told her that Vincent was to be put away. Not only the health visitor, but also Vincent, had suddenly turned bad in Mrs Adams's mind, under the impact of ending. Mrs Adams's first reaction was an angry discarding of both relationships – she was going to drop Vincent as she herself felt dropped now by the health visitor. There are some echoes of this in Bob's session (Chapter 4) when the train 'sank in the middle of the deep sea'. Graham also responded with renewed bitterness when Mrs L began to discuss her leaving; he felt cheated by the electricity board and exploited by other authorities. But both Mrs Adams and Graham were able with help to get in touch with more positive feelings.

Gloria, aged eighteen, had been in care for much of her life and was having counselling sessions with Mr T about the new independent life she was about to start. She had told him how sometimes residents from her old children's home had been invited to stay with ex-workers from there who had left the service and now had their own homes. Mr T was known also to be about to change jobs and there was some evidence that Gloria would have liked social contact with him. She asked in a session if counsellors spoke to you or cut you if they met you in the street. In this instance it seemed necessary to clarify with her, however painful it felt to both of them, the boundary between a personal relationship and the professional relationship that they had. It was important that their shared, useful work relating to ending could continue with recognition of the true situation, which included the crossing of a major boundary in Gloria's life, namely ceasing to be a child in care. It was necessary for Mr T to grasp the transference aspect of Gloria's pain and relate to her feelings of being 'cut out' of his life, as well as feeling cut off from her past surroundings. If a client can be helped to express negative feelings about an ending to a worker, further realistic work may follow concerning the relinquishment of the actual relationship. The client's experience of such work can then enhance the quality of her own inner resources.

MOURNING IN RELATION TO ENDING (AN OCCUPATIONAL THERAPIST AND GILLIAN)

We have talked about endings in relation to weaning. Klein (1940) wrote that the baby, around the time of weaning, 'goes through states of mind comparable to the mourning of the adult, or rather, that this early mourning is revived whenever grief is experienced in later life'. We shall now see how therapy helped a child come to terms with her mother's death, by working through her feelings about the ending of the therapy itself.

Gillian had become withdrawn and apathetic following her mother's death, and had severe psychosomatic symptoms. She was also showing learning difficulties at school. After a year, when her symptoms still persisted, an occupational therapist working in a hospital clinic was asked to see her regularly as an out-patient. Gillian was then twelve. Eighteen months of twice-weekly sessions with the occupational therapist helped her greatly, and her disturbing symptoms disappeared. But it was not until the therapist began to discuss the possibility of ending their work that Gillian started to provide material relating to death and mourning.

She had always been an eager participant in their work, and from being silent and withdrawn, refusing to go to school, she had become happy and active at home and at school. Her severe psychosomatic symptoms had also gone. Her therapist talked to Gillian about the possibility of finishing their work together.

In the following session, Gillian started a game. She and the therapist, Miss P, were at the seaside, and Gillian was searching for goldfish. There were some gold-looking used coins in the playroom which Gillian said were the goldfish. She caught them and put them in various bowls filled with water, for safe keeping. As the game developed, Gillian would be deliberately careless with the goldfish, keeping them out of water too long while transferring them to another bowl. Miss P was given the role of warning her that they were dying, or complaining that they had died; Gillian rescued some of them just in time. Then she put them in the back of a car, and they drove hurriedly over a bumpy road; the water splashed out from their bowls and they died. Gillian told Miss P to tell her dad about the danger to the goldfish; Miss P was then to play the part of her dad, and forbid her to put them in the back of the car. However, Gillian went on with it, and at the end of the game left the goldfish dead. Miss P found the game very moving, and said to Gillian that the game was about death, that Gillian felt responsible for the fish but they had died, and that this must be very frightening.

The 'gold' fish obviously stood for something valuable, beautiful and loved, and the game seemed to be about how do you keep the goodness and love alive. Thoughts were aroused about Miss P's obligation to be careful about her work and not to rush the ending. Gillian was also showing Miss P how she needed her help in the task of holding on to, and internalizing, a good relationship; Miss P had to have the role of warning Gillian about her carelessness, and about the dangers of her behaviour. This links with the concept of good objects in the inner world (Chapter 14). Gillian's play also threw light on what some of these dangers to her good objects were: the deliberate carelessness sounded like a denial of the value of the relationship ('What does it matter anyway? Who cares?') The rush and hurry in the car sounded like a 'manic' defence against the sadness of ending. Putting the fish in the back of the car, where it was impossible to see what was happening to them and where they could not be looked after, sounded like relegating something or someone to the back of one's mind. Perhaps it was also linked with pushing something out of sight and memory into one's bottom (rather reminiscent of Bob's play (Chapter 4) where the issue of ending is also discussed). Gillian seemed to have a strong conception of work needing to be done over the ending, to help her get it right. She was anxious that she would not be sufficiently caring towards anything or anyone whom she loved and valued. (This is an example of 'depressive' anxiety which we discuss in Chapter 14.) She was also quite clear that responsibility for her good objects' safety in her inner world lay with *her*.

This last point is very important, since it is the source of hope in our work. In any discussion of this type of work with people unfamiliar with it, the objection is often raised that whatever good we do is bound to be undone by the unfavourable home circumstances, or the disruption of the next fostering breakdown or residential placement if in care. The importance of the external world should never be minimized, and indeed the interaction between inner world and outer experiences, the modification of the one by the other, carries on throughout life. Nevertheless, it is also possible that a child's courage, belief in goodness, and trust can be strengthened, so that he can make use of any good new experiences that come his way, and not continue in a vicious circle of mistrust, cynicism, distortion, and destruction. One way of evading the pain of grief and mourning is through twisted, bitter lying about the reasons for the ending and the nature of the lost object. Alan's sullenness, and his suspicious questions about Mrs. O's motives for ending, and his throwing the torn box at her, was a way of evading his sadness by distorting her into someone hateful. But this means that nothing good is left inside him, nothing worth holding on to or fighting for. As he said, 'You might as well forget it. It's best just to forget.' Compare Sam's frame of mind at the start of his sessions (Chapter 7); the apparent 'goodies' in the battles were not clearly different from the baddies; they became just baddies in disguise, and everyone ended up getting killed; the prevailing feeling was one of emptiness and desolation.

Sam's therapy continued long enough for him to be able to distinguish between goodness, love and courage on the one hand, and destructiveness, envy and cowardice on the other. There were also signs that he was beginning to develop within himself some of the good qualities. In Alan's case his worker was not going to be able to carry on with him. Some of Alan's anger reflected his feeling of being thrown away by Mrs O; one of her tasks in the therapy was to acknowledge his bitterness and disappointment and take responsibility for some degree of justification of these feelings.

Miss P had asked some questions about timing her ending with Gillian. Was she being overprotective if she decided to continue with the therapy after Gillian's symptoms had gone? In the discussion, other workers gave examples of clients whose symptoms had disappeared fairly quickly once therapy had started; it seemed likely that this was because the conflict was being brought into the therapeutic relationship and no longer needed to be externalized as a symptom. Stopping therapy at that point would be likely to provoke a recurrence of some form of symptom, since there would not have been time for anything to be changed in the inner world. There needs to be time for the work of internalization to be carried out; this is discussed further in Chapter 14.

Another question about ending relates to the worker's anxiety about the child's external situation, which may be very precarious. Should she prolong therapy as a support? Here again it should be possible to assess whether the client has yet developed sufficient inner strength to make the best of what his home and school setting can offer.

One essential is to give the child or client time to work through the whole gamut of reactions to the ending; even if an ending is premature, it can still often be planned, as Mrs O did with Alan. The feelings about the ending often have to be borne by the worker before the client is able to experience any of them himself. There has to be room for the various denials and defences to take place, and to be recognized. But the relationship is not a crutch, to be offered in perpetuity as a means of hobbling through life. A client has to be helped to internalize the relationship; often the last and most important stages of this work can only begin when the problem of ending is brought clearly and firmly into the centre of the sessions.

The positive outcome of ending can be that the client is enabled to mobilize his own resources; as we see in Chapter 11 ('Love, separation and loss in weaning'), it can provide the stimulus for further growth.

Part 4

The Relevance of Early Relationships

Chapter 10

A New Life: Early Developments

THE PLACE OF BABY OBSERVATION

Asking our course members to spend an hour a week observing a baby seems on the face of it inappropriate: some members have limited experience of working with children and may feel it is not relevant to their work; many have had children of their own; some, like health visitors, have had extensive training and experience with babies. Similarly, in what way is it helpful or relevant to quote as often from events in the first years of a child's life, as we have done in this book?

One answer might be that being in touch with how a baby relates to his mother can help us understand the non-verbal communications of some of our clients. Nicholas's emptying his box (described in Chapter 8) seemed to link with emptying his mind, a repeated evacuation; and he emptied it by throwing its contents at Mrs D – this was the nature of his relationship with her in their first sessions. It helped us to think about Nicholas's behaviour when we compared (and contrasted) it with a baby evacuating his unmanageable feelings into a mother, through crying (see the description of Gita below). If an observer has lived through a painful time of a mother trying to help her baby over some bad experience, she will have seen how the mother responds, and how in time the baby's distress is relieved. (This second part was what seemed to be so missing in Nicholas's experience when he first came into therapy.)

Being able to see a baby in his family setting over a period of a whole year gives the observer an opportunity to see how problems can occur, and become resolved. Something could be learned of the interactions that take place between mother and baby that help a baby master a particular anxiety, for example, in the descriptions of baby Ewan and the bath below. We learned from Dean and his mother (Chapter 11) how one feeding couple struggled with the process of weaning. Learning about several babies and their families in a group can help us realize that there is no one right way to go about bringing up a baby; what matters is how that particular couple, and that particular family, find their way together to resolve the problems.

Some of the babies observed had older brothers or sisters who at times experienced feelings of envy or jealousy towards the new baby (Chapter 11). The observer had the opportunity of being in touch with the envy and jealousy of the siblings, and with the mother's sometimes painful feelings in these moments. This experience might also enable the observer to deepen her perception of such feelings and can form a useful backcloth for relating to children such as Rupert (Chapter 7).

It is valuable to be able to see the normal growth and functioning of relationships, but also to see the similarities to disturbed behaviour. When we are first confronted with a disturbed child, as the student nurses were with Ginette (Chapter 6), we are likely to feel this behaviour is totally alien to us, and quite meaningless. Observing a baby can help us think about a more primitive level of mental functioning, where feelings are linked to a part of mother's body, not yet to mother as a whole person (see the account of Amy's colic later in this chapter); or where inanimate objects can be imbued with mental qualities. Ewan (see below) fixed his attention on the television screen which seemed to perform a function for him of 'holding him together' while his mother was out of the room. There have also been examples of how a baby imparts 'goodness' or 'badness' to another person. When Amy was sat suddenly on the observer's lap (see below), she suddenly experienced the observer as a very frightening person, though previously she had been giving her smiles. So we have the chance to see moments of a baby's experience, which would be considered evidence of disturbed behaviour if they were the dominating features of an adult's life. It is possible to see mental processes in a baby that form an unconscious, quite unrecognized undercurrent throughout life for most of us, but which may illuminate our work with our clients.

The observer also necessarily has to watch a great deal of apparently meaningless activity, especially in the first weeks of a baby's life. Having the patience to keep observing and to try and hold on to what was seen, and not to dismiss it as meaningless ('Nothing much happened: he was awake but I didn't see him bathed or fed' as the outcome of an hour's visit) was important. That willingness to experience events without being able immediately to ascribe a meaning to them is surely an essential part of any attempt to work individually in a counselling or therapeutic relationship. This seems particularly relevant to work with silent children, such as Andrew (Chapter 8). There the worker had to bear much that she could not understand, but gradually came to see some meaning in his finger play, as well as in his silence. In our comments on the baby observation we try to think about meaning, and be sensitive to what the baby may be feeling, though we emphasize the need both to wait for further evidence and to review our thoughts again in the light of further experience.

The observer is also liable to feel quite a range of strong emotions in herself. Some of these will arise from her own personality and her situation in life – anxieties about being an intruder, feelings of rivalry with this other mother, feelings of being excluded from a private, loving closeness between two other people. Other feelings may be evoked in her by something the mother or the baby (or someone else in the household) does in connection with her. Amy's mother suddenly put her baby on the observer's lap; this happened on other occasions, and it seemed that mother was saddling the observer with something, perhaps to do with who was successful at not arousing Amy's tears. Amy also aroused in the observer the feeling that she was in fact doing something bad to Amy, such was the quality of Amy's protests at being on her lap.

The observer may experience a feeling, often quite painfully, but not know where it has come from. Being able to think about herself in relation to this feeling, and recognizing what comes from her, and what on the other hand is put into her by the baby or family, is not only a valuable experience that helps with similar situations with clients; it also offers the observer a chance to grow as a person. Gaining some insight into our own motives and impulses, though painful, is essential if we are to try and enhance our capacity for insight and empathy.

Sometimes there is a quite unexpected result from observing a baby and his family. Some mothers have told the observer how much it has meant to them to have someone really interested in their new experience: someone with time to listen, who does not cap everything with stories of their own, and who does not feel obliged to criticize or give advice; someone who is ready to listen when things go wrong but also ready to share in the joy of a happy experience. The observer herself thus may be experienced as fulfilling some of the functions of a 'container' for mother or, as in the visit with Emma described in the next chapter, for the family.

BEGINNING A NEW RELATIONSHIP

The baby observations described here were undertaken by course members who were permitted by the family to spend an hour weekly, normally in the family home, in order to follow whatever the baby was doing in the family setting, in practice usually with the mother, although others could be present. The observer had no task other than to observe, and had explained to the parents how he or she would value learning at first hand about the development of a normal baby in his family setting as a help in his or her studies. Some members felt that going to observe a baby in his family setting would be a very intrusive thing to do, or to have done to one; others not. Someone questioned if the observer would be professionaly to blame if things went wrong in the family and she did not intervene. People felt unsure about their role as observers. Should they hold the baby if invited to? Could they ask questions? Could they choose where to sit, and be free to move to see the baby better? Would they come back to the seminar and be told they had done it all wrong? And would they be able to make any sense out of what they saw on their visits?

Some of their anxieties seemed to have their parallel in the family's experience of a new baby. One mother had told the observer at their first meeting that she had been concerned what her milk would be like for her new baby: would he take to it, would it suit him, would he manage to thrive on it?

A health visitor on the course had found one young mother in tears because her six-week-old baby son cried every evening from 7 p.m. till 10 p.m. She felt it must be because her breast milk was not right for him; it must be upsetting him. She had tried feeding him a bottle but he had 'sicked it out right across the room' and then cried more than ever. The health visitor had seen the baby put on weight rapidly since the birth and was able to satisfy herself that there was no physical trouble that needed attention; he was a healthy thriving baby. It seemed as if mother was struggling with her own anxieties, beset by them as well as by what may possibly have been communicated to her by the baby.

Several observations of newborn babies showed the baby relating only to a part of his mother – her voice, or her hands, or her breasts that fed him, and not yet able to relate to her as a whole person. Mothers sometimes experienced chaos and confusion in the early weeks. And it was difficult for the observer to remember the baby's behaviour since his movement seemed so random, disjointed and haphazard – nothing seemed to hold together. First sessions in work with a disturbed child can feel similarly fragmented, chaotic and confusing.

A 'PROPER' BABY (MRS WILLIAMS)

Mrs Williams, when meeting with a course member to discuss having her baby observed, mentioned how, when on pre-natal visits to the hospital, she had looked anxiously at some of the newborn babies she had seen and questioned whether they were 'all right'. She considered postponing the observation because 'the baby did nothing but cry and mess'. It seemed that she felt overwhelmed by a feeling of not having had a 'proper baby', although the little boy was healthy; maybe she felt he was more like the messy product a little girl would produce than the baby of a real mother. She did, however, accept the observation, and in later days when talking to the observer thankfully compared her current pleasure in her thriving son to her earlier experience of frightened misery.

Pregnant mothers cannot have an external experience of the baby they are carrying within them and anxieties about the nature of the baby may not always be able to be set aside immediately on the birth of a healthy baby. We can see how Mrs Williams's worried preoccupation existed before her son's birth and continued until she was able to gain some real experience of his viability and her own capacity to feed and care for him. We know that anxieties in therapy take time to 'work through' too. The willingness of the observer to accept the crying and messing baby as a real baby and as suitable for baby observation, together with the experience of the observation itself, may have been experienced as containing by Mrs Williams and hence useful developmentally for the couple. Parents, although also aware that their child needs help, may find it difficult to allow the intervention of a professional worker, perhaps because it arouses a sense of potential loss in their own relationship with the child, or brings forth increased anxieties about being blamed; they may feel some inadequacy in the child or themselves is being confirmed, and may need help with this.

These examples from infant observations perhaps help us to think about the beginnings of relationships with a client: how for both the worker and the client there may be anxieties about what they are bringing to the relationship and how they will be received. Len's worker (Chapter 1) spoke of needing courage to embark on a new approach; there were also instances of clients coming to a new agency, whose preconceptions of it differed considerably from the reality.

The next example shows how a mother (who was here the 'client' of a hospital) can be vulnerable to anxious feelings on starting her relationship with her new baby; it also shows how workers may defend themselves against the impact of a client's anxiety by institutional defences, as we also discussed in Chapter 6.

A YOUNG MOTHER IN A MATERNITY UNIT (MRS STONE)

An observer called by prearrangement to visit a young mother in hospital with her seven-day-old baby. The observer paused to admire the baby girl sleeping in her cot; the mother, Mrs Stone, replied sadly that yes, she slept all the time. The baby hardly ever seemed to rouse for a feed and never sucked for long before going back to sleep; now, she was still losing weight when she should have started to gain, so they were putting her on a supplementary bottle. Mrs Stone said she had so much hoped to breast-feed but she was feeling hopeless about it now. The observer, worried, asked about help from the hospital staff. Mrs Stone began crying and said she knew they were all very kind really; the trouble was, there were so many of them and you had to ask the right person the right thing. She had asked a nurse for a clean nightdress for the baby, as only the staff were allowed to go to the linen cupboard, but was told 'the junior nurses will be bringing them round'. Later on in the day the nightdresses still had not come. This young mother did not know how to tell which were the junior nurses; she asked for clean nappies another time and was told, 'I'll have it seen to'; again, she had asked someone too senior. But when she asked for help in encouraging her baby to suck, the nurse said 'I'm only a student; you'll have to ask staff nurse or sister.' Some other jobs were only carried out by nursery nurses, yet another category.

Jobs were evidently apportioned out within the hospital hierarchy, which sounds reasonable enough, but this mother had no means of knowing which job went with which rung of the ladder, or how to tell a nurse from a sister. No doubt her own rather shy nature contributed to the problem. But it seemed a pity that just when she was desperately struggling to learn how to be a mother, she should also be expected to unravel the intricate sign systems, rituals and taboos of the hospital.

Another problem was that staff disappeared unpredictably on leave or on breaks between shifts. After she had left the hospital, she told the observer she would know how to manage next time: sisters wore the dark blue dresses, staff nurses light blue, agency nurses dark green, student nurses blue striped, nursery nurses green striped, and she was able to joke about it. But the observer left on that first occasion feeling very concerned about this 'lost' young mother who had not been helped to get a relationship going with her sleepy baby.

It can be a delicate matter for a mother and baby to establish breast-feeding. The mother is new to caring for the baby in the outside world, and the external baby is new to her too. Mrs Stone was a vulnerable young mother, unsure of how to carry out her new responsibilities and unable to get the help she needed from the hospital for herself and her baby. She obviously felt confused among the many rules of the institution and the fragmented nature of the service. It was a pity that the hospital organization could not enable its staff to perform more of a mothering function for her so that she could feel her needs and those of her baby were gathered in and listened to by one person.

One can imagine how sensitive attention on the part of professional workers might have helped that nursing couple to develop their relationship. We have spoken of the importance of having a clearly defined and held setting for our clients in our places of work so that a child, for instance, knows that his therapy time will not be interrupted by lengthy conversations between mother and therapist. But we should not be so rigid that we exclude the possibility of relating to the parents, foster-parents or care workers who may have brought the child and thus risk giving the impression that our institutional 'system' comes before people's feelings. If for some reason they have not managed to be in regular contact with a worker themselves, they may need help in finding someone to talk to without intruding into the child's session. Ahmed's foster-mother (Chapter 2) is a case in point. All the examples in this section seem to underline the need for sensitivity and tolerance in beginning new relationships in our work.

PRIMITIVE WAYS OF COMMUNICATING (AMY)

Anxieties about not understanding a new baby, and not having an answer to every problem that arises, can take many forms. When the observer arrived for her first visit to Amy (then aged two months) and her mother, she found the health visitor there too; mother and the health visitor were discussing Amy's frequent spells of prolonged crying. The health visitor suggested it was colic; mother was clearly under considerable stress because of the unrelenting crying, which also carried on through the night. The observer thought it might be an example of something she had read, where-so-called 'colic' was said to be due to an over-anxious mother over-feeding her baby.

The leader suggested we might hear about what happened during the visit and try and see what we could learn about Amy and her experiences from that rather than have any preconceived theories. Amy did indeed start to cry during the observation and continued for some while; she did not respond to mother's soothing cooing voice, or to mother's gentle touch as she changed her, or to being held in mother's arms. On the contrary, she kept turning her head from side to side, and avoiding looking at mother while she was angrily crying. It looked as if Amy was being attacked by a bad inner experience which she was trying to get rid of by her crying. The group discussed whether we need to, or can, draw a distinction between physical and mental pain in the experience of a two-month-old baby. Only the actual breast-feed calmed her; she was then able to look at her mother for the first time in the observation, not with a smile, but very intently looking into her eyes.

It seemed as if Amy did not have any conception of mother as a whole person through most of this observation, but was only able to relate to the breast that fed her. But once she had reestablished this relationship to the breast and was feeding, she was then able to look 'very intently' into mother's eyes, as if she were now aware of her as a whole person.

Mother, health visitor, and perhaps the observer too, felt an urgent need to find an explanation for Amy's crying. Something of Amy's primitive anxiety was getting into them, and something of mother's own anxiety about whether she could cope with her first baby. Sometimes in our work we may feel an urgent need to come up with an answer, but that may prevent a slower, more patient attempt at real understanding. We may need to hold on to the uncertainty and wait for more evidence.

In the setting of observing a baby, we are not required to do anything, we are there simply to learn, so this can be a chance to try and develop a state of relaxed attention without the hounding of a need to make an effective contribution.

Amy, aged four months on this occasion, was sitting on her mother's lap on the sofa, with the observer next to them. Mother was making cooing noises and smiling at Amy while chatting with the observer, and Amy looked relaxed and attentive. Amy kept turning to look at the observer with great interest.

When the doorbell rang mother swiftly and unexpectedly placed Amy on the observer's lap, explaining as she hurried off that it was so cold in the hall and at the front door. Amy watched her mother leave the room, then looked at the observer, no longer interested and friendly but now quite apprehensive in her expression. Amy turned back to the door mother had left through; mother returned at this moment and took Amy back.

Once back on mother's lap, Amy seemed again very cheerful, making lots of happy-sounding noises, smiling at her mother and turning to smile at the observer.

After fifteen minutes or so of this happy 'conversation', mother as quickly and unexpectedly as the first time put Amy on the observer's lap; she had seen the same caller returning, and sure enough the doorbell rang. This time mother was out of the room for longer. Amy again looked at the observer with a solemn, intent look for a short while, then began to cry. The observer tried to soothe her by walking around holding Amy over her shoulder, but the cries become louder and louder.

Mother came back and took Amy into her arms; the crying stopped at once. After speaking gently to Amy, and explaining that she would be at the front door for a few minutes more, mother placed Amy in her baby bouncer facing the sofa.

Amy was at once unhappy again when mother left the room, not crying as loudly but vigorously moving her arms and legs as she cried. At one point she pushed so hard against the front of the sofa where the observer sat, that she actually moved herself, bouncer and all, back from it a few inches.

Mother returned to the room but then the phone rang; as mother answered it, Amy cried even louder. Mother placed a humming top down for Amy to watch, but Amy frowned at it while she continued crying. With one hand holding the phone, mother tried to draw Amy's attention to the row of swinging toys on the front of the bouncer. Amy looked only briefly at them, and though her arms and legs were still moving vigorously as she cried, she seemed to avoid moving or touching them deliberately. Once finished on the phone, mother picked Amy up again and peace was restored.

The group discussed together what Amy's experience might have been during this sequence of events. One worker suggested that Amy might have been 'mourning' for her mother when she saw her go; but the observer said the crying had not been a sad wailing; it had been more like screaming. Another group member wondered if this was Amy demanding attention, and perhaps finding that if she cried each time, mother would always pick her up. But the observer said it had felt as if the crying was directed against *her*, not against the mother. In fact, she said, it had made her feel somehow guilty, as if she had been doing something dreadful to Amy, and she had had to explain to mother that she had not been doing anything! Amy had seemed very interested and almost pleased to look at her as long as Amy was on mother's lap; but when mother gave her to the observer and left the room, she acted as if the observer had become someone very frightening and bad.

So the outer reality of a friendly visitor was changed in Amy's perception – Amy was putting into her some terrifying characteristics. This was an example of projecting something bad into another person and then feeling attacked by it. The group, in the discussion, brought several examples of children or clients who had experienced them, or something in their room, as bad and dangerous. They recognized and had shared the observer's irrational feeling of being guilty and responsible; this linked with other discussions about projection as a form of communication.

The sequence of events also gave the group an opportunity to explore the difference between 'mourning' and what Amy was experiencing. Amy was not sadly sobbing at losing her absent loved mother; she was frightened and screaming to protect herself from someone (felt to be) bad who was present. In fact there was a total contrast between an ideal mother who instantly consoled her when she picked her up, and a totally bad other person whose every gesture was an attack. The opposites of love and hate, ideal and persecuting, were poles apart, split between two different people. And there was nothing left in Amy's mind of a loving, good mother to tide her over her anxiety; she acted as if she felt completely abandoned to this frightening experience. The two were not brought together in her mind. Contrast the example of Emma, over a year old, described in the next chapter, who could be seen struggling to reconcile the bad and the good as both being aspects of her one loved mother.

In the last observation we saw how Amy experienced intense anxiety when her mother left the room. It did not seem as if she was anxious about the loss of her loved mother, but rather that she felt exposed to the possibility of attack from a visitor now felt to be dangerous. (The distinction between depressive anxiety and persecutory anxiety is discussed in Chapter 14.) In the next observation we discuss, it seemed as if she was controlling the comings and goings of various objects and claiming the right to deal with them as she wished. Maybe she was dealing with her fear of being attacked by assuming omnipotent control over the people and objects around her.

Some of the controlling, aggressive behaviour of children described in Part 3 (Annabel, Nicholas and Colin) could be better understood as a means of protecting themselves against a deeper anxiety. Behaviour that in Amy's case was a transitory phase in normal development can help us understand the more entrenched disturbances of an older child.

SEPARATION AND CONTROL (AMY)

Amy, now eight months old, was sitting on the floor with mother and the observer. She was smiling, chuckling and making talking noises as the two adults spoke together. Mother said she was still breast-feeding as they both enjoyed it, and she would carry on for as long as Amy wanted it. Amy was waking once or twice in the night to be fed but settled straightaway afterwards. She was having little bits of solid food as well. When mother left the room Amy seemed happy to continue exchanging sounds and smiles with the observer.

Mother returned with a mug of tea for the observer. Amy looked at it intently but it was out of her reach. She leaned forward to reach the observer and grabbed briefly at a button, and sat back, only to lean forward again and try to grab the observer's face, then her hair. Mother warned her that Amy's little nails could really scratch; indeed mother's face had some scratch marks on it, and at other visits Amy could be seen tugging really hard at mother's hair. Her mother did not check her over this.

But when Amy reached again to grab at the observer, her mother gave her a fluffy ball to distract her. Amy handled this, letting it drop and picking it up again. Several times the ball rolled away from her. Amy then stretched herself forward or sideways to retrieve it. When it was too far to reach, mother pushed it back to her. Once Amy found she could just reach the loop on the end of the ball. Sometimes she put the ball to her mouth and sucked or mouthed it briefly.

Eventually she reached for a magazine on the settee. Mother laughingly said she loved ripping things up; sure enough Amy set about tearing it – sometimes into little bits, sometimes whole pages at a time. This was evidently enormous fun and involved much chuckling and generally throwing the smaller bits of paper all over the place. Sometimes again she put one or two pieces to her mouth but did not protest when mother gently removed them. By now the sitting-room carpet was becoming covered in the shredded litter.

Amy's mother said Amy stayed awake now till after her father came home and liked to play peep-bo with him; he hid behind the sofa and reappeared for her, which delighted her. She was usually ready for bed after that but sometimes stayed up till 11 or 12 p.m., which left mother feeling tired and annoyed at not having any time to herself.

Amy was visibly happy and thriving, and her mother was relaxed and enjoying her; this was the prevailing feeling. Within this setting, the group explored what Amy's mental and emotional experiences might be during this scene. The observer had been conscious of leaning towards Amy in response when Amy first reached out to her, but when she felt Amy tugging at her face and then her hair this was done with such force it was quite painful and the observer was glad when her mother passed Amy a ball and she herself could retreat a little out of reach. It seemed clear that Amy's grabbing was done with intent, just as she intentionally let the ball go and then reached out for it repeatedly; and her excited shredding of the paper was also a repeated theme.

It looked as if she was enacting a scene where an object is put down and retrieved by her and therefore controlled by her in its comings and goings; and as if she claimed the right to grab whatever she wanted and even demolish it (the paper). Both times these things (the ball and the paper) went to her mouth. Perhaps she was experiencing mother's breast that fed her as something separate from her, but still totally under her control and there for her to handle as she wanted.

Amy's mother was lovingly indulgent towards this little baby, but she did express a wish to have her late evenings free of her. Perhaps she would move soon towards setting some boundaries for Amy with regard to herself, her time, and her living space. Amy did already seem to be working at the knowledge that mother was a separate person but perhaps would need help soon in recognizing that mother was not totally under her control. We had seen this mother and baby adapting towards each other in the past, and it was a brief phase we were observing, not an entrenched problem. But it gave the group an opportunity to think about the need for boundaries and the way in which boundaries can serve a purpose enabling growth to take place. If there is nothing to limit a baby's greedy impulses, then the baby is deprived of the chance to develop concern, or the sort of love that spares the object, and gives it freedom to go. If a baby is allowed to cling to a belief in a world that is exclusively hers, that holds no frustration or loss, this encourages a delusion of omnipotence; it also hinders a baby's chance to develop her own inner strength and her capacity to take in and develop goodness.

The value of boundaries in our work with clients has been discussed in many places in this book. The example of Rupert could be mentioned, who needed help in recognizing the rights of Dr M's other patients.

THE MATERNAL FUNCTION AND REVERIE (GITA; KEVIN)

The concept of containment has been frequently mentioned in this book in connection with the worker's role.

There is nothing automatic or easy about the process of containment or about a mother's growing capacity to understand her baby. The couple involved (mother and baby; worker and client) have to work at it together, often involving a great deal of anxiety. Sometimes with our clients, we are faced with a containment that went wrong, or that never took place, and the consequences of this are described in other sections. But here we can look at a sequence between a mother and baby which must happen over and over again in any ordinary 'good-enough' family, and in the course of any ordinary development. Something is wrong for this baby; how does she experience it, how does she convey it, how does her mother respond, how do they reach a solution?

Gita, a three-month-old baby, was coming to the end of a happy, harmonious breast-feed. She sucked gently, her hand resting softly on her mother's arm. As the sucking finally eased to a finish, mother gently laid her on the couch on her back. (There was no attempt at bringing up wind.) Gita lay with her head towards her mother who was murmuring to her, and gurgled back in response, making quite definite little noises. After a little while her movements became less gentle and her vocalizing sounded a bit distressed. Her mother moved Gita's position and this seemed to ease her for a little while; then her noises once again became more anxious or perhaps angry. Her mother took her on her lap, and after a few more efforts of moving her about and making her comfortable, and wondering whether she was fretting after an injection, mother put her back to the breast again. The baby began sucking rather frantically and her arm began to thump her mother's jersey violently and it became quite clear that feeding wasn't what she really needed. Her mother laid her again on the couch; Gita seemed to be pressing down really hard, followed by quite an explosion in her nappy. This seemed to ease her for a little while but then the agitation started again. Her mother tried her on her tummy over her arm, then picked her up and held her quite close to her. Gita now made some really loud screams, and carried on screaming hard, her face getting very red and con torted. Her mother held her very calmly and gently patted her back for a little while. Gradually the screams subsided and mother laid her down on the couch again, on her tummy. Gita made a sudden loud burp, and then seemed settled.

We cannot be sure what Gita was experiencing when things began to go wrong, but it may have been an internal discomfort increasingly caused by wind in her stomach. At any rate it disturbed her happy 'conversation' with her mother after a feed they had both enjoyed. When her mother tried seeing if a new feed was what she wanted, Gita's behaviour was strikingly different from the earlier one. She did suck, as if she too felt that might be what was needed, but with desperate gulps and eventual angry hitting of this 'wrong' breast. When her mother held her close to her, Gita really screamed; this sounded like a violent evacuation of something wrong and bad from inside her. It sounded as if she was passing a motion into her nappy. But the physical evacuation was not enough, and not the solution. We might have wondered whether a change of nappy at that point would have helped her, but the distress and agitation were there before the soiled nappy. In any case it seemed to be her mother's continued calm holding her, and gently patting her, that gradually quietened her. Following that, she was able, relaxed, to bring up the wind that had perhaps been the initial pain inside her. It was as if her mother's ability to remain unflustered, and yet gently concerned, through her desperate screams, had somehow 'taken' her bad experience and made it tolerable; the overwhelming anxiety went, and she relaxed enough to let the wind come up.

The unconscious mental activity that was taking place in Gita's mother's mind is perhaps an example of what Bion (1962a) has called 'reverie'. A mother does not necessarily immediately understand the cause of her baby's crying; an understanding may gradually evolve, perhaps mainly at an unconscious level. This is discussed further in Chapter 12 ('Projective identification and communication') and in Chapter 13 ('The concept of containment').

Gita's screams were an attempt at physically evacuating bad pain from inside her, but since her mother was there and responded, they were also a communication. One of the group asked whether the drive to communicate was there from the beginning of life; perhaps a baby has a preconception of something which receives? In any case this experience of Gita's was obviously one of a series of interactions with her mother stretching back months to her birth, so the sequence of pain→distress→crying→being understood was one that must have happened many times. The slow emergence, from this repeated sequence, of a capacity within the baby to hold on to, and tolerate pain (mental and physical perhaps cannot or need not be distinguished here) will be discussed when we look at baby Dean's experience of weaning. And also the slow emergence of a capacity to communicate in a less drastic way, by symbols and eventually words, will also be discussed.

This sort of interaction between a mother and baby does not always take place, perhaps because of mother's illness or unavailability, perhaps because of some difficulties in the baby which make it impossible. The group heard about another family where an older baby seemed only able to enact irritability and restlessness and where there was little or no evidence of any capacity to communicate between him and his mother, or him and any other adult. The family had come to the children's centre because of concern over Kevin's slow development. Kevin was eighteen months old, the only child of a couple, Mr and Mrs Rogers, who had both attended schools for the educationally subnormal.

Kevin's mother, Mrs Rogers, was at the centre with him, accompanied by Mrs Rogers' adoptive mother who lived some distance from the family but visited several times a week. All three were in a large playroom with other mothers and children, and nursery nurses. Kevin and his mother had been at the centre (mornings only) for just over a week.

Mrs Rogers sat with Kevin on her lap, facing away from her. She passed Kevin to grandmother, who sat him on the floor. Kevin swivelled round on his bottom and started to make irritable noises, threshing his arms and legs. Grandmother picked him up and handed him to Mrs Rogers. Kevin twisted his body around, looking at the other women and children in the room and struggling, and Mrs Rogers put him back down on the floor. Grandmother picked up a cup and gave him a drink. Kevin did not try to hold the cup, and after a sip threshed about with his arms. Grandmother picked him up. Kevin twisted to look at two mothers talking nearby. Grandmother held his arms down and put the cup to his lips again. Kevin screwed up his face, threw himself about on grandmother's lap, kicking and arching his back. Grandmother put him down on the floor. He pivoted round and tried to open a cupboard door, gave up, stretched out his hand for some bricks but again gave up when they were out of reach, and pulled at a doll.

All this time Mrs Rogers was smiling and looking at the other mothers and children. Kevin picked up a tin lid and a spoon. A nursery nurse put a doll down in front of

Kevin, chatted to him a bit, and gave him a plastic cup before walking away. Kevin explored the cup, turning it upside down and back again and then pretending to drink. He picked up a tray, turned to watch another child, and began again to make irritable noises, throwing out his arms and legs angrily. Mrs Rogers picked him up and held him over her shoulder, talking to him. Kevin held out his arms to his grandmother, who took him on her lap. His grandmother offered him a drink; he threw his arms out indicating he didn't want it. His grandmother put him over her shoulder. Mrs Rogers was looking at the other children. Kevin struggled to be down; his grandmother kept him on her lap and showed him a large teddy.

Kevin patted the teddy's face, put his head on its face, pushed it away and laughed. Grandmother looked weary but tried to keep him amused on her lap. His mother left the room and returned holding a fluffy toy which she held out to Kevin, who had been put back down on the floor. Kevin ignored it. Mrs Rogers watched the other children, smiling.

Food was brought for the children. Kevin grasped the spoon and managed to get some food into his mouth. Mrs Rogers helped him. His grandmother watched for a time, then supervised, and finally took over feeding. She tried to press him to finish his dinner; he turned away. It was time to go; Mrs Rogers waved goodbye to the staff.

Mrs Rogers was dressed in clothes almost identical to Kevin's grandmother's, and looked older than twenty-two. She was said to take very good physical care of Kevin. At the case conference it was reported that she had been 'sorted out' with a coil; it was recommended that Kevin attend a day-nursery with a physiotherapy and speech therapy input. Mrs Rogers was visited by a social worker.

We refer later (Chapter 13, 'Failures in containment') to the difficulties Kevin's mother herself may have been having to face, which may have made it impossible for her to develop any capacity for reverie and containment. The little boy's own mental and emotional development was clearly affected; it was impossible to be sure at that stage how far this was due to his relationship with his mother and how far there were other contributing factors. But certainly there was an unhappy lack of the sort of understanding that was obviously developing between the other mothers and babies described in this chapter.

One may question why we give such a detailed account of this interaction. We think such malfunctioning may highlight the qualities of containment and may also be worth thinking about in relation to mental and emotional retardation.

We can surmise that sustained help might be necessary to help Kevin relate mentally to his feelings about other children, rather than perhaps just irritably excluding them. Perhaps this was why the children's centre proposed active referral to various units for Kevin, although it would obviously be difficult for anyone attempting to work with a child lacking experience in sustained meaningful relationships. Action was also taken in 'sorting out' his mother's sexual life. There were differing views as to how all this was appropriate. Sometimes action can be a way of professional avoidance of staying with the painful deficiencies in a relationship and not knowing whether they can be helped by slow, careful attention over a period of time.

PRIMITIVE ANXIETIES AND THEIR RESOLUTION (EWAN)

Seeing how a baby struggles to cope with the ordinary anxieties and stresses that occur in the course of his day can help us think about defence mechanisms used by our clients, and to some extent present in all of us, though inaccessible and unrecognized because they are deeply unconscious.

Ewan was the fifth baby born into a busy family where there was much affection and love. Ewan's time alone with his mother was inevitably less than was the case of Amy and Gita, who were both first babies. In the following descriptions, he was using a way of coping with his large and noisy siblings that seemed to involve firstly blotting out any awareness of their existence, and secondly fixing his attention on the TV or the ceiling light. This enabled him to manage through what was clearly a stressful situation, as if the light he fixed on gave him some stability or cohesion.

Baby Ewan was six weeks old, sitting in his baby 'recliner' chair in the sitting-room with two of his older brothers. The television set was on, but the two oldest boys were more occupied with some toys. They were tending to squabble over who had what, making quite a lot of noise and bumping into Ewan's chair quite often as they ran past. Ewan seemed not to respond to the noise and movement of his brothers at all. He was sitting half-turned, staring at the screen. From time to time he started to cry, but stopped very quickly. Sometimes he moved his arms and legs, looking as though he was struggling backwards. After a while mother came in, and said Ewan looked 'fed up'. She lifted him out of his chair.

From Ewan's intermittent fretting on that occasion it was obvious he was under stress; he tried to cope with it on his own by blotting out and denying any awareness of his active, rumbustious brothers, focusing limpet-like on the light. His mother rescued him before his precarious control broke down completely.

Two weeks later, when Ewan was eight weeks old, he was in the sitting-room with his father and three of his siblings. He occasionally looked at his father but largely stared with a blank look at the TV screen. Again, he seemed to be excluding his brothers from his consciousness and contriving to be unaware of their existence.

A month later, when he was twelve weeks old, Ewan was sitting with his brothers and sisters after a feed while his mother cleared up in the kitchen. The TV was not on; three of the older children were sitting at the table drawing. Ewan's 3-year-old brother frequently went over to Ewan, kneeling over him, making sudden approach movements and noises. Ewan seemed discomfited by this, showing an initial interest, then turning away, and making as-if-about-to-cry faces. Ewan sat twisted in his chair so as to look upwards at the ceiling light.

It seems that Ewan was finding his boisterous older siblings too much to contend with. No doubt a bit of jealousy lay behind some of their rougher attentions to him. Several times he seemed about to be overwhelmed by tears. What seemed to help him to manage was a source of light – either the television set, or the ceiling light, particularly when his mother was not immediately present.

The whole process of having a bath seemed to arouse intense anxiety in Ewan. It was the only time the observer saw him really crying. When he was six weeks old, after a happy time spent with him in the sitting-room, mother began to take off Ewan's clothes for his bath. 'He won't like this!' Sure enough, Ewan began to cry as the clothes were removed over his head. She picked him up gently and invited the observer upstairs to watch him bathe. His mother collected some cotttonwool and carefully wiped his eyes and face. He began to get upset. He clung hard on to his mother. She spoke to him soothingly while beginning to put him in the water. He cried and flung his arms back and pressed down with his legs, still crying hard. She soaped and moved her hands over his body smoothly. He calmed a little. Then she lifted him out and cuddled him in a towel and he stopped protesting. They went downstairs again. His mother held him on her lap – he seemed very relaxed. She began to dress him and he let her do this easily. He was getting sleepy.

A week later, when he was seven weeks old, Ewan had again been content, until his mother started to undo his nappy on her lap, prior to a bath. He began to cry lustily. His mother wrapped him in a towel and picked him up to go upstairs for his bath. She realized that he was going to protest and talked to him as she dipped him in quite quickly. 'Sh, sh, it's lovely really'. Ewan cried loudly and a tear squeezed from a corner of his eye. His jaw quivered. He arched and struggled backwards, kicking hard with his feet. He was clutching mother's sleeve. He looked frightened and distraught. Soaping his body didn't stop him crying, but having water on his head made him pause and blink and listen to his mother's voice: 'There, there'. When she splashed water on to his chest, though, he cried again and was quickly removed and wrapped in a towel and patted dry.

In both these observations Ewan clearly felt frightened and unprotected without the covering of his nappy and clothes. Being placed in the water aroused increased anxiety, and Ewan could be seen fighting against this catastrophic experience by arching his back, struggling backwards, kicking down with his legs, and screaming. The one thing that seemed to afford any hope of rescue was his mother's arm or sleeve which he clung to throughout. The feel of her hand gently soaping his body did seem to calm him a little in the first week, and her gently soothing voice in the second week. It was as if her presence helped him through what was still a very bad experience.

The following week, his mother said she had been trying out ways of making it easier for Ewan, and he now had his bath in the sitting-room with the family. (He was now eight weeks old.) She placed him in the bath by the fire. He didn't seem to mind. Then mother let go of Ewan so that he was on his own in the bath, half-immersed, but with his head and shoulders out of the water. Ewan turned to his mother and slowly seemed to relax a little. She explained that she had found Ewan seemed to like it when he was allowed to be alone and unheld in the water. When his mother went to wash Ewan, she held his head and he started to look as if he would cry and struggle. She soaped him and let him go again – again he seemed to relax and float. Brother Michael splashed water on to him and Ewan made a splash with his fist, copying Michael.

Two weeks later, when Ewan was ten weeks old, his mother said 'He likes his bath now, and doesn't mind it when his clothes are taken off.' He pushed up with his feet from the ledge at the bottom of the bath. The pushing became stronger, almost kicking, and he let his arms splash down into the water. Eventually he was jumping so strongly that the water splashed out of the bath. He seemed to enjoy the slippery movement. His mother seemed to enjoy watching his antics and laughed. '*Now* he cries when he's taken *out*!'And sure enough he began to cry as she lifted him out into a towel.

The next week (Ewan was eleven weeks) he seemed to feel the bottom of the bath with his feet, and began to make jumping movements, enjoying swishing up and down. His play got more and more vigorous – pushing into the corners and twisting about. He was watching his brothers as he did this. His rhythm began to build up waves in the bath and eventually a wave splashed out of the bath. After a lot of fun in the bath, with his mother kneeling and laughing with him, she took Ewan out and quickly wrapped him in a large towel. Ewan started to cry loudly and vociferously, his jaw quivering. He didn't stop as he was rubbed and patted dry, but began to quieten as fresh clothes were put on him for the night.

In the subsequent weeks the observer saw Ewan beginning to delight in his brothers' activities and joining in with them, vigorously splashing water in the bath. Clearly the earlier need to blot them out of his mind had gone, at any rate in these observations when mother was also present.

Ewan's evident enjoyment of the splashing, kicking and bouncing up and down in the water suggests an extra element of delighted triumph in his behaviour, perhaps related to the experience of an anxiety overcome.

It was clear from the whole sequence of observations that Ewan's mother had acted as 'container' (Chapter 13) for his anxiety, and had managed to remain calm in the face of his screaming protests. A less secure mother might have experienced these as an attack, or as 'wanting his own way', and responded accordingly. Parallels come to mind with negativistic children or clients (Chapter 8) where it is easy to respond to the aggression and overlook the underlying anxieties.

PARENTAL ROLES

The experience of being a pregnant or breast-feeding mother is of course an exclusively female one. Many fathers do, however, look after their infants in the daytime in the same way as mothers do, and also share in night care. It is thus possible to think of interactions between small babies and their fathers – or other carers – which are similar in function to some of those we have described with mothers. Fathers of new babies may also perform a containing function for the mother by giving thoughtful attention to her doubts and anxieties. A mother such as Mrs Williams, beset by doubts concerning her own capacity to look after her infant, may be helped by a partner who not only pays attention to her worries, but believes in her capacity to be a loving mother.

In the next chapter we include further observations of relationships between infants and young children and their mothers and fathers and see how these contribute to the developing identity of the child.

Chapter 11

Infant Development in the Family Context

It was very apparent, through all the description of babies growing up in ordinary families, that emotional growth is not straightforward, inevitable and easy, like a flower unfolding. We discussed in the last chapter the vital importance of a mother's role in understanding the baby's emotional experiences and making them bearable. In this chapter we shall be looking at some of the experiences of a baby and small child in more detail. The developing relationships formed in the first three years contain very intense feelings, and in some of the observations we were able to see the (often painful) struggles of a baby and young child to come to terms with these.

LOVE, SEPARATION AND LOSS IN WEANING (DEAN)

For small babies, the feeding relationship is usually the centre of their waking experience, and for older babies feeding and being fed is usually a time of closeness with the mother or caring adult. We heard many observations where it was plain that the baby and mother were sharing a warm, loving relationship in the feeding (whether breast or bottle) and that baby was taking in not just nourishment but also the mother's caring and love. The feeding relationship seems to be the prototype for a capacity to take in goodness, to internalize the good qualities of another person.

Because of the love and closeness of the feeding situation, however, and its link with the baby's need for food in order to survive, the experience of having to wait for a feed, or having to accept a change to solid foods, and the gradual withdrawal of the much-loved breast or bottle, can all give rise to painful feelings. The baby has to experience his separateness from his mother and has to struggle with his inability to control her comings and goings.

These feelings have been paralleled in many of the therapeutic relationships described earlier in this book. Most of the significance in Nicholas's sessions (Chapter 8) centred around the coming and going of his worker. Rupert (Chapter 7) found the ending of each session a painful time. Feelings evoked by the ending of each session were significant in many of the descriptions. It is not always easy for a worker new to this approach to appreciate the importance of the relationship she offers, or to realize the deep feelings stirred in the client by the times and endings of their sessions together. The often intense feelings surrounding the early feeding and weaning experiences in infancy are the foundation for later relationships and may be evoked again by aspects of the interaction between client and worker.

Dean, the first child of a young couple, gave us the opportunity to observe and think about some of the intense feelings involved in both feeding and weaning. For the first six weeks he was fed more or less on demand, roughly every three hours. The observer noticed that his feeding usually followed the same pattern: he sucked from the first breast with great enthusiasm and excitement, gasping for breath between gulps, concentrating his whole attention on the feeding. After being winded, his behaviour as he sucked from the second breast was quite different: he sucked much more slowly, often looking intently at mother, stroking her breast or moving his hands gently around her breast or his face. Sometimes he made little contented noises during this second part of the feeding. After a feed he sometimes went to sleep; sometimes he sat on his mother's lap looking up at her, smiling at her and making little noises in response to her gently talking to him. Each time his initial urgent need for the breast was succeeded in the second half of the feed by a slower, gentler, more relaxed and loving relationship to the breast. When he sat on his mother's lap after the feed both seemed very close.

Dean's mother had however said several times that she did not want him to get too exclusively dependent on her. She was keen to help her husband with a business he ran from their home, and when Dean was six weeks old, she decided to put him on a regular four-hourly schedule. From then on, she said that Dean was always hungry at feedtimes; she also mentioned long and trying miserable periods every evening, when Dean cried and she got tense and anxious.

In an observation when Dean was ten weeks old, his mother told the observer she wanted to put off feeding him for a little while, and stood holding him away from her. Dean did not cry, but by sucking movements and little cries made it plain he could not forget his hunger. His mother gave him to a friend to hold; for a moment it looked as if he were going to protest, but then he briefly settled, looking across at his mother. When he started crying she took him back, and put him to the left breast. He sensed as soon as she took him what was coming, and was quite alert with expectation and breathlessness when the breast was offered. He latched on with a gasp and sucked very hard. He was then briefly winded, and fed hard at the second breast; after five minutes he lifted his back and mother at once sat him to wind him. He looked exhausted by the feeding, flopping against mother's chest and panting to regain breath.

This new pattern continued over the next weeks; Dean was very tense through all the feeding, with his arms and legs going 'as if he were climbing a mountain'. At thirteen weeks, for example, when he was put to the second breast he continued to feed in a desperate way – gulping a couple of mouthfuls, turning aside to catch his breath, then back to the breast, all the time moving his limbs energetically, kicking against mother with his legs. This feed again ended abruptly. Some while later Dean was sitting in his baby chair while his mother was busy about the flat. He began to get his hands to his face and held one or other hand there; finally he got his thumb to his mouth and sucked it. He removed it suddenly with a whimper, but then returned it to his mouth. He sucked and licked it for some minutes, watching his mother move to and fro; eventually he began fretfully crying.

He appeared to be trying to adapt to his mother's wishes and needs by holding on and managing not to cry as he waited for his feed; however, when it did come, the franticness that had been there from the first was now extended to the whole of the feed, and there was no pleasurable playtime at the breast. When he sucked his thumb and then rejected it with a whimper he was seemingly still hankering for the earlier relationship, when he was given the breast when he wanted it, and could stay with it longer.

When he was three months old his mother introduced him to new foods, and his supper was a meal of solid foods. He began sleeping through the night. The observer did not see any more breast-feeds. His mother sometimes commented that Dean wanted to be talked to all the time, otherwise he started yelling. In several observations Dean seemed not to settle when left in his baby chair or on the mat, but it was striking how he always followed his mother with his eyes. When he was three and a half months old and mother finally picked him up after he had been crying, he snuggled into her bosom as if checking it was her and later he snuggled into her for about five minutes, really pushing and rubbing his face into her bosom and making some half-hearted feeding motions. Dean was making great strides in other skills at this time, learning how to use a baby bouncer for instance, pushing himself up vigorously with his legs and fixing his mother (who was sitting watching) with his eyes all the time. He seemed to be doing it for her sake.

At four months, Dean's mother spoke of him having 'tantrums'. She thought he might be teething; he had also a nappy rash. He was having a lunch of cooked foods now as well as supper. He seemed restless and unhappy throughout the observation. His mother lifted him from the chair, sat down with him facing her and began to bounce him gently up on his feet. He was definitely unhappy and soon broke into really miserable crying. His mother stood up saying 'Oh, you are miserable,' and held him up to her shoulder. He snuggled and pushed his head into her neck and bosom and seemed comforted.

At four and half months, his mother said she had been trying to get him to cut down on breast-feeding during the day more. He had been getting more and more miserable. Finally he had 'gone on strike' and not eaten at all, and she had realized that it was too much to expect and decided to set about the weaning more slowly. He had after all given up the night-time feed voluntarily. At five months, Dean was visibly glowing and happy; it was also noticeable that his mother and he both enjoyed his nappy change and clean-up, and this now seemed to have become the focus of the happy interchanges between them that had previously followed each breast-feed.

At five and a half months, his mother said she would like to stop breast-feeding but could not induce Dean to take a bottle or a feeder-cup. He now had a morning and an evening breast-feed, with fluids from a spoon during the day. His mother was again commenting on his 'tantrums' which she said happened quite often. In the observation Dean was trying to put everything into his mouth; he grabbed a wooden toy once and thrust it into his mouth, but in his violence had hurt his lip on the edge of the toy. He gave himself up to crying bitterly. His mother took him, and he cried and burrowed into her bosom for a few minutes, but could not calm down.

His mother was going ahead with reducing his breast-feeds; however, she recognized then she was asking more of Dean than he could manage, and slowed the pace for him. Dean was finding it difficult and painful to accept the increasing restriction of his time with the breast, and the weaning seemed to have become something of a battle with him in mother's mind when she spoke of his 'tantrums'. For Dean, the breast-feeding had visibly not just been something that satisfied hunger; he had taken in love with the milk, and had 'spoken' to his mother's breast and played with it; the breast had a special meaning and intensity for him which was not entirely carried over to mother as a whole person.

At six months, Dean was having his lunch, sitting up in his high chair. While his mother was dishing up the feed and bringing it over he got so excited he could hardly contain himself and was almost crying with anticipation and suspense. The first few mouthfuls of vegetable mash, slurped down, were interspersed with cries, then he gave little moans between mouthfuls, a mixture of pleasure and desire. He was fairly tense throughout the meal, concentrating on getting the food in and down. At the last little bit he demurred, turning his face away from the spoon. He put his thumb in his mouth and sucked quietly for a moment or two.

At six and half months, he was sitting on a friend's lap, sucking apple juice from a bottle. His mother said he would still not suck milk from a bottle, however. As he sucked he was looking across at his mother all the time. When he was put on the floor, he ignored the toys but sucked at an empty baby oil bottle and at an empty feeder-cup. Then he moved, and reached out to his mother's skirt; for a moment he sat holding it and sucking his thumb. Then he picked up some torn paper and sucked his thumb solemnly while holding the paper to his cheek. He did this for some while; then he put a small piece in his mouth, sucked it, and spat it out again. His mother lifted him up into his high chair, saying he could have his tea early if he was so hungry. While he was waiting in the chair he was watching his mother with an expression of desperate anxiety as she cut bread and buttered it, as if he was simply longing to get something into his mouth. Several times he put his thumb in his mouth and sucked for a moment but seemed not to find this satisfying. When the bread came, he crammed bits of it into his mouth, taking them out and fingering them, and putting them back in.

Dean's longing for the breast was evident throughout. When he reached over to mother's skirt and clutched it while he sucked his thumb, and all the times when he nuzzled into her chest, it was as if he were mourning for a love that had gone.

He certainly developed other skills, perhaps partly in compensation, and developed other relationships with his father (see this chapter 'Developing feelings of identity' and 'The growing family and father's role'), and in that sense the weaning could have acted as a stimulus to further growth.

When he finally accepted a bottle as something to drink from (though not milk, only apple juice), he seemed to be trying to work something out about bottles: that he could pick them up and put them down when he wanted to, that he could claim them and use them or not as he wanted to; and his thumbsucking at the end, holding his mother's skirt, seemed to make it clear that he was also working something out about that other sucking, which was not always there when he wanted it, and was not under his control.

He did seem to be trying to spare his mother his demands, and tried to contain his wish for the breast by settling for a substitute (the thumb, other relationships and activities). The desperate anxiety was transferred to other food. But, his tummy full, he just turned his head away; there was no loving interplay during and following the feeding. Instead, he sat alone in his high chair and sucked his thumb for a moment.

It is easy enough to recognize a baby's delight in breast-feeding, but it is probably harder to recognize the intensity of feelings linked with weaning, and the sadness and loss a baby has to struggle with at the ending of that relationship. Perhaps it was more hurried than usual in Dean's case; but similar moments can be observed in most babies' development.

In a later observation we catch a glimpse of an anxiety that forms part of the cluster of feelings around the weaning process – an anxiety in the baby's mind that he is not lovable enough, not good enough, and that that is why he is turned away from. Dean was in his bouncer, and some friends were in the room with him and his mother. The adults were eating apples, and Dean looked longingly at the apple, waving as if willing it to him, saying 'Mma'. A friend waved back, and Dean waved again. The friend clapped, and it became a great pleasurable game. Dean waved, expecting and hoping for a response, which he got. There was endless waving and much laughter from the grown-ups. Each time he waved, Dean looked with extraordinary apprehension, almost as if he were thinking 'Is it going to work again?' 'Does she really want to notice me still?' (There are further observations of Dean later in this chapter under the heading, 'Developing feelings of identity'.)

Another baby of seven months, Sandro, had just been given a drink from a feeder-cup at his evening feed, instead of a breast-feed, for the first time (though he had had the feeder-cup at other times of day). After the feed he stood on his mother's lap, making talking noises and fingering her necklace. Then he gave her a slobbery kiss on her neck; she drew back in pretend disgust and said jokingly, 'Oh darling! How messy!' The little boy burst into tears and would not be consoled; he wept and wept, and his mother was quite distressed at the extent of it. Her disapproval of his slobbery kiss had obviously hit very deep, and may have met with a latent anxiety that yes, he *was* unlovable, and that that was why he was being fobbed off with a feeder-cup, and being deprived of one of his few remaining breast-feeding times.

STEPS IN INTEGRATION (DICK)

Dick unlike Dean, had always been bottle-fed but it was obvious that for him being weaned from the bottle carried with it very similar feelings of letting go a very close, special relationship with his mother. Over the six months covered by these observations he could be seen struggling with conflicting emotions, and oscillating between development and regression.

At the time of the first observation described here, he was eight months old; he was used to being fed solid food and enjoyed most of it, but he still had a bottle at mealtimes. On this day, he had been happily together with his mother and the observer, then his mother left the room to get his food. Dick's face fell, he looked sad and miserable, and began crying. When his mother returned, he whimpered to her. She said, 'Oh, he's been weeping real tears!' When she left the room Dick showed sadness, something the observer had not seen in him before and something that evidently surprised his mother too. It contrasts sharply with Amy's feeling of persecutory anxiety when her mother left the room (Chapter 10 'Separation and control').

Dick's mother took him on to her lap and held the bottle for him to suck from. While he sucked he gradually turned round to look at the observer. When the dog came in, Dick broke off sucking, stared unsmiling at the dog, and started to chew the teat, looking angry at the interruption. Eventually he turned back to his mother and started sucking again. After a while he stopped, let the teat fall from his mouth, put his thumb in his mouth and started chewing on that. His mother quickly withdrew the bottle, saying his teeth were hurting him, and put him in his chair. Dick looked surprised and about to cry.

When he chewed the teat and then chewed his thumb it looked as if he was testing and experiencing what his teeth could do: did they inflict pain? He may have been exploring his own biting aggressive qualities and their effects. He was surprised and upset when mother took his bottle away, and nearly cried. It might have seemed to him as if she withdrew the bottle because of his biting.

His mother started to spoon-feed him. At first Dick took the food from the spoon slowly and she asked him if he didn't like it. Dick gradually took the food more quickly, opening his mouth to receive the next spoonful before his mother had it ready. When the dog came towards him, Dick banged hard on the side of the chair as if he again resented the dog being there. He looked down towards his blue teddy which his mother picked up and gave him to hold; she murmured something, smiling at him. He beamed at her, clapping his hands together, and let go of the teddy which fell in his chair. He rubbed his leg against his mother's as he fed and made talking sounds to her to which she responded. He then dangled the teddy in front of the dog, and his mother told him to stop teasing him. A moment later he made a grab for the dog, who removed himself quickly.

Perhaps he saw the dog as a possible rival for his mother's attention and love, and was teasing and triumphing over him by saying something like '*I've* got the soft cuddly teddy-mummy now, and you haven't'. If he was giving expression to some feelings of rivalry, it implies he was beginning to be aware of his own hostile feelings.

When Dick had eaten most of the main course, his mother gave him the bottle, commenting to the observer that she could not get Dick to hold it and feed himself. Dick did everything else with it; he rolled it, pulled the teat, and scratched the tray with his fingers where the milk had dribbled. Then he picked the bottle up and dropped it over the side.

He was investigating it (tipping it and rolling it), but there was also an element of attack and banishment (pulling the teat, and then dropping the bottle over the side of the chair). He may have felt mother was trying to 'drop' him by insisting he hold the bottle himself. He was obviously very reluctant to hold it himself; evidently he loved and wanted the continued link with mother who should hold the bottle for him.

When this observation was discussed in the group, members felt that Dick was experiencing love towards his mother but also some anger and resentment against her, and that he was struggling with these two conflicting emotions, aware of them both as feelings he had towards the one person. This is very different from what Amy experienced when her mother left the room and she cried hard and angrily at a different person: the one (the mother) was idealized, the other (the observer) was totally bad. Dick's emerging capacity to bring together loving and angry feelings towards the same person, his mother, led to the dawning of sadness and depressive anxieties. That is, he may have felt she left the room or withdrew the bottle or suddenly put him off her lap and into the chair, because she did not want him any more, owing to his aggressive attacks (the biting, chewing and banging).

Sometimes Dick seemed to avoid these painful feelings by trying to control his mother and have her at his beck and call. He seemed to insist at moments that she must be there to hold the bottle and was not to have her freedom. It was an ordinary domestic scene which nevertheless gave glimpses of sadness, possessiveness, anger and love.

A month later Dick's mother had put him in his feeding chair and held his bottle for him while he drank. His hands were in the air as he started drinking, his fingers as if plucking the air. Then his right hand went to the bottle and his mother said 'That's right, you hold it'. She tried to let go but Dick looked at her reproachfully and made no attempt to hold the bottle. Then after a moment or two mother picked up his left hand and placed it on the bottle, and as he seemed to take hold of it she said he should hold it while she went to get his food.

Once she let go of it, the bottle in his hand went into an upright position. He pulled a face and made a protesting cry as he gulped at the teat. Then he took it out of his mouth and put it back again in an upright position, still sucking it. Then he started to cry, with a bad-tempered or frustrated sound. His mother called out that she was just coming.

She returned with his food and they smiled at one another, Dick sometimes chuckling as well. As she approached Dick she tipped the bottle up, holding it for him. Dick gave vent to his feelings by chewing on the teat with his teeth. During one such moment she withdrew the bottle and started to feed Dick with the solid food. Dick took the food but started to stiffen and shake and make little protesting noises after he had taken the food into his mouth. He repeated this later and started to bring some of it out in the process. She laughingly told him not to splutter it over her and she remained good-natured throughout his protests.

Dick's mother was very gentle with him and also looked quite sad at times when he was protesting and chewing the bottle or refusing the solid food. She said to the observer that she did feel sad at times, not having a totally dependent little baby any more.

In an observation a month later Dick picked up the bottle on his own and drank from it, looking from his mother to the observer and back again as if to make sure both adults could see him doing this. It seemed as if he were trying to achieve some separation from his mother in the feeding situation. After his meal he struggled to walk off across the room on his own; perhaps this was also to indicate that it was he who was making the separation from his mother, not the other way round. He seemed ready to try moving on from being mother's little dependent baby.

At twelve months he was also trying to use a spoon and feed himself, sometimes holding a second spoon that his mother had as well. After the meal he walked around holding his bottle by the teat, then put it on a ledge and pushed it out of reach. He then climbed on to a stool and got it back; he tipped it over and left it. He fetched a little bike and gave it a push but then lost interest and lay on the floor doing nothing for a while. Then he tried to climb up and sit in his pushchair; finally he snuggled into his mother's lap.

Dick's behaviour here again suggested struggles about managing not to be the 'little baby' any more. When he clutched both spoons he may have been trying out what it feels like to be the mother with the spoons. The observer also reported that there were times when he looked as if he was 'being father', 'working' with a hammer for example; these seem like primitive forms of identification, a subject described in greater detail below. And when he pushed the bottle out of reach and then climbed up to get it, perhaps he was also oscillating between feeling ready and not ready to be weaned. He made an attempt to be a 'big boy' with the bike, but gave up, and the observer had a feeling of despondency underlying his actions. He reverted to being the little one who is pushed in the pushchair and sits in his mother's lap.

At thirteen months Dick was drinking from a feeder cup and feeding himself fairly skilfully for part of the meal. When his mother lifted him from his chair he went to get his soft blue teddy, poked its black nose, tugged its ear, then hugged it to himself very tightly, burying his face in its fur. He sat it on the sofa; it toppled over, and he sat it upright again, just as his mother had helped him to sit up when he was smaller; here he seemed to be 'mothering' the teddy.

Dick seemed to be expressing many varied and conflicting emotions in his behaviour over these six months. This suggests he was in touch with his feelings and struggling with them and experiencing the problems they posed him, rather than denying their existence. Mary, who will be described later in this chapter, seemed in contrast not to be aware of many of her feelings of envy and rivalry until they erupted in the form of soiling. Dick's ability to move between development and regression was quite different from the rigidity of behaviour of some of the children described in Parts 1 to 3 who seemed very 'stuck' in their repetitive disturbed behaviour.

WORKING THROUGH A PAINFUL EMOTIONAL EXPERIENCE (EMMA)

Emma was the first, and much wanted, child born to young parents. Her mother had breast-fed her, keeping the breast-feeding going after her return to part-time work when Emma was five months old. Emma was looked after at a friend's house while her mother was at work. Thought her first year of life it was striking how perceptive Emma's mother was of her needs, and how much both parents enjoyed a warm, physically close relationship with Emma. Emma herself seemed to have adapted to the routine of going to a baby-minder, after an initial difficult two-week period when she had a constant cold and 'seemed to go downhill', as her mother had put it. The observer had seen several 'reunions' between Emma and her mother when it was apparent how happy both were to see each other.

One time, however, in the second year of the observation when Emma was fourteen months old, the observer arrived in the middle of a family crisis; it was the only time she had ever seen Emma cry.

Emma's father opened the door to me, looking harassed. I could hear Emma's cries as I walked down the hall and into the kitchen. She was sitting in a low baby chair. There were tears running down her cheeks, her nose was running and she was ramming an empty plastic bottle into her mouth. Her mother was standing with her back to her, peeling potatoes at the sink; she said Emma was crying as she had just had to grab her from the baby-minder and she hadn't had time to cuddle her. She had had to rush back from work and start clearing up and cooking straightaway as some relatives were arriving unexpectedly following an accident. She herself was looking rather desperate and said she had called to Emma that she 'would have to get on with it'. Emma was still crying loudly. She glared at me. All her face was wet and she was pushing at her mouth and rubbing her hair with the back of her hand. Her father and mother were explaining the crisis to me and discussing how they were going to cope; then Emma's father said, 'Why don't *I* do the potatoes?' and her mother lifted Emma out of the chair; Emma put her arms round her mother's neck and gradually she quietened. Her mother held her while she stirred some food that was on the cooker. Emma turned a pink damp face from her mother's neck and smiled at me.

Emma's mother sat her on her high chair and started to feed her from a large dish of baby food. Emma said 'Biccy', but her mother laughed and said she could finish her first course first. Emma ate with great enjoyment, savouring every mouthful thoughtfully and occasionally smiling at me. Two of the visitors arrived and Emma's mother suggested they should go into the sitting-room.

Emma's father left to meet the other relatives and her mother took Emma from the high chair into the sitting-room. Emma was holding some pieces of biscuit and her mother sat her on the floor, sitting herself by the relatives. I went and sat by Emma, who was facing her mother.

Emma's mother suggested that Emma should show me her new puzzle toy and fetched the toy box. Emma waved a yellow plastic fish at her mother and said 'fish'.

Emma picked up a piece of the puzzle toy and glanced at it. Then she turned and crawled over to her mother who was deep in conversation. Emma pulled herself up on her mother's legs, whimpering and rubbing herself on her mother. Mother went on talking but put her hand behind Emma's head and put Emma's face beside hers.

Emma turned round and looked at me smiling, but still making moaning noises. Her mother rocked her gently and slowly Emma quietened. She lifted her back to the toy box, saying 'Come on, come and show (the observer) your new toys.' She returned to her visitors and again Emma glanced at the puzzle toy, picked up a piece but then dropped it, looking back at her mother.

She went back to her mother and crawled up on to her lap, putting her arms round her neck. Her mother went on talking. Emma put her hand gently into her mother's mouth and ran her fingers along her teeth. Her mother lifted her face and kissed Emma and Emma patted her cheek, saying 'Aah'.

Emma's mother rocked her gently, returning to the conversation. Emma fingered one of her mother's ear-rings and then looked round to her mother's other ear-ring and said 'two'. She pushed herself up on her toes, rubbing her head into her mother's neck.

Her father could be heard coming down the hall. He had brought other relatives and introduced them to me. Emma turned and pushed herself into mother.

Her father said he'd take these guests into the study as it would be easier. Directly he left the room Emma launched herself from her mother's knee and hurried into the study. Her father was standing talking to his visitors. Emma ran to him and put her arms round his legs, pressing her face between them. He talked softly to her, telling her about the visitors, that they would love to see her. She turned and looked and smiled at them, still leaning on her father. He walked with her and squatted by her, still talking and including the visitors. Emma smiled and turned and walked from the room and went and stood by her mother who was still in the sitting-room. Her mother smiled when she saw her and said 'She's including me in what's going on next door.'

It had been plain from previous weeks that Emma had managed to adapt to her mother's regular absences, and had settled down with the baby-minder, but always cherished her reunion with her mother; today this had had to be forfeited. Her mother was taken aback by a distressing family crisis and had been fairly sharp with Emma. This was a small ripple in the pond for this happy, close-knit family, and Emma had clearly got over it well before the observer left. But perhaps it is possible to learn something of how Emma experienced the crisis; how her perception of her mother changed; and how she made peace with her again afterwards. An adult can usually (though not always) hold on to his knowledge of someone else as a good loved friend, even in the middle of a quarrel; but it seemed clear here that Emma had completely lost touch with any reality of her mother as a loving, caring person. Emma was attacking her own mouth with a hard, empty plastic bottle. Instead of her mother's gentle attentive feeding, the mother that had shouted at her now seemed to be experienced as something hard and painful ramming into her mouth. The good mother was lost in Emma's inner world and completely replaced by a hard, cruel, attacking one. Her mother was, herself, still the same person, loving but at the moment short-tempered and unavailable. A 'splitting' such as Emma showed here between her good, loved mother and the bad one, and her devastating experience of feeling attacked by the bad one, are phenomena of the paranoid-schizoid position, discussed under that heading in Chapter 14. Emma also glared at the observer, endowing her with bad characteristics too. This was similar to Amy's behaviour with the observer when her mother left the room (Chapter 10).

But her father's offer to help with the cooking enabled Emma's mother to rescue Emma. His offer may have evolved from their talking the problem over together as they explained it to the observer; we will return to this below. Emma responded at once, putting her arms around her mother's neck. Once her contact with her good mother was restored in the external world, Emma's internal world of love and trust began to be restored, and she was even able straightaway to make friends again with the observer.

But the bad experience was not to be forgotton and blanked out. We can see Emma working it through, remembering it, trying to link it with this loving mother she had regained, needing over and over again to 'tell' her mother about it, sharing the bad experience with her mother ('whimpering' and 'moaning') and finally perhaps reaching the insight that the two completely separate, incompatible, mutually exclusive mothers (the cruel, hard, empty-bottle mother, and the mother with the soft lap and round cheeks) were the same. She ran her fingers along her mother's (hard) teeth, perhaps locating there the hard words, the hard bottle; and finally established the 'two' ear-rings, out of sight of each other but nevertheless part of the same mother. It seemed then that the work of thinking about, and digesting, this experience was completed and Emma had grown a little and developed as a result. This was in contrast to Mary's behaviour described later in this chapter.

We catch only a glimpse of the parents' interaction with the observer. She had shared their anxieties over separations and illnesses several times in the previous year. Here it seems at least possible that their sharing the desperate situation with her enabled them to find a solution and that she had in some way acted as a maternal 'container' for them.

STRUGGLING WITH JEALOUSY AND RIVALRY (PETER; MARY)

Sometimes a second baby has been born towards the end of a two-year observation period and sometimes the family of the baby to be observed already had an older child, not yet of school age, who had been at home during most of the observations. Preparing for the arrival of a new sibling, the birth and first months of the new life in the family are all major events in the life of a small child. To some extent these children have all been 'displaced' as the baby of the family, and we have been able to learn a great deal about how intense their sense of pain and loss can be at times as they struggle with strong feelings of jealousy and of being left out. We have also seen how a mother's understanding and support, and sometimes especially a father's, can enable an older child to come to terms with these feelings, and make considerable strides forward as a result of the new experience.

Peter, aged fifteen months, had been a very cherished, 'ideal' first baby. While his mother was feeding his two-week-old baby sister, he kept running into the kitchen and fetching himself a biscuit. She said that the day before he had disappeared into the kitchen during his sister's feed time, and she found later that he had opened and emptied all the cupboards. She showed the observer a pink frilled pram rug she had been given for the new baby, and mentioned Peter's 'blankie', actually a pram rug too, that he was going to keep as his own. Peter at once hurried behind the sofa and scooped up a large fawn-coloured soft rug and held it to himself. Then he curled up in a foetal position on the floor, fingering the blanket while he sucked a thumb, with a sad, faraway look on his face. His mother said he often curled up on the sofa like that with his 'blankie' next to her while she was feeding the new baby.

David, aged five, felt that he was a schoolboy when his brother was born, and decided that he had outgrown his toys; he 'only liked cars and Lego' and he had decided to donate the teddies to the new baby. However, when the baby was five weeks old, David suddenly remembered a rather ugly soft plastic Donald Duck with a squashy beak that he had loved chewing as a baby, but had not played with for a long time. Now he announced he 'needed it most importantly'. He became more and more unhappy and frantic as it was searched for, finally bursting into tears when his mother said it seemed to be lost.

Although David was much older than Peter, and felt himself to belong to the world of school, and masculine interests, nevertheless seeing his mother tending the new baby, and seeing him feeding at the breast, had at a deeper level revived his intense possessive love for his mother and for her body, and had also confronted him with the renewed loss of this special relationship. But unlike Peter, he was not quite consciously aware of what he had lost and what he longed for. He experienced his loss in a very concrete way. It was displaced on to a long-forgotten toy; yet the pain and sadness were as real for him as they had been for Peter.

Sally, aged four, had been watching television and paying no attention to her mother who was feeding her four-week-old baby brother in the same room. When she left the room to bath the baby, Sally wanted to come too, but was told to stay in the sitting-room with her grandmother (perhaps because baby John had not yet got used to being bathed, and her mother, flustered, knew he was likely to cry a lot). Sally turned from the bathroom door in silence but her face looked sullen and near to angry tears. When John was bathed and dressed and back in the sitting-room looking quite sleepy, Sally's mother gave him to Sally to hold. Sally held John's head quite rigidly in her hands, with a set, grim look on her face, so that John started to cry. Her mother spoke gently to Sally and tried to 'rearrange' John on her lap, but Sally pushed him away.

The parents of both Sally and David were able to recognize the feelings of loss, of being left out and displaced, and could accept the intermittent hatred of the new baby that sometimes accompanied them; over the next months they were able to support Sally and David, and it was obvious that each child also felt a lot of pleasure and joy in their new siblings as well.

Mary's experience seemed rather different. She was three and a half and Robert was two when the next baby in their family was expected. Robert had been premature and ailing for the first few months of his life. Their mother had had to rely on Mary 'managing' from a very early age. Mary, a conforming, intelligent girl, had adapted by developing verbal skills very early, enjoying 'educational' toys and turning more and more to her father when he was at home.

Mary's mother, heavily pregnant with the third child-to-be, was in the garden with both children. Robert was swinging fairly wildly on a low baby swing. Mary was calling to everyone to see how good she was on the scooter, rolling down a slope on the grass with gathering speed. The next time down, Mary's scooter headed straight for the baby swing, and although everyone leapt up, Robert catapulted out of the swing, on to his hands before his mother or the observer could catch him. Mary had also leapt off the scooter and very lovingly without being asked kissed Robert and said she was sorry. In fact Robert seemed unscathed, did not cry and got straight back on to the swing. Robert began swinging violently. Mother told Mary to put away the scooter 'and fetch a quiet toy'. This Mary did without a word but gave a sideways rebellious look at her mother.

She fetched out a Lego tray and began making a castle; she obviously knew how to do it well and was showing the observer that she did, explaining why the bricks had to overlap, and so on. Robert did not like being left out; he got off the swing and demanded the observer's attention by climbing on to her lap, turning her head with his hands away from Mary and telling her to look at his appliquéd Rupert suit. Mary left the Lego and stood by the observer showing off her new sundress. Their mother then noticed that Robert was holding his trousers and wriggling about on the observer's lap; this to her meant that the potty was necessary. She brought it out into the garden and Robert grinned at the observer as he did a wee. Mother was delighted and praised him as she straightened his suit. Mary was standing quietly by, looking on. Mother left the garden to empty the pot and to get the tea.

In the meantime Mary had told the observer all about their new baby; how he was in mummy's tummy and would come out soon and she was to help choose the name. She took her rag doll out of a toy pram in the shed and said this was her baby boy, and as she cuddled it she said she was going to help her mother with the new baby. Robert cried '*Me* baby, *me* baby!' but Mary said, 'No, our new baby is in Mummy's tummy.' Mother called them in for tea, but Mary indicated she wanted to go to the toilet by bouncing up and down and holding her hands between her legs. Mother said 'Go along then, but hurry up!' Mary disappeared upstairs. Later on, her mother said with exasperation that she found that Mary had used Robert's pot, passed a motion as well as wee'd, and then emptied the pot on her bedroom carpet. She said Mary had been clean and dry for some while and was well used to using the lavatory, not the pot, but had become 'really naughty' in the last few months.

It seemed that Mary felt her mother was not available for her in a special sense. It was as if what she missed was not the soft feeding mother, as Peter did, nor her mother's time and attention, as Sally did, but more a mother who could take and accept her mess. Robert was helped to use the pot, and praised for it. This busy, tired mother not unnaturally hoped that her eldest child could look after herself, especially with the prospect of a new baby's nappies looming so near. But Mary seemed to be demonstrating not only that she still needed the pot, and mother's assistance with her clothes, like Robert, but also that she felt the need to pay her mother back, to punish her, by dumping the excreta on to her (literally on to mother's carpet) whether she wanted them or not. Perhaps her feelings of jealousy over Robert had had to be suppressed and deflected rather than accepted and understood (her mother had been in hospital and had then had to devote herself to Robert in his first few months because of his illness); perhaps there had never been the work of communication and understanding between them over Mary's feeling left out; the concrete 'mess' of her urine and faeces could then also be the tangle of her feelings, never accepted and so never sorted out. And the mother who fails to listen (for whatever reason) can so easily be perceived as the mother who refuses to listen and who therefore in the end has to have it flung at her. Mary herself had developed as a conforming 'achieving' little girl going for educational toys rather than fantasy play; perhaps this had been partly her way of defending herself against recognizing her own 'messy' baby self with its painful feelings. The underlying feelings are quite apparent in Peter's craving for biscuits and blanket, but in the case of Mary's soiling the feelings are not immediately recognizable. So much of what is dismissed as 'difficult', 'naughty', and 'spoilt' behaviour is a concrete substitute for an inner, too painful emotion. It has its reflection in the apparently mindless acting out of older children or adolescents. Mary's deliberate soiling has its echo in the symptoms of some of the children who are referred for help. Her mother's exasperation reflected her affront at this deliberate naughtiness; a communication that went wrong has become an attack.

DEVELOPING FEELINGS OF IDENTITY (DEAN; PETER)

We have seen how the good aspects of a baby's inner world are built up from his ability to take in, and identify with, his mother, her caring and concern for him and her ability to understand and contain his fears and anxieties. We have also discussed how the children and young people we work with may be able to take in and internalize something of ourselves and something of our ability to contain and modify mental pain. It may be helpful here to look at some examples of a baby and a toddler exploring a father's qualities, and beginning to internalize and identify with them. There is plenty of evidence that a baby notices, and responds to its father in the first few weeks of life in quite a different way from his response to mother. (See also the observation of Ewan briefly 'taking in' his father at eight weeks old, Chapter 10).

In the observation of Dean (whose feeding experience was described at the beginning of this chapter), Dean was two weeks old and alone in the room with his father. Dean seemed to experience him as a 'not-mother', an experience to be endured, or at best a palliative, but never an object of interest in his own right.

Dean was yelling loudly when I arrived, a good deal of energy going into it, with his legs, arms and head all moving. His father was starting to change his nappy, which he did gently and carefully. The nappy was full of faeces and Dean seemed relieved to be rid of it. The fury of the crying died down and while his father got on with cleaning up his bottom – cottonwool, warm water, cream – Dean cried intermittently in between searching for the breast. He turned his head from side to side, looking and straining with arms, hands and head, the mouth seeking something to suck. The putting on of a fresh nappy took a long time and Dean was frustrated by his fruitless searching; he started to yell again, kicking and wriggling violently, raising his abdomen off the table and generally not making the task of fitting the nappy any easier. This was finally achieved and his father picked Dean up in his arms and held him up against his shoulder, where he stopped crying. Dean blinked across into the room, still trying – but with less earnestness – to find something to suck.

Contrast that with the following observation, when Dean was about three months old, sitting on his mother's lap and getting rather tired towards the end of the afternoon.

Dean grizzled a bit; he was not very happy or comfortable. Mother tilted him forward, his stomach supported on her hand, and he looked happier. His father came into the room at this point, watched closely by Dean as he talked briefly to his wife and then left the room to answer the telephone. When he returned Dean shouted 'Ah, ha' and raised his arms; his father took Dean on his lap; there followed an absorbing 'conversation' between father and son, who was sitting up facing him. Father made a noise, then Dean made a similar noise; father repeated it and waited for Dean to respond. It was hard to know who was imitating whom, but both were enjoying the game. Dean's father then put him into his baby chair. He held a circular rattle in front of Dean, who struggled with immense concentration and effort and eventually got hold of it in one hand. Dean talked to the rattle, very pleased with his achievement. He then spent some time trying to get the rattle to his mouth, kicking actively with his feet to help his hands along. He managed to suck at the rattle for a bit, then transferred it to his other hand, at which his mother exclaimed that he had not done this before. All this time Dean was concentrating tremendously hard, his tongue often protruding, while he tried to organize his activity with the rattle. Eventually he became rather distressed, apparently unable to get rid of it, and finally threw it to the ground with an air of finality.

A few weeks later:

Dean was sitting in his little chair holding his ring rattle, watching father who was moving about the room. His father approached and talked to him for a bit. Dean responded with expressive breathing and blowing bubbles. 'That's very good,' said his father. Dean moved the ring to his other hand, breathing hard with concentration and all the while reacting with crows and gurgles to father as he moved in and out of Dean's vision. He squatted down again and stuck his tongue out and winked exaggeratedly at Dean, who watched very carefully and stuck his own tongue out a little way. His father then left the room. Dean looked disappointed and sad. He dropped the rattle. I gave it back but he dropped it again quite deliberately down by his side, twice more.

Dean's absorption with his father in these observations seems to be linked with an urge to achieve new skills, and mastery of his environment, based on imitating and identifying with his much-loved father (notice that the observer will not do as a substitute). Peter, (referred to also in the discussion of older brothers and sisters) 'suddenly developed a passion for climbing' after the birth of his baby sister. He struggled repeatedly to get on to and over all the furniture in the house. His mother said he clapped his hands when he had achieved something, as this is how his father praised him when he managed something difficult.

While his sister was being dressed Peter climbed all over the ottoman and tried to look out of the window. He climbed into the wardrobe next and eventually managed to dislodge a key from the wardrobe door. He took this key over to a large plastic box that his mother had locked because it contained medicaments and lotions for his sister's bath. Peter tried to sort out the lock of the box with the key from the wardrobe. When they all went downstairs, Peter pushed a chair against the French window, climbed on to it, and looked out into the garden from that height. He tried to reach up to a high shelf nearby with forbidden objects on it. He went over to another small window and climbed on to the coalbox there. The following week he placed a chair against the French window again and stood on it, trying to get the key out of the glass door. While his sister was being fed, Peter was continually climbing up over furniture and pulling at out-of-reach objects.

Next week, while his mother was collecting things for his sister's bath, Peter was climbing about on the arms of an armchair, then from there on to the radiator, then hanging on to the window-handle. His mother described the kind of behaviour he now entered into all the time. She stretched her hand out round the whole of the room indicating things he had climbed, including a very high chest, from the top of which he had taken things, and the windowsills (the windows all had safety locks). On all occasions, his father was not there, perhaps Peter was struggling to acquire skills that he seemed to link with his father. There was sometimes a frenzied quality to it, as if he were desperately needing to be a young man in order not to be aware of being his mother's (now displaced) little baby. In the next observation we see how shattered he was when this temporarily broke down.

It was evident that Peter was very pleased to have his dad at home. He watched his father getting the fireplace ready for having a fire. He was carrying a little booklet around with him and his mother asked him what it was. He came close to tearing the outer cover, and his mother said 'No, you can't have that, go and take it to Daddy.' Peter intently watched while his father laid and lit the fire; Peter clutched one of the sticks of wood. His father emptied the coal bucket; Peter struggled to pick up the big bucket and carry it out to the kitchen. He carried the bucket back, and stood watching the flames with shrieks of joy. When his father went to refill the bucket, Peter followed him, and did so again a short while later when his father went to use the telephone.

Both had been gone for quite a while when Peter could be heard suddenly bursting out crying in the front hall. His mother went to fetch him, and brought him back in, with tears streaming down his face. He would not let her comfort him, crying hard while his face got red and blotchy. His mother comforted him as best she could but he would not stop until his father came. The trouble had evidently been something to do with the booklet and the telephone call. Peter was gradually comforted by his father's voice. When he was quiet his mother laid him on the sofa and covered him with his baby sister's rug. It immediately became evident how conscious Peter was of the experience of having Sasha's rug on him; he lay there quite still holding the booklet and said just once 'Sha-sha' and his face took on a slightly glazed expression. He sucked his thumb and just lay there savouring the experience.

That seemed to be an attempt at identification that had not really succeeded; it seemed to be based on a denial of the real differences in age, size, and everything else between him and his father, and so it was bound to be break down sooner or later, with humiliation added to the frustration and despair. Nevertheless, some of the skills Peter was struggling to attain really were becoming his; taking in some good aspects of a loved person, and identifying with this good person inside oneself, is a process that carries on throughout life. At the end of the last observation, Peter seemed to be projectively identifying with his baby sister Sasha, the one who is little and helpless and covered with mother's soft warmth and love; it was almost as if being *Peter* was too painful and unbearable at that moment.

Peter's attempt at identification with his father seemed to consist in his 'becoming' father, and he was no longer in touch with his own littleness, dependency, jealousy, and so on. To that extent the identification was not really a helpful one. (We discuss projective identification in Chapter 12 and introjective identification in Chapter 14.)

THE GROWING FAMILY AND FATHER'S ROLE (IRIS; FARALA)

The Johnson family had three boys and then a little girl in fairly quick succession. When baby Iris was born her brothers were approximately five, three and two years old. Their father, a businessman, has managed to postpone some of his trips in order to be at home to help his wife as much as possible in the months following Iris's birth. He seemed particularly to make himself available for the boys when their mother was preoccupied with the baby. In an early observation, when Iris was only a few weeks old, their father and an older visiting cousin gathered the boys together while their mother was feeding Iris in the garden. He organized a game with some balls in which they all wanted to participate, showing pleasure and interest. Their attention seemed to wander at times, however, and the game, including some of the balls, drew nearer and nearer to mother and Iris, without any adult comment being made. At one time the 3-year-old seemed to be giving a rather desultory solo demonstration of how he could bounce the ball, whilst the 2-year-old went off in the vicinity of his mother and the baby, apparently to retrieve a ball. In this 'retrieval' he knocked the little hammock in which Iris had now been placed, but neither she nor her mother seemed to notice. He then banged the hammock more directly; Iris cried and was picked up, and her brother briefly scolded. Nevertheless, with their father's help, the game was resumed and played with some enjoyment.

The Patel family had a little girl, Farala, who was three when her baby sister Madhur was born. During an early observation her mother was preparing to feed Madhur. Farala watched, kissed the baby, and then placed herself on the sofa next to mother and baby in a curled-up position, one hand touching her mother and the thumb of the other hand in her mouth. She watched the feed, during which the mother talked in a way that seemed to include both children. Their father, a teacher, also tried to be at home as much as he could to help. He returned home that day when his wife was still feeding the baby. He offered to make the tea and asked Farala if she would like to help. She said she would and got up eagerly to go with him.

These are brief illustrations of how two families in their own way related to the feelings of older children shortly after the birth of a new baby. Both families also drew the observer's attention to interests and skills of the older children, and encouraged them to show the observers some of their toys and their achievements. Both families also spoke of not wanting the older children to suffer unduly on account of the new baby. The observations illustrate parental concern, and help us to be aware of the needs of the older children and the particular contribution of fathers at such a time.

A father, even if he cannot be physically present as much as might be wished, may be able by his help and understanding to offer containment to the mother in her attempt to respond to the enlarged family and their feelings. Mrs Patel told the observer how she enjoyed discussing her day with the children with her husband, and that this seemed to relieve some of the strain she found with now having two children to care for. The support that one less directly involved worker can give to another in a similar way is discussed in Chapter 6 ('Headteacher and care worker in a residential school'). The observations also underline the importance, and the individuality, of both father and mother. One can also see how a father may help children to get in touch with a wider range of feelings, helpful to development. We saw the pleasure Farala had in being able to do something with her father. This may, perhaps, have given her some relief from the intensity of her emotions about the new baby. In this instance she may have been trying to manage to love the new baby by actually feeling herself into the feeding situation of the baby and mother. If so, the one-to-one relationship with her father could enable her to feel responded to as the actual 3-year-old that she was. She would also have had the opportunity of using her skills to experience herself as different from the baby; this could have helped her to develop her perception of herself as a wanted and even possibly useful little girl, as opposed to trying to avoid feeling herself as solely a displaced baby.

In the Johnson family we also saw the pleasure with which the relationship with their father was taken up at the start of the ball game, and the pleasure also from participation within it. This example also illustrates the provision of an opportunity to develop skills and be like their father. It is also apparent here that the relationship with him need not be perceived as something replacing that with their mother, but as something different and individual that exists in its own right with its own contribution to family life. (In saying this we are not implying that a father cannot carry out so-called 'maternal' functioning; we are simply drawing attention to the difference between parents and, of course, other carers.)

The burden of bringing up a child alone is a heavy one. If the mother forms a new partnership this is not necessarily better, as we saw with Sam (Chapter 7) who was beaten and abused by two stepfathers in succession.

When Miguel's mother remarried (Chapter 8) his new stepfather proved very supportive. However, Miguel also had the arrival of a new baby to contend with, and the painful experience of seeing this new baby receive the love and care which he himself had never had may have proved too much for him to bear.

Changing patterns in family structure – the aftermath of divorce, the arrival of step-parents and step-siblings, single-sex couples as parents, one-parent families – have been reflected sometimes in the work we describe here but these patterns are not themselves its main focus.

The birth of a new baby is a major event for an older child. His place in the family is changed and his sense of identity affected. Although he may experience some pleasure and relief that a new baby can be born safely in spite of his own jealousy, he no longer occupies the same position in the family and he inevitably suffers pain and loss.

The observations help us to think about ways that seem to be developmentally helpful in approaching this pain. We can see one of the little Johnson boys showing some aspect of his feelings in the rather desultory bouncing of the ball, and his little brother's open display of jealousy accompanied perhaps by a wish to have his feelings noticed. Farala's close involvement in the feeding situation may have been keeping feelings of jealousy at bay. As we saw with the other brothers and sisters of the new baby, it is important for parents to notice and find some way of being in touch with their children's unavoidable suffering. This will probably contain elements of jealousy which is not always a socially acceptable emotion. Not noticing, albeit accompanied by attentive concern in other areas, can be felt as a not wanting to know, and the pleasurable provision of other activities as a mere uncaring deflection. We saw in Chapter 1 how important it was that Wayne's possible pain should find a place to be thought about.

We have looked here briefly at early moments in the lives of families where there is a new baby. Observers are privileged in being able to follow the developing interactive processes of such parents and their children and to see how they manage to relate to the joys and sorrows that a new birth brings. As we have said before, there are broad developmental needs, but there is no set or 'right' way for all families to relate to them.

Part 5

A Review of Themes and Concepts

Chapter 12

Inner World, Phantasy and Primitive Communication

Note: We spell 'phantasy' with a 'ph' to indicate that this refers to an unconscious process, or one very near to it, as here, to distinguish it from the fantasy (spelt with an 'f') activity of daydreaming, which is conscious.

INNER WORLD AND PHANTASY

We might begin by asking not only 'what is the inner world' but also how do we know there is such a thing, and of what relevance is it?

Children are often brought for help because their parents, or possibly their school, are concerned about their behaviour. So it may be asked in what way is a child's inner world relevant, since it is his behaviour that needs altering? Similarly adolescents and young adults may ask for help because of problems in relationships with other people, so how is it relevant to consider what may (or may not) exist in their own private unconscious life?

Perhaps we could consider an adolescent girl, Mamie, who was intelligent and was expected by the school to do well in A-levels and go on to higher education. Mamie left school at sixteen against her parents' wishes, took an unskilled job, and started a relationship with a young man whom her parents suspected of taking drugs. Mamie had several successive relationships, all with men who were at odds with society and in trouble in some way or other. She came to a counselling service eventually and through many stormy sessions it became plain how much Mamie experienced the counsellor as a hostile 'mother' who disapproved of and enviously criticized her love relationships. These elements were not present in the counsellor's words and behaviour but only existed in Mamie's perception of her. Mamie also began to be aware how much she was belittling and denigrating herself as someone too degraded to have a 'good' boyfriend. Mamie's behaviour had been determined by forces and conflicts of which she was quite unconscious. We not only have relationships with people in outer reality; we also have relationships with unconscious figures in our inner world which shape and influence our behaviour in the outer world.

How does our inner world come about, how is it formed and modified? Klein (1952) describes how this inner, or internal, world is built up by a process of introjection (a taking in) and projection (a putting out) starting from very early in life.

The baby observations described in Part 4 may provide some examples. Amy, when two months old, was angrily crying and seemed to be avoiding looking at her mother, as if her mother were something bad that was causing or heightening Amy's anger and distress. Later, when she was four months old, she was put on to the observer's lap and began crying in a way that made the observer feel she had done something dreadful to Amy. In both these examples Amy's perception of the other person (her mother, the observer) was of a bad, hostile object. Amy perceived them as bad because she had projected into them some qualities of badness. This may seem an elaborate description for a common enough, and transient, moment in a baby's life. But a similar mental event can happen with an older person sufficiently often, as we saw with Mamie, to distort any relationships he or she may make.

Projection often (though not always) consists in putting bad qualities into another person. Introjection, inversely, consists often in taking in something good. Amy's screaming, in the first episode, ended when her mother put her to the breast; Amy then looked intently into her mother's eyes while she fed, and peace was restored: it seemed that Amy was 'taking in' the goodness of the milk and also the goodness of her mother's loving glance.

Our unconscious inner world, throughout life, seems to consist very concretely of phantasy objects. There are of course impulses, physical sensations, and emotions, which may or may not be conscious. But they also have inner unconscious representatives. The baby does not experience just the physical pain of hunger; the hunger is accompanied by an unconscious mental equivalent. We can sense something of this in adult life if we have a physical illness. It is rare for the discomfort to be purely physical; we can sometimes become aware of an accompanying mental phantasy, for example that we 'deserved' to be ill, that someone made us ill or gave us the illness, or that the illness will last forever. Common speech reflects the linked identity of physical and psychic events: we speak of devouring someone with our eyes, or digesting a piece of news.

Meltzer (1978) refers to Klein's very concrete conception of this internal world as being 'in many ways her least spoken about and perhaps greatest contribution to psycho-analysis'. Heimann's description of it is graphic:

> An inner world comes into being. The infant feels that there are objects, parts of people and people inside his body, that are very alive and active, affect him and are affected by him. This inner world of life and events is a creation of the infant's unconscious phantasy, his private replica of the world and objects about him. Thus it forms part of his relation to his environment, and he is no less affected by the condition and activities and feelings – imagined by himself though they are – of his self-created inner objects than by the real people outside himself. Sensations, feelings, moods and modes of behaviour are largely determined by such phantasies about people inside the body and events in the inner world. . . The phantasies about the inner world are inseparable from the infant's relation with

the outer world and real people. It is only a limitation of our means of description which makes it appear as if there were two distinct entities which influence one another, instead of one whole, one multi-faceted interacting experience (Heimann, 1952).

Isaacs (1952) writes, 'a phantasy represents the particular content of the urges or feelings (for example, wishes, fears, anxieties, triumphs, love or sorrow) dominating the mind at the moment'. Such phantasies, she makes clear, refer to unconscious processes, originally experienced at bodily sensation level before the infant has the power of language. We see this illustrated in the above examples from the observation of Amy. One of the many graphic examples Isaacs gives is of a twenty-month-old little girl with very little speech development who appeared terrified of a flapping, broken sole on a shoe of her mother's. The shoes were put away. It was not until she was nearly three that she put into words her anxiety: she asked where they were and said 'They might have eaten me right up.' Phantasies continue throughout life in all of us as an undercurrent of our mental lives. 'All impulses, all feelings, ... are experienced in phantasy which give them *mental* life and show their direction and purpose' (Isaacs, 1952).

The continuous existence, yet changing nature, of phantasy in the inner world is illustrated by the observation of Emma in Chapter 11. It shows how phantasies are influenced not only by external experiences, but also by the recipient's own response to them. We saw Emma at first ramming the hard, empty bottle into her mouth. This appeared to represent a phantasy of how she had inside herself a cruel, hard, attacking mother, which would indicate her response to the unhappy episode with her mother. It was not that her mother had attacked her with the bottle, but that Emma's phantasy now was of being so attacked. This is a representation of the mother that was at that time real for Emma in her inner world. In the course of the observation we were able to follow how she seemed to bring this earlier phantasy into contact with her later experience of her mother's loving care. Not only did she experience a different aspect of her mother in the external world, but worked at putting together this felt-to-be-cruel, hard 'empty bottle' aspect of a mother with that of the loving one with the soft lap and round cheeks. Not only was Emma in a restored, peaceful relationship with her mother, but the phantasy of a mother in her inner world would be changed too.

A child, or adult, relates to a world inside himself as well as to the external world. The nature and state of this inner world can alter his perception of, and relationship to, the external world. This happens for instance when a baby suddenly turns away from a friendly and familiar observer in fear (as Amy did). And conversely of course a good new experience in the external world can help to modify our inner world.

The existence and development of an inner world depend on there being, first of all, some distinction between the self, and other people. Secondly, there needs to be some concept of an inner space inside oneself, and inside another person, which can contain phantasies. Bick's work (1968) and Bion's concept of containment (1962a) both throw light on these aspects of mental life and will be discussed later on in this and the next chapter.

PHANTASY AND ITS EXTERNAL REPRESENTATIONS

Since the anxieties, impulses and phantasies of which we have been speaking are unconscious, it follows that they cannot very readily be observed. There may be some reflection of them in a child's play, however, or in his drawings, or in what he can tell us about his fears.

Justin was referred to a clinical medical officer when he was ten years old because of his nervousness and anxiety in many situations which were hindering his development at school and increasingly dominating family life at home. His father had left home a few years ago ostensibly for work reasons and Justin was brought up by his mother and her older sister; he had regular contact with his father, who also returned home periodically.

In his first meeting with the medical officer, Justin drew two large elephants with a smaller one behind them. The doctor said this looked like a family, perhaps? Justin answered, apparently irrelevantly, that he was terrified of worms and would prefer them to die underground. Then he drew a plan of his bedroom, and explained there was a locked cupboard by the door which was his father's; he wondered what was in it, it frightened him to think about it. He was too frightened to ask his father about it, he didn't know why. He went on to describe how frightened he was of the banisters but didn't know why. The doctor asked him to describe the banisters for her: he said they were like Egyptian mummies marching up the stairs. He added that he couldn't go upstairs on dark nights without his sister (four years older).

Later on he added that he felt he must guard and protect the locked chest which has his father's things in, but worried that there was a dead person in there. He had missed seeing his father in the summer; he added that his mother hated his father. He then talked about a shower arrangement in his room which he never dared to use in case it flooded the room.

It seems clear that Justin was preoccupied and disturbed by the relationship between his parents; he knew very well that something was wrong, but it had never been openly talked about or acknowledged in the family. But Justin's mental life contained not just quarrelling parents; there were also dead people with frightening powers, and it was his anxiety about these that had taken over his everyday life and produced his symptoms. The dead person associated with the chest, the dead mummies on the stairs, the dead worms, were all creatures of Justin's inner world. Their formation was certainly influenced by the unhappy and unresolved situation between his parents (and by Justin's own feelings and perceptions about it) but they now had an independent inner reality.

Here was an unhappy and emotionally handicapped boy. In the session he indicated the nature of his inner world and the terrors it held for him. But he did not know their actual content; that lay in his unconscious phantasies. He was also terrified to find out; curiosity seemed dangerous; a potentially cleansing shower seemed dangerous. How could one reach him? Separate help for his parents would obviously be desirable; it is possible that this could lead to some change in the parents – an acknowledgment of the difficulties alone could provide Justin with a more open and honest environment. Change in the parents, however, would not in itself attend to Justin's inner reality, which is part of him. Therapeutic work might be able to help him to think about and bear some of his anxieties. Bearing in mind that Justin was afraid of putting any curiosity he had to the test, a worker would have to be ready to recognize with him that her attempts at understanding could also be felt to be dangerous, as well as potentially relieving. In other words one needs to be aware from the start that there would be a transference component to the relationship (Chapter 15), in which the therapist could be felt to be setting off a dangerous enquiry, even perhaps felt to be 'worming her way' into his mind.

We can thus see how from the beginning of an attempt to help therapeutically, there is likely to be a projection on to the therapist from Justin's inner world, just as there was from Amy to both her mother and the observer in early infancy. How the projection is received by the worker and made available for reintrojection by Justin is relevant, just as Amy's and Emma's mothers' response to their babies' expression of painful feelings was relevant. (We shall discuss the receipt of such feelings by the mother and the worker in Chapter 13 under 'Containment' and 'Failures in containment'.)

Justin was seen by the clinical medical officer for assessment, so she probably encouraged him to use his time with her by using toys or by doing a drawing. His choice of what to draw was at all events completely spontaneous, and was his first real communication to her. When the doctor suggested his drawing might be linked with a family, he did not give the sort of reply based on external reality that one might expect from a 10-year-old; he told her how terrified he was of worms, which was clearly something to do with his phantasies and his phantasy life. If the worker has some understanding of a child's phantasy world and is receptive to what he can tell her about it, she can then begin to understand something of his inner life and aspects of his personality that are linked with it. In Justin's case the doctor had been told he was failing to make progress at school in his education, and that his behaviour at home was nervous and inhibited. She was able to include in her assessment not only this description of his external behaviour but also something of his inner conflicts, as shown in the phantasies he described to her.

Justin's drawing and talk had much in common with a child's spontaneous play – a form of communication that we now want to discuss further.

COMMUNICATION THROUGH PLAY

Children seem to use play from a very early age as a spontaneous means of working out their relationship to the world about them, and to other people, and as a means of overcoming difficulties, whether physical or emotional. Indeed a child who seems unable to play is quite rightly usually a cause for concern. Play seems to be a first step in symbol formation, and thus in the ability to digest, work over and think about an important experience.

Klein (1975a) and Winnicott (1971) have written about the meaningful nature of children's play. Its value in normal development is widely known. A feature mentioned by Winnicott (1964) includes 'a being honest about oneself'. This aspect could be observed in some of the babies we have discussed and is also relevant for therapy. We saw Emma's meaningful play when seeking out her mother's second ear-ring; how she was not only actively engaged in an external search but also in an internal communication which sought to relink her divided perception of her mother and re-establish a loving, trusted figure in her inner world. This play took place in close proximity to her mother, and was partly communicated to her, Emma seemingly needing her mother to hear about some of her recent unhappy feelings. The pain she had felt apparently had to be openly and honestly recognized, and this interaction seemed to be relevant to the restoration of a 'good' mother.

Infants can also be seen experiencing their feelings when playing by themselves. Dick (Chapter 11, 'Steps in integration') placed his bottle on a shelf out of his reach and then retrieved it, seemingly 'working' on his feelings about weaning; another time he was thought to be experiencing his feelings of rivalry and jealousy by tantalizing the dog in mother's presence and earning her mild rebuke. On a different occasion he seemed to be 'being' the dog, circling around and growling, perhaps defending what he felt was his territory in a dog-in-the-manger manner against possible rivals.

In the examples we have given here, Emma used play to work over her experience of, and phantasies about, an external event, helping her to acknowledge the unusual and distressing events of the day and finally to set them aside. Dick appeared to be giving expression to his phantasies about current, relevant issues in his life, honestly experiencing some of his less sociably desirable qualities. Both infants seemed also to have some inner resource that enabled them to play actively themselves, the play in itself contributing to the quality of their lives. Through such play in everyday life children can be in touch with their own feelings and have the chance of working over events inside and outside themselves. Sometimes an adult presence seems to be needed, sometimes not. Amy, Dick and Emma were ordinary children living in families where development was encouraged, and who also had their own drive to develop.

Many of the children we see in our work will have had less propitious external environments, where there may have been less opportunity for distressing events and phantasies being worked through in the course of ordinary living, and many children discussed in the first part of this book have had, like Justin, a fairly entrenched phantasy life. Some too may have not sought to grapple overtly with whatever problems there were. Whatever may have gone on before, the prime need remains for us to use ourselves as a vehicle for the understanding of their feelings. Play is a medium through which these can be communicated to the therapist, and the work of the therapy is to provide a new opportunity within this relationship for understanding and change.

To enable our clients to have the opportunity of being 'honest with themselves' we will have to allow space for experiencing and working through unhappy, negative and less socially desirable feelings. This will have something in common with the space available to the infant Emma to express, and have attention paid to her 'hard feelings' about her mother, and for Dick to be in touch with his conflicting feelings about growing away from being a baby, his possessiveness and rivalry towards potential siblings.

Part of the play may be based on recognizable external events, but much will be an external representation of internal phantasy life. As much of this is unconsciously based, children in therapy, as in everyday life, will not be able to tell us directly about its meaning, although they may be able to talk about the actions or events they portray in it. For Justin the idea of a family seemed to be associated with worms and death; he could not explain what he meant in words, but he could go on to draw a plan of his bedroom.

Edward (Chapter 2) through his play showed how the 'magic' of which he consciously seemed so proud, could lead to undesired results. When we bear in mind the unconscious basis of phantasy life, we can appreciate that although Edward for example was able to talk about a 'cops and robbers' chase and convey anxiety about the outcome, he would not be able to explain his feelings. Through his play, however, he may have portrayed an underlying hope that the worker would be able to collect together and hold some of his conflict when he changed the robbers' van into a refuse collection truck.

Play, then, has meaning and is a vehicle for the expression of a child's phantasies, that is to say the unconscious thoughts and feelings that underlie actions. Gillian (Chapter 9) played with the 'goldfish' coins, saying they needed to be kept safe in bowls of water, but then was very careless about leaving them out of water each time they were transferred to another bowl; the therapist was given the role of warning her so that she rescued them in time. At the end, Gillian in her play portrayed how she drove off too hastily with the goldfish in the back of her car and they died. This play symbolized her anxiety about keeping a good relationship alive through gaps and endings, and was related to the proposed ending of the therapy as well as to her mother's death.

Sam (Chapter 7) alternated between softer moments playing with a furry toy dog, soft puppet, or the dolls, and aggressive controlling times when he was an autocratic war general; his play enabled him to explore the gentle, loving side of his nature that was beginning to emerge in contrast to the hard, destructive part.

We can experience, think about and use play and drawings as a basis for communication with the child. This may help the child to be able to relate his feelings in a more verbal, and (in time) more self-understanding way. An increased verbal capacity in some instances is an outcome of therapy, rather than one of its prerequisites.

Play in therapy provides an opportunity for a meeting of the phantasies of a child or young person's inner world with a new external object, the worker, with the possibility of change arising from a new version of the 'multi-faceted, interacting experience' of which Heimann speaks. When we look back at some of the work discussed in this book we can see that this has led to changes in the clients, not just in their behaviour, but in how they felt about themselves and their inner world. We saw, for example, that Gillian had not only shown marked improvement in her symptoms and behaviour in the external world; she also demonstrated graphically at the end of therapy how she valued the good objects in her inner world.

PRIMITIVE STATES OF MIND AND ADHESIVE IDENTIFICATION

We have discussed the nature of the internal world, and how its phantasy content can be expressed through play, both as part of normal development and as a therapeutic communication. We want to look now at some aspects of how this world is built up and can change, using the baby's early experiences as a model.

It is hard to know anything about the mental states of a baby in the early weeks and months of life, although evidence has been collected of a great range of mental and emotional activity in small babies, for example by Bower (1977). It is difficult to know the content of these experiences, but if similar ways of relating to objects or people can be followed through from these early weeks into later childhood, it may be possible to understand something of the processes involved. These primitive states of mind survive into adulthood, though they are largely unconscious.

Some of the children and young people described in this book could only relate to people in very primitive ways. If something of their mental state is not understood, clients are liable to be dismissed as bizarre and beyond help. Ginette (Chapter 6), Colin (Chapter 7) and Nicholas (Chapter 8) come to mind as examples. Some of them too lack the capacity to play and so have a limited ability to communicate, with a corresponding need for adult work in developing understanding.

We saw earlier in this chapter how the building of the internal world is reliant on there being enough difference between self and object to allow internal space for taking something in. One of the most primitive ways of relating to an object, perhaps in the absence of such space, seems to be a clinging, or holding, especially in stressful moments. The baby, in its infantile unintegrated state, seems to feel a need to 'stick to' or hold on to certain objects, such as a bright light or a sound. It is as if the object can be used to hold the baby together against feelings of great, possibly catastrophic, anxiety of falling apart. Bick (1968) writes of a 'frantic search for an object – a light, a voice, a smell or other sensual object – which can hold the attention and thereby be experienced, momentarily at least, as holding the parts of the personality together. The optimal object is the nipple in the mouth, together with the holding and talking and familiar smelling mother.' This latter contact carries the implication of a potentially deepening relationship.

Baby Carol was a few days old when first seen by the observer. She was being carried into the kitchen from the bedroom on her mother's shoulder. She looked comfortable there, and seemed to be looking around. Unexpectedly, mother put her on the observer's lap and left the room to open the front door to an older sister. Carol stared at the observer and then moved her head to fix her eyes intently on the brightly lit wall. When mother came back in, the observer spoke, and Carol turned to look at the observer's face, and smacked her lips. Mother said she looked as if she was hungry, and took her from the observer to feed her.

When Carol stared at the wall, she may have been holding on to the bright light as a way of dealing with her anxiety at being suddenly put on this stranger's lap. Ewan (Chapter 10) was also described over several observations when he was six weeks and eight weeks old, as fixing his gaze on the television or the ceiling light. He seemed to use this as a primitive holding mechanism, and as a protection from the potentially overwhelming noise and activity of his brothers. Indeed, he seemed to blot out their existence. These babies seemed to cling to something with their eyes, perhaps to keep themselves together and protect themselves from falling to pieces under the impact of too strong an experience.

Bick (1968) also refers to the physical function of movement as an alternative way of feeling held together prior to having a sense of being held within one's own skin. A small baby of about a week old was seen by one observer in hospital constantly wriggling her body as the attention of the nurse who was holding her was given to someone else. Many apparently random movements of small babies may serve this need. By their very nature all these phenomena may not be readily noticed and are difficult to describe.

Babies relating in such ways have mostly been observed gradually developing a deepening relationship with their mothers. Baby Ewan used the television screen when his mother was not there to fix his attention; the bathing sequences originally described in Chapter 10 show a deeper kind of interaction. This is discussed in Chapter 13 under

'Containment'. The word 'deeper' is used deliberately to show the contrast with the shallow, two-dimensional feel of adhesive identification. This concept is a relatively new one, based on work by Bick (1968) and Meltzer (1975).

An example from an older child may help to clarify the concept. A nurse in the group described a 4-year-old boy, Ricki, who attended a nursery group in a child assessment centre. Ricki never played with the toys or made any relationships with the other children or grown-ups. If one of the other children cried, Ricki would make a crying noise too. If a child shouted with anger, Ricki shouted – but it was just a noise, with no feeling behind it. He was echoing or mimicking the other child. If he saw a child having a quiet cuddle on the lap of the nurse assigned to him, Ricki would hurry over, push the child off, sit himself on the nurse's lap, and put his arms around her neck – but without any affection or warmth; after a second he would leave her lap and go to some other activity. He sounded like a child who was only capable of 'adhesive' identification.

We saw how Nicholas (Chapter 8) used adhesive tape and a sticky star, as if these could be ways of joining people. Adhesive identification has an essentially bodily or sensuous, rather than thinking connotation, and perhaps Colin (Chapter 7), when twirling his toy, may illustrate this point. In such an instance its use signifies a retreat from more painful ways of relating. It is, however, probably a normal developmental occurrence, and also liable to play a small part in the everyday life of ordinary children and adults. A coming together of phantasies in the internal world with an external situation seemed to have led to its use by an adolescent at her first interview; initially all she seemed able to do was to look around the room, as if she were hanging on to the walls with her eyes, without speaking. Only after recognition of her anxiety about being in a strange place was she able to speak and use the time profitably. In talking about her early life she told the worker how she had as a tiny baby been placed in an institution.

As a general phenomenon in social life adolescents often insist on the same clothing as their peers, down to the exact details of the currently fashionable style. A feeling of being part of a uniform adolescent identity can serve as a kind of holding-together skin, in the period of transition from the containment of family life and move towards adult status. Copying, with the intention of being the same as the object, may be an indication of adhesive identification, and may be quite different in intent from copying based on trying to take something in from the object. The countertransference feelings of the worker are likely to be a guide to what the client is conveying to us. This is discussed in Chapter 15.

Adhesive identification may have the primary purpose of holding the fragile self together rather than communication, but in its sticking to others, can involve them in this need. We now turn to projective identification, also of primitive origin, but in which there is an implicit notion of a projection being received and 'taken in' by someone else.

PROJECTIVE IDENTIFICATION AND COMMUNICATION

Projective identification as a form of communication has been referred to in many contexts in this book. As the term 'projective' implies, it has to do with putting something outside oneself. This process, first described by Klein (1946), involves the omnipotent phantasy of, in her own words, 'splitting off parts of the self and projecting them on to, or rather into, another object' (Klein, 1955). One can see two components in this: firstly the projecting, or putting out, of part of oneself into someone else, and thus largely losing touch with it, and secondly, the identification, which relates not only to who one feels one is, but to where one feels one is.

We discuss in this section the predominantly 'projective' aspect. Attempting to put oneself into the mind of another in this way can be part of ordinary communication. We try to put ourselves into the minds of our clients in the service of understanding what it is like to feel their feelings and to be them (but do not intend to extend the process to the point of losing touch with our own feelings). Nor do we try and stay in their minds with any intent of 'being' them in the sense of taking their identity. This latter problematical area we shall discuss later when we refer to the identification aspect of projective identification in Chapter 14. Throughout the book we have referred to the process of containment and we describe it further in Chapter 13. Bion developed this concept from Klein's description of projective identification. As part of the process of containment Bion (1962a, b) describes how the infant can by projective identification arouse in the mother fears of which he may wish to be rid. In so splitting off and projecting his feelings the effect for the infant is to feel that the feelings in question, and the part of himself feeling them, are now located in the mother. It is as if the infant wraps his pain in an envelope of part of himself and sends it to the mother. This can then be seen to be a communication. And we shall see from our study of the concept of containment in Chapter 13 that if the communication is usefully received by the mother she will attend to it in her reverie.

Both mother and baby experience the effects of this. For a period of time the baby has lost his fears, but he has also lost a feeling part of himself; the mother herself now experiences feelings deriving from her baby which she did not previously have. But if the containing process goes well, the baby receives back the projected part of his personality together with his fears in a more bearable form. This seemed to take place between Gita and her mother (Chapter 10, 'The maternal function and reverie').

Some forms of projective identification contain other elements as well. Dean, described in Chapter 11 ('Developing feelings of identity'), was two weeks old. It was several hours since his last feed and he was yelling and kicking while his father tried to change his nappy. The yells and kicks might have been a communication about the absence of the feeding mother. His father stayed calm and gentle, and when he lifted Dean on to his shoulder at the end, Dean settled and stopped crying, perhaps experiencing his father as having provided containment for his pain.

But Dean could have experienced his father as a hostile sort of anti-mother, failing (or refusing) to feed him; he might have experienced father's attentions to his bottom as an invasion or attack by this anti-mother, which had to be repelled with yells and kicks. His father could well have experienced the yells and kicks in turn as rejection and might have felt unwanted and accused (as the observer did with Amy when mother left the room, Chapter 10, 'Primitive ways of communicating'). Many parents who have subjected their babies to non-accidental injury have said afterwards that they felt the baby was attacking them with its screams. The projective aspect of Dean's behaviour could have been intended to rid himself of pain, or it could have been intended to hurt the object (his father).

The attacking elements of projective identification are usually very obvious. Mrs D for example felt attacked and battered by the many sessions when Nicholas flung things at her (Chapter 8). And being used as a dumping ground for unwanted pain is usually easily recognizable (as with Annabel in Chapter 8). But it is important also for the worker (as it is for the mother) to be alert to any elements of communication that accompany the attack. We may feel in a session that we are useless; we need to think then whether some of the client's own feelings are reaching us via projective identification. If so, this gives us a chance of experiencing his emotions and helping him with them. The client, however, will have split these feelings off and projected them and therefore will not at that time feel that they are his. It is only the worker who is in touch with them. We can think of the belittlement and feelings of uselessness that Mrs L had to bear initially from Graham (Chapter 9). When we have thought about it inside ourselves it may become clearer that the projective identification into us may also have some other purpose such as to hurt or to control us and we can try to relate to that aspect.

A frequent use of projective identification is to avoid experiencing separation, but here again there are different qualities of meaning that can be conveyed. One baby may cry to impart his fear of being left alone because of some disaster that may ensue; another may angrily be putting a part of himself inside the mother to make her stay. Similarly a client will often bring up some new and pressing materials just when it is getting towards the time for his session to end. The worker is made to feel that his material is so urgent that she must overrun the allotted time in order to attend to it. The worker may feel extremely anxious as a result of the client's communication, or may alternatively feel attacked or threatened by it. The quality of her feelings at that point may enable her to feel what the ending of the session means to the client. The same is of course also true of material coming just before holiday breaks.

We shall see, when discussing 'splitting' in the paranoid-schizoid position in Chapter 14, how bad parts of the self are split off and projected, enabling the idealized part to develop. Sam, discussed in Chapter 7 and also referred to earlier in this chapter, had been referred for stealing (among other problems), but when he was concerned about the safety of his box, he claimed that other children using the room might steal it. In that way he was projecting the 'robber' part of himself on to them. It is also possible for good parts to be split off and put into someone else, in order to keep them safe from the subject's more aggressive feelings. Graham (Chapter 9), despite his handicaps, difficult situation and offences, may have initially been able to interest the consultant in his plight partly by means of projective identification in getting the latter to feel some of his more positive qualities, which only became more evident as the work with Mrs L developed.

Unfortunately, as we have indicated, the term projective identification can be used with varied emphasis or meaning which can lead to confusion. For the sake of clarity we reiterate that it can denote getting rid of feelings into another person, together with the part of oneself that has these feelings. This is the sense in which the term is most commonly used in this book, and which we referred to above, when we emphasized the 'projective' aspect. But the same phrase can also refer to 'getting inside another person's skin to become them'. This use of the term lays most emphasis on the 'identification' aspect, and will be discussed in Chapter 14.

Chapter 13

Containment, Mental Pain and Thought

THE CONCEPT OF CONTAINMENT

We are indebted to W. R. Bion for the development of the concept of containment in the sense that it is used in contemporary psychoanalytic writing. He refers to the relationship between a mother and baby and describes what he calls maternal 'reverie' as the 'psychological source of supply of the infant's need for love and understanding', and suggests that this reverie is an expression of her love in non-physical terms. He describes it as a state of mind which is 'capable of reception of the infant's projective identifications whether they are felt to be good or bad' (1962a). It seems clear that we shall soon be back in the realm of infant observation to find examples of 'reverie' such as we discussed in relation to Gita and her mother in Chapter 10.

But let us look a little more at the theoretical exposition first. The mental mechanism of 'projective identification', as we have discussed in the previous chapter, is derived from Klein (1946), and relates to the feeling of detaching from oneself a part of oneself imbued with particular emotions and locating it elsewhere. As we saw, this process can be used for various purposes. Bion (1962a) describes what he means in the context of containment:

> Melanie Klein has described an aspect of projective identification concerned with the modification of infantile fears; the infant projects part of its psyche, namely its bad feelings, into a good breast. Thence in due course they are removed and reintrojected. During their sojourn in the good breast they are felt to have been modified in such a way that the object that is reintrojected has become tolerable to the infant's psyche.

Bion (1962b) further describes projective identification in this context as meaning

> behaviour reasonably calculated to arouse in the mother feelings of which the infant wishes to be rid. If the infant feels it is dying it can arouse fears that it is dying in the mother. A well-balanced mother can accept these and respond therapeutically: that is to say, in a manner that makes the infant feel it is receiving

its frightened personality back again but in a form that it can tolerate – the fears are manageable by the infant personality (1962b).

We can see how important the communicative aspect of this activity is. The infant wishes to be rid of the fears, but they can be received as a communication by the mother.

Using this theory Bion has developed the model of an idea of a 'container' into which feelings are projected, the latter being the 'contained' (1962a). We can see that this is an activity shared by two individuals, the infant's fears being conveyed to the maternal 'container' for the loving work of maternal reverie to take place, and then returned to the infant for reintrojection, in other words for him to take back into himself, but in a more tolerable form.

This shared activity is of enormous importance for the infant's development. In the first place, as we have seen, fears may be 'contained' in the maternal 'container' and then taken back by the infant in more bearable and meaningful form. In addition to this the infant, if all goes well, takes in the feeling of 'being contained'; of maternal space having been available for his anxieties to be borne and thought about. He will thus be able to take back not only his own anxieties but will gradually introject, or take in, what Bion calls the contained-container apparatus, and develop his own containing processes and space in his inner world.

In infant observation we can find many examples of containment in action. Let us look at the observation of baby Ewan (Chapter 10). Some form of maternal reverie may have taken place not only at Ewan's actual bathtime, which had been causing him so much distress, but also in between, as illustrated by the arrangements his mother later made for his bath, and her comments to the observer. When observed with his brothers in a number of observations, he was reported as looking blankly at the television screen, or focusing limpet-like on the light. This may be an example of the holding together described by Bick (1968) and discussed in Chapter 12 ('Primitive states of mind and adhesive identification').

In the observation of bathtime when Ewan was seven weeks old, mother was clearly aware of his anxiety from the start and attempted to communicate this to him. When Ewan was so frightened, the drops of water on his head did seem to help him to be in touch with, and take in, his mother's voice. In the subsequent observations we saw how his confidence had increased and how he seemed to be more of a 'person'. It seems clear that there had been more than a 'holding together', vital though that had been for him. Anxiety had been communicated to his mother, who had been able to 'introject, harbour, and so modify the baneful force of emotion' (Bion, 1959). Ewan in turn it seemed was able to take something back into himself that contributed to his capacity for play and experiment. In other words, one could say that there had somehow been containment, with ensuing development.

The above example also illustrates how the containing process can be composed of what may on the surface seem to be very small pieces of attention. Learning to tolerate painful emotions with the help of maternal reverie is an important step forward for the growing infant. We can see the close similarities between such maternal reverie and the kind of containment offered by the worker. In Chapter 10 we saw how Gita attempted to evacuate her pain into her mother, but because of mother's presence her cries were also an effective communication. Similar communication, it seemed, had taken place since Gita's birth, and each event would have made its own 'painstaking' contribution to Gita's development. This may be a salutary thought for us when we perhaps feel discouraged, or are criticized for the length of time it may take to work with some of our clients.

In the minor family crisis in Emma's family (Chapter 11), it may be that the presence of the observer helped the parents to feel that their crisis was being understood and thought about. The parents, in the context of their urgent response to a sudden external event, initially seemed less closely and sensitively in touch with Emma's feelings than usual. It seems possible that their experience of the observer's interested concern over the previous year of their ups and downs with Emma, together with her current accepting and uncritical attention to their current crisis-laden feelings, may have helped them to feel more able to reach some solution to the immediate problem. (The potentially containing role of the observer in infant observation is discussed more fully in Chapter 10.) In the course of the reported observation of Emma one can see how Emma's whimpering to her mother about her earlier distressed state of mind was contained by mother and this containing mother was reinstated within Emma's inner world.

Examples of containment in contact with clients can be found throughout this book. Sometimes workers may describe what may, in the instance in question, be the same thing by a different name, such as 'reflecting back'. We prefer however to avoid the terms 'mirroring' or 'reflecting back' because they can be used to describe an activity that does not include the emotional depths of really taking in and feeling a client's pain.

We saw in Chapter 1 how Jerry found a place in the therapeutic experience for his chaotic and confused feelings to be expressed and thought about. The containing nature of longer-term therapeutic contact can be illustrated in the account of the work with Graham (Chapter 9). We read how Mrs L helped Graham to feel that she was really taking in his bitterness, but at the same time found a way of helping him to understand that he now had an opportunity to lead his own life. By stalwartly struggling to think about his feelings in the context of their relationship, Mrs L gave Graham the chance of taking inside himself an experience of someone who could try and work with difficulties, as opposed to attempting to get rid of them by blaming 'the authorities'.

When working with Harman in the residential school (Chapter 6) Mr F, the worker, did not react and enact the 'white bastard' role with which he was imbued, but tried to stay with Harman's feelings and to perceive their meaning. He did not act towards Harman as if the latter was just being abusive, naughty or mad, but continued to relate sensitively to him. He was open about his immediate thoughts of practising 'saintly indifference' or physical domination, which may have been projected expectations from Harman. Instead perhaps one could say that Mr F practised some 'infant observation' as he became aware that Harman was clinging on to him tightly, despite protesting that he wanted to be let go. Furthermore Mr F responded by insisting they go in, presumably relating to the communication of the 'infant Harman' as opposed to the 11-year-old protestor. He also tried to stay with the situation, and did not attempt to provide some 'answer' based on pseudo-understanding. In this work Mr F was supported throughout by the headteacher. The latter was respectful of the fact that it was Mr F who was actively engaged in the encounter with Harman, but was very much in touch with Mr F's feelings arising from it. This support from the headteacher for Mr F was reminiscent of some infant observations where a father has been seen to be supportive to a mother in containing the anxieties coming from or concerning a baby or young family.

The inter-relationship between baby and mother is potentially paralleled by that between client and worker in that the client may successfully 'arouse in the worker' feelings of which he would like to be 'rid', but as a result of their sojourn in the worker may be able to reintegrate these feelings in a more bearable form. We remember that containment is an expression of the mother's non-physical love for the baby, which includes a willingness to receive 'bad' projections, and in her reverie to understand that these can be a communication. We are aware that Harman must have aroused plenty of feelings in Mr F and that he and the school staff were clearly being containing in receiving them in the way they did and not reacting to them untherapeutically. It may be that through a continually thoughtful approach of the headteacher, Mr F and other staff, some children may be able to take back into themselves and reintegrate some of the feelings they arouse in the staff. But it must remain an ongoing task for the staff to monitor such events as took place between Harman and Mr F and think about what may seem to be conflicting needs of Harman, the other children, the staff and the educational needs of the school.

With infants, much of the containing communication will take place in non-verbal form, as part of the mother's, or other carer's, ongoing responsive attention. Ongoing thoughtful attention by an observer, as we have described in infant observation, also seems to have a containing aspect which it would be inappropriate for the observer to verbalize. However, even in the case of quite small children such as Jerry, it does seem useful to try and put some of one's understanding into words; the child has a chance of taking into his inner world more of a thoughtful process. This communication has to be related to the function of the setting. Clearly workers in a school such as Mr F, along with the headteacher and the other staff, will have to think very carefully as to how they can carry out their multiple tasks in relation to the children they care for. Mr F may have had varied tasks to perform in relation to Harman within the school, which would have made it inappropriate for him to speak to Harman as if they were in a more sequestered clinical setting. The needs of staff who are the recipients of many felt-to-be unbearable feelings in the service of a containing approach also have to be considered. The discussions in Chapter 6 ('The containing function of the institution' and 'The work group') are relevant here.

FAILURES IN CONTAINMENT

Bion (1959) believes there is a preconception of a containing maternal process and describes a patient's resentment when he feels cheated of his expectations. What can go wrong between a couple when a function of containment seems called for?

On the one hand, a mother may have difficulty in accepting the infant's projective identifications. If an infant projects a fear that he is dying, it is insufficient for a mother just to respond dutifully with her presence; from the infant's point of view she needs to take into herself the experience of the infant's dread, and yet keep a balanced outlook. If this does not occur, the infant feels that the fear of dying is stripped of such meaning that it has, and he thus 'introjects not a feeling of dying made tolerable, but a nameless dread' (Bion, 1962b). This would be so whether the mother reacted to the feelings 'either by denying them ingress, or alternately becoming a prey to the anxiety resulting from the introjection' (Bion, 1959). When the projections are actually not taken in, the infant will reintroject and have inside himself an internal object that 'starves its host of all understanding' (Bion, 1962b).

Unhappy developmental outcomes can occur when there are difficulties within the baby. Bion sees the capacity to tolerate frustration as being, to some extent at least, innate, and he talks of a baby indulging in 'excessive projective identification' when this is lacking. An example of this could be a baby so determined to be rid of his painful feelings that he could omnipotently feel he was evacuating them by, say, his cries and motions, so that the need for the presence of a mother to receive the pain as a communication would be bypassed; hence there would be no opportunity of modification of pain by maternal containment, but simply an evasion of it by evacuation. A baby (or client) with a greater toleration of frustration could bypass the potential joint containing work of the couple and substitute an omniscient, know-it-all approach with unfounded moral assertions of superiority (Bion, 1962b) with a very false feel to it.

Envy, as well as jealousy, is part of the human condition and is present in most relationships to some degree. Klein (1975b) in *Envy and Gratitude* describes the struggles which may arise in ordinary development around these opposing emotions. Very worrying with regard to developmental outcome is the baby with inordinately strong feelings of 'hatred and envy of the mother's ability to retain a comfortable state of mind although experiencing the infant's feelings' (Bion, 1959). If his envy spoils his appreciation of the containing ability of his mother, he cannot take in any therapeutic maternal response; he thus receives no containment and is left with his fears unmodified.

Problems in the infant or the mother (and by extension in the client or the worker) have been set out separately for the purpose of initial clarity, but of course it is in the interaction of the couple and their effects on each other, internally and externally, that the outcome lies.

We have seen a number of difficulties around the process of containment in examples given in other chapters. Turning to the account of Mary in Chapter 11: Mary defecated into her younger sibling's pot against mother's wishes and then emptied it on to the bedroom carpet. At one level one could just say Mary was being naughty and behaving badly towards her overburdened mother. But it also seems that she was demonstrating her feeling about having a mother who in her view did not accept her mess, a mother without a containing facility, a space in her mind, for Mary's tangle of emotions, with their components of jealousy and feeling left out. Here we can see the difficulties for a heavily pregnant mother to respond to the more infantile needs of her young children, as well as the inability of the older child to contain these herself under the pressure of doubled feelings of jealousy. Mother to Mary at that time may have felt not like a container but more akin to a 'brick wall', 'denying ingress', to what she may have felt were her legitimate needs.

Bob (Chapter 4), when he learnt that only five minutes of his session were left, reacted by a spate of activity, ending with the mother and auntie dolls being put in the bathroom, auntie now with her feet in the oven, and the baby being put in the toilet. It seemed that Bob was conveying to the worker a culmination of feelings already touched on in the session about not being contained. His representation was of a maternal world which would be totally overcome by any feelings about ending coming from him, and would just let him sink in a muddle within it. He did however end the session with thoughts about the next one, although needing to confirm when it was (contrasted to earlier reference to his next session being on Friday). Here it seems he may have had a little hope that the worker might be able to keep him clearly distinguished in her mind, and not just in some catastrophic muddle. His mother was known to have had poor health throughout his life, there were troubles in the marriage and some serious illness among his siblings which may have affected his experiences. Although we cannot know what his infancy actually was like, we do see in the session that he carries within him an experience of a mother who is overwhelmed by what she is being asked to feel. As we said in Chapter 12, the inner world consists of concretely experienced phantasies – here, an internal mother who could not contain Bob's chaotic feelings. This internal mother would of course be partly formed by his experiences in infancy and childhood with his own mother, but inner world figures are not just simply replicas of our external experience, but are affected both by what we make of the experience ourselves, and by subsequent relationships. In the work of the therapy, glimpsed in the session, there was a chance that a containing experience with the worker could be experienced and taken inside himself, so that there could be some change in Bob's inner world from a mother who was 'a prey to anxiety', to a mother with some of the worker's capacity to respond with her reverie to his projective identification.

Aspects of 'non-containment' in mother and worker alike, which of course may be part of an interactive process with a child or client, can also be described in everyday terms. There can be a 'sieve-like' aspect of non-containment, in which a communication seems to run through, rather than into, a mother or maybe a worker; 'in one ear and out the other', a kind of pseudo-listening that does not really take in and pay attention. This may have been Kevin's experience of Mrs Rogers and maybe Mrs Rogers' experience of the grandmother (Chapter 10). One can also describe a kind of 'teatowel' version of pseudo-containment, in which there is an apparent wiping away of feelings of distress, as opposed to paying attention to their possible meaning. As we saw in Chapter 6 ('A young mother in a maternity unit'), an institution may lend itself to this kind of functioning.

There is also the possibility of what might be seen as very kindly maternal functioning, soaking up distress as a kind of 'nappy' or 'sponge', but which takes away some of its meaning. Perhaps the social workers involved with Wayne (Chapter 1) were so concerned to spare him pain that they may have acted in this way. Workers and mothers may also, sometimes due to misplaced kindliness, sometimes to inattention, find themselves serving as some kind of dustbin or 'dump' for pain.

The wiping away or soaking up of a painful experience is not the same as a therapeutic bearing of a feeling of pain and trying to help the sufferer to modify it. A baby may wish to be rid of the pain, and the mother may find herself responding as a teatowel, nappy, sponge or dustbin. Maybe the baby evokes this response; maybe her own personality inclines that way. Clients, just like infants, may make excessive demands on the environment for pain removal. We remember how Myra, discussed in Chapter 1 ('The client's initial perceptions of the worker and the setting'), came for one interview, poured out her troubles, and then failed to return for her next appointment. In a real containing process, it is always a necessary task for the recipient of projective identification to examine the feelings aroused in her as an indication of the meaning of the communication. As a result of inward reflection and examination of the countertransference (Chapter 15), a worker might become aware that the client was wishing her to operate in one of these 'analgesic' modes discussed above, and might be able to talk to him about this.

The results of the 'non-containment' are of course important not only for the infant but also the client. Where there is a 'sieve', 'teatowel', 'nappy' or 'dustbin' response, the chance of an introjectable model of a functioning container is passed over. If the non-containment is of the 'brick wall' type, denying access to the communication, the client is liable to take away a version of felt-to-be deliberately non-understanding object. A therapeutic service cannot necessarily offer help to all the clients who come to it. The help offered may not be what the client initially asked for. It is important however that we try and discuss this with our potential clients in a way that does not make them feel met with a brick wall, particularly as some of them may be struggling with such an expectation.

If a mother is 'sieve-like', or is totally overwhelmed by her infant's communication and falls 'prey to the anxiety', the infant is left with an experience of a non-containing container. A number of our clients have had disturbances in their relationships with mother figures in their early life and if their worker becomes ill or suddenly leaves they may well feel she had been similarly overwhelmed. If the client is suddenly discharged (cf. Bob above), this could have a similar effect. There can of course be mothers, and perhaps workers, who project their own infantile anxieties and unconsciously look for help from their child or client, thus reversing functions. A worker also has to be aware that, although she may be working in a containing manner, the client may feel in the transference from his inner world (discussed under transference in Chapter 15) that this cannot be the case. Betty (Chapter 7) felt that the mess she had created under the influence of her envious feelings had 'gone everywhere' and would therefore have damaged the worker's containing function. This sort of feeling can of course usefully be worked with in therapy, where an old expectation may be reworked in the context of a new experience.

Work with clients who have had or feel they have had minimal containment in their earlier years can be rewarding but difficult. On the one hand, as Bion (1959) points out, there may be gratitude for the current experience which gives this opportunity; but the worker must also expect to be attacked as the transference representation of an earlier object for not fulfilling this function. She may also be attacked for not having been there earlier. The experience of the worker thus may have a paradoxical feel to it. But a worker who is prepared to receive the projective identifications of such a client and pay attention to his communications, including his complaints, may provide a real experience of containment for him which he can take in and make use of. This seemed to happen for Rupert (Chapter 7) and Graham (Chapter 9), among others. A clearly bounded setting, in time and space, is an important aspect of the work. It parallels the containing space in the worker's mind and her continuing willingness to struggle with what comes. These are all needed by the client to provide an opportunity for him to test out his experience of his internal world, including its non-containing aspects, in relation to his current experiences with the worker. It is therefore clearly important for the worker to be able actually to function as a container, however she may be perceived in phantasy.

We imagine that readers will have their own examples with which they can illustrate these points. The concept is of course relevant not only in the directly therapeutic context of which we have written, but in many other areas, such as education and the upbringing of children. We think that its 'discovery' by Bion is one of the most useful developments in psychoanalytic theory in recent years, because of its hopeful aspects for development and its wide range of application.

THE CAPACITY TO TOLERATE MENTAL PAIN

Many of the children and clients discussed in this book have suffered unusually deprived childhoods where they were exposed to excessive degrees of unhappiness, rejection and physical ill-treatment. Obviously anyone working with children does everything possible to avoid exposing a child to that sort of suffering. However, it does not follow that a child should be protected from all experience of pain. If the reality is there, if a parent has a disabling physical condition or terminal illness, this is an inescapable fact and something the child needs help in coming to terms with rather than evading. Much more minor situations of stress occur in all families.

When Emma was left sitting in such a distressed state (Chapter 11) it was obviously something that had come about through exceptional circumstances. Normally her parents would protect her from such a degree of mental distress that she clearly could not manage on her own. Deliberately and repeatedly exposing a child to mental pain would have to count as cruelty. But is it then true that babies and children should be protected from every measure of emotional pain where possible?

In the chapter on older brothers and sisters we saw how several small children struggled to cope with their feelings of jealousy when a new baby was born. The following experience of Romero was rather different. He was the first child, and much awaited son, the only one to carry on his rather elderly father's name. The household routine was arranged to suit Romero. When he was nearly two his baby sister was born. Romero had paid no attention when his mother told him she was expecting a new baby. Now, she told him Lisa was 'someone for him to play with' so that he need not feel jealous. The little girl, Lisa, by four months seemed exceptionally quiet and placid. While mother was feeding her, Romero tunnelled behind mother on the sofa, then squashed himself on to mother's lap as well as Lisa, and finally bounced up and down on the sofa next to them. It seemed that as far as mother was concerned, no boundaries needed to be set for Romero, there was no area called Lisa's that he needed to be excluded from. Mother sat Lisa in her reclining chair and placed this in the pram, saying now Lisa could see what was going on. Romero pushed the pram along the hall, building up quite a speed, and the observer was aware of a sense of anxiety. Mother said that Romero loved to play with Lisa, and he was so interested in her; she said she had had to stop him exploring Lisa's eyes and eyelashes, as the area round was getting quite red.

We may wonder whether it was true that Romero did not need to feel jealous, and whether in fact a lot of his behaviour was not the outcome of unrecognized jealousy. How far was it really helpful to Romero to allow him to invade so much of Lisa's space and become so much the linchpin of the family? In the same way Vincent (Chapter 4, 'A health visitor's work with a young mother') had been allowed to invade his mother's privacy in the bathroom, toilet and bed. Leaving this aside, was Romero's mother wise to avoid arousing jealousy, as she saw it?

Her feeling seemed to be that jealousy, like falling downstairs, or even like whooping-cough, can be avoided by careful management. Perhaps there are parallels here with children seen in individual therapy. A specialist teacher working individually with disturbed children in a primary school described the problems that arose because the children she worked with individually always saw each other going to her for sessions (Chapter 9, 'Problems of a premature ending'). Each child's rivalry and feelings of being shut out were obviously heightened in these circumstances, but there was no way of avoiding this, and it would not have been a good solution to allow children to interrupt each other's sessions when they felt left out.

Another worker in her first individual session with a little girl had been asked not to give her access to the locked cupboards in the room, which contained boxes of equipment, painting and toys kept for other children also seen individually. The cupboards, and her exclusion from them, became the focus of the child's anger and jealousy in her sessions. Some questions then arose in the discussion group: why not allow her access to them? Was it just an empty rule? Couldn't her jealous feelings have been avoided by allowing her to see into the cupboards? Similar issues arose in the case of Anthony (Chapter 3, 'Boundaries and confidentiality') and in the discussion on Rupert (Chapter 7), who wanted the other children's pictures taken down from the room where he saw Dr M. One aspect of this problem has been taken up in (Chapter 3, 'The physical setting' and 'Boundaries and confidentiality'); the other children's possessions do need to be safeguarded, just as Lisa did need some sheltered space free from her brother's intrusions. What concerns us here is the need to recognize and acknowledge the feelings of curiosity, greed, possessiveness, anxiety and jealousy in all these examples.

Why is this necessarily preferable to evading these feelings? Sometimes when a toddler falls over, an adult will jolly him out of his pain by bouncing him, swinging him around or offering him a toy as if he was to be distracted from his pain rather than being helped to bear it. Similarly it seems that Romero was being deprived of any chance to recognize the pain of feeling displaced. This can be compared with the hesitations of the social workers in the case of Wayne (Chapter 1) who tried to avoid letting the boy see the real circumstances of being taken into care, 'in order to avoid causing him pain'.

When discussing containment earlier in this chapter we have seen how a mother may be able to bear feelings and gradually make them tolerable for the baby, and that in this way the baby's inner world is in turn enriched and strengthened so that he slowly develops his own inner strength. Something of this process seemed to be happening in the work with Nicholas (Chapter 8); with Colin (Chapter 7) when he was helped to recognize his feelings about the disrupted sessions; and in Dr N's work with Sam (Chapter 7) when for so long she had to bear the feelings of being the stupid, confused, unwanted little child. If Romero's mother fails to help him recognize and experience his jealousy, he is being deprived of a chance to come to terms with it.

Evading mental pain in the long run seems to lead to psychic disaster. A child like Bob can develop a physical symptom (the soiling) which in turn evokes dislike and rejection from those around him (he refused school because he was called smelly). Nicholas seemed sunk in apparent 'idiocy' and elective mutism, beyond the reach of his mother or his teachers. Rupert was in a vicious circle of lying and stealing which in turn lead to yet another foster-placement breakdown. All these children seemed stuck, with no way forward, when they were referred for individual help. We have seen how, in the process of normal development, an anxiety mastered is a great stimulus to further growth (see Ewan's elation when with his mother's help he overcame his fear of the bath; Chaper 10). Taking away the frustration, anxiety, or in Romero's case jealousy, that are part of normal life deprives the child of the chance to grow and develop. It seems important that the caring adults involved should not collude in evading the pain by any of the many means available. Evasion simultaneously becomes the absence of, or negation of, truth. 'Healthy mental growth seems to depend on truth as the living organism depends on food' (Bion, 1965).

THE EMOTIONAL BASIS OF THINKING

Some people who come to us for help seem able to think about their emotional experiences. A young widow may be able to describe directly her pain and grief and get some relief from sharing it. More often, however, what they talk about, or in the case of children what they do, seems unrelated to the troubles we might expect them to be bringing us. A child who has been to a number of different foster-homes and is now in a short-stay children's home with a large turnover of staff, where we are told he is subject to bullying, instead of sharing with the worker anything about this, apparently rejects her offer of friendly interest and throws her toys across the room. Being able to experience mental pain, and think about it, is not something that arises naturally, like being able to see, or even like learning to walk.

It is something that only arises gradually, in the context of a relationship with a loved and trusted person, in the way that we have described under 'Containment'. Probably the happy, contented moments between a small baby and a mother are not a stimulus to thought; they can be enjoyed in the present. The frustration of being hungry and waiting for a feed, or a bad experience of indigestion after a feed, on the other hand, are painful sensations that somehow have to be dealt with. A mother who can hold, comfort and feed that baby modifies and gives meaning to his chaotic experience. The baby can then take in something of his mother's capacity not only to tolerate pain, but also to make his chaotic experiences into elements of emotional experience that can be thought about. Klein (1952) had already described the capacity to internalize goodness, and the capacity of introjection, which exists from the beginning of life. Bion (1962a) describes how primitive emotional sensations, sense impressions and feelings of hunger, anger and so on, have to be retained in the mind before they can be thought about. They have no meaning for the baby when he is getting rid of them into the mother by crying. His mother's acceptance and understanding of his distress restores the feelings to the baby in a more manageable state, by having made sense of them. She gives the baby not only an introjectable experience of containment but also a rudimentary capacity for containing and thinking about his experiences. It is by means of what Bion calls the 'alpha function' in the reverie of the mother that she makes the chaotic infantile experience into one which has elements that can be thought about.

Perhaps it is the absence of the good, loving, life-sustaining mother that first needs to be encompassed emotionally and mentally. When this good mother has gone, a baby may first experience her as replaced by a hostile, attacking 'bad mother'. Something of this seemed to be what Amy was experiencing (Chapter 10) when her mother left the room and she was alone with the observer. The observer, whom Amy had until then perceived as friendly, suddenly found Amy treating her as if she had cruelly attacked her. At a later stage a baby needs to move on to recognizing that the 'cruel', not-there mother is the same as her loving, attentive mother; that is, that her mother remains the same person, even if she is away or unavailable for a time.

Emotional experience does have to be thought about to be filled with meaning. A preliminary stage in thinking seems to be the capacity to have unconscious phantasies, to dream and to form symbols, which the baby is in a position to develop as a result of his experience of his mother's alpha function. Emotional experiences can then be worked over in dreams, phantasies and symbols, and it can become possible to remember experiences and think about them. This seemed to be something that Nicholas (Chapter 8), for example, seemed unable to do. On the other hand Emma seemed to be thinking and working over her upsetting experience and perhaps even symbolizing the two opposed qualities of her mother (the flustered shouting one and the gently loving one) when she fingered the two ear-rings and said 'two'.

Thinking of this kind is rooted in, and arises from, the relationship between two people, when one comes to understand the other, not superficially but as a result of painful emotional experiences. Bion (1962a) calls this thinking 'K' (for 'knowing' another person). The earliest experience of 'K' is maternal reverie. We have often referred to the thoughtful and containing function of the worker, and it is particularly a thoughtfulness related to the bearing of emotional pain that we have in mind.

THE EVASION OF MENTAL PAIN

The experience gained from listening to observations of a baby's development has helped us to understand some of the ways in which stress, anxiety or mental pain can be evaded until the capacity to tolerate and think about them can be developed. Ewan (Chapter 10), for instance, was often seen completely ignoring the existence of his noisy, active older brothers who darted in and out of his vision and bumped into his chair without his apparently being aware of them.

This was obviously just a stage in the development of a normal baby. But blotting something out from consciousness and then failing to think about it may become a more persistent trait. In Chapter 10 ('The maternal function and reverie'), we heard about a young mother who had been classified as of low intelligence, and was in an assessment centre with her small boy. She seemed quite impervious to his behaviour. Kevin was irritable and did not settle to anything, but there was no communication between him and his mother. He never seemed to make it plain what the trouble was; it was as if he knew something was wrong but had no expectation of anyone or anything that could deal with it. (This could be contrasted with Emma's crawling over to her mother to look for solace and understanding, Chapter 11.)

Mrs Rogers herself seemed quite unaffected by this very fraught morning (though the grandmother looked exhausted). Mrs Rogers was unavailable to help Kevin sort out his feelings (mentally unavailable, though physically there and picking him up); she herself seemed also to be empty of the feelings one would have expected her to have. What did she feel when grandmother picked Kevin up, or when Kevin rejected mother and held out his arms to grandmother, or when grandmother disagreed with her way of feeding him and took over? She seemed quite untroubled, and kept her smile, apparently incapable of an appropriate emotional response. It would be difficult to explain this as just due to her low level of intelligence; she seemed to have failed to develop on a feeling level as well. We do not know enough about her to know what lies behind this, but in the observed context people seemed to be running her life for her and acting as if she had no feelings and no rights (grandmother knew better about feeding Kevin; the authorities apparently knew better about her having another baby since they had 'sorted her out' with a coil).

Getting rid of painful feelings is one way of avoiding the pain; but the capacity to develop and come to terms with one's life is also lost as a result. Colin (Chapter 7) came back to his sessions after a series of breaks and cancellations, and began by sending a helicopter-toy whirling off across the hall, whirling off himself after it, before they had even reached the therapy room. When his teacher-therapist told him not to, he replied 'Yes miss', giggled, and whirled off again after it. Later on, after he had conveyed a feeling of great terror to the worker, he stood giggling; then he speeded up a tape till it became meaningless and giggled again. 'My mum smacks me when I giggle and then I can't stop ... something makes me do it.' His mother obviously felt maddened by the emptiness of the giggling. Later on he said (about himself) 'It's silly.' The silliness, the giggles, the mindless whirling away are all ways of getting rid of terrifying inner experiences, but at the cost of becoming mindless and mentally empty. In Colin's case the worker was able to re-establish a relationship with him in which he perceived her as somebody able to receive the shock and terror, experience it and put it into words for him – part of the ongoing work she had been doing with him over many sessions and a first step towards enabling Colin to tolerate his feelings instead of evading them.

The physical ways of getting rid of things from one's body may be by evacuation (of faeces and urine), by spitting saliva, or by driving out sounds (screaming; passing wind; belching). These concrete ways of evacuation are also at the most primitive level the mental channels of evacuation; indeed for a baby physical and mental cannot be neatly separated. As we have seen, evacuation of a bad experience can also become an evacuating-into-a-container, a form of communication, a projective identification, leading to the development of a capacity to think; but it can also remain evacuation, and become ever more violent. Mary's tipping her excreta out over her mother's bedroom (Chapter 11) seemed an example of that, but it had not yet become entrenched and the family might well come to help her sort it out in time. For Nicholas (Chapter 8), evacuation of every experience before it could become a thought had stripped his mental life till there seemed to be nothing left. Mrs D in attempting to give meaning to his mental evacuations is performing 'alpha function' for him.

There are other more subtle ways in which the capacity to tolerate and think about emotional experiences can be attacked. A member of a discussion group described an incident in a hostel for disturbed adolescents. One of the older adolescents seemed to be trying to sort out a violent quarrel that was taking place late at night between four others, and he had taken on the apparently helpful role of 'umpire'. In fact, however, he was subtly inflaming the other adolescents; he also provoked an argument between the two care staff which somehow extended the quarrel to them and to the staff structure of the hostel. His apparent behaviour as a helpful, mature member of the group was a form of hypocrisy that got in the way of any real understanding.

Cynicism and lying are other forms of attack on emotional truth, described by Bion

(1962a) as '−K' ('minus K'). Sam (Chapter 7) brought into the forefront his envy and suspicion of the other children Dr N saw. If he could claim (untruthfully) that he 'knew' she let other children get at his box when he was not there, this was an excuse for killing off his growing gratitude to her, and his sadness at missing her; it was an excuse for returning to the vicious circle of lying and stealing that had characterized his former relationships. A lie gets rid of the painful truth and the anxiety about it, but at essential cost to the personality. Some aspects of these phenomena are present to some degree in all of us. People who are considered perfectly normal may nevertheless have a permanently suspicious attitude, always ready to see bad in something. Others are always trying to prove their point instead of being in search of the truth. Others use specious arguments. These are all ways of avoiding mental pain. Not being able to digest and use an emotional experience is harmful to the personality. It leads to aridity and emotional sterility.

We need to live through and not evade or deny major emotional experiences, otherwise we gradually become progressively unable to sustain living emotional relationships with other people. If we evade the experience or block it off in any other way, we deprive ourselves of the truth about it and truth seems to be essential for psychic health. This was why for example it seemed so important that someone should help Wayne (Chapter 1) acknowledge and bear the truth about his father's illness and about his placement away from home.

The consequences of refusing or evading understanding are far-reaching. Learning in any true sense can only arise out of doubt, uncertainty and the frustration of not knowing. The temptation for the therapist is to evade this painful uncertainty in many ways, for example by resorting to a familiar explanation or by applying a new theory parrot-fashion. It is more difficult to tolerate the anxiety until we have the chance, with the client's help, to understand what he is showing us.

Chapter 14

Development in the Inner World

THE PARANOID-SCHIZOID POSITION AND DEFENCES AGAINST ANXIETY

The ability to project feelings concretely on to another person has been a central concept in this book. Sometimes, as we saw, feelings containing hostility are projected with a view to their being understood by the mother; but if the projected feelings consist of active hatred and aggression, the baby (or older person) will as a result fear the return of an attack from something or someone hostile in the outer world. This seemed to be the case for Amy (Chapter 10 'Primitive ways of communicating'). In an observation when she was four months old, her mother suddenly deposited her on the observer's lap. She reacted with quite recognizable anxiety the first time, and sustained crying the second time. The observer was made to feel as if she had done something dreadful to Amy. Amy pushed herself away from the sofa where the observer sat; she was pushing away a presence, or an experience felt to be bad and dangerous. At this stage Amy was making a definite distinction between something familiar, safe and idealized (her mother) and something felt to be bad and dangerous (the observer). Making a split between ideal and bad seemed to operate as a necessary defence for Amy in a situation of anxiety.

A baby in the first few months of life is likely to attempt to keep his good experiences separate from his bad ones, good objects separate from bad ones, and the parts of himself that relate to these separate from each other. This splitting allows a space for goodness to be sought, perceived and to grow with some safety within a bounded part of the self.

We saw in Sam (Chapter 7) a child who could not manage to separate good from bad; both were hopelessly confused in his mind, leading to despair. With the help of Dr N he was able, almost literally, to 'sort things out'; he had a more clearly defined picture in his mind of those he saw as definite 'baddies', such as other children whom he felt would steal from his box if given the chance. But he also had a more positive feeling about himself and his own, less confused identity; it now seemed worth putting his name on his box and at least hoping that Dr N would safeguard the contents. One could also see his soft, idealized 'Boo Boo-like' self coming to help an idealized Dr N. The projection of Sam's bad feelings outwards was at this stage a step forward in his infantile development, enabling his immature psyche to have the chance of having and taking in loving relationships, protected both from his own hatred and from feelings of chaos and confusion. Sam had been able to move forward from his confusion to making a clear split between an ideal kind of goodness, and badness. He could not, however, as yet risk the soft baby feelings that enjoyed being pushed in the pram by Dr N to be in touch with more aggressive feelings; when he heard the war cry he had to 'turn into a soldier again'.

This is the 'splitting' of the paranoid-schizoid position; it is as if parts of the self and objects were separately bounded. The term paranoid-schizoid position was introduced by Klein (1946) and is used to describe this cluster of phenomena: a relationship to part objects (that is, to parts of people), the splitting of objects into ideally good and persecutingly bad, and the splitting of one's own feelings into idealized love and unmitigated hatred. In both cases good is unmixed in any way with bad. Unfortunately the name makes no reference to the 'ideal' side of the split; the 'schizoid' part of the term refers to the split, and 'paranoid' to the bad feelings which have been 'split off' and projected outside, thus arousing 'paranoid' anxiety about their return. We saw how the observer was made by Amy to feel frighteningly bad. The experience of fear may be avoided by omnipotent denial, as we saw when Ewan (Chapter 10) blotted out his perhaps frighteningly boisterous brothers. Such splits and denials are part of the normal development of small babies and tend in favourable circumstances to lessen with time. Indeed Ewan, despite his distress, was seen struggling to take an interest in his brothers' activities when he was twelve weeks old. One may from time to time hear in the course of one's work, however, of a child now giving rise to worry, who is reported to have been 'such a good baby'; here maybe 'splitting off' or denial of anxieties went on for too long.

Understanding these states of mind can help us in our work. It was easier for the worker to bear the onslaught of Andrew's negativism and silence, when she could see that he ran to his mother after the session with a new love and helpfulness (Chapter 8). Previously all his relationships had been spoilt by sullenness and hatred, but it seemed now that he could make an effective distinction between good and bad, and could trust the worker to cope with his bad feelings. If the bad feelings remain with the worker in this sort of split between good and bad they are available for understanding. The home situation has a chance of amelioration, and support for the therapy is not at risk of being undermined by negative behaviour at home. It becomes easier to work with the negative transference (see Chapter 15) if the value of splitting between good and bad is recognized. It is also important to remember that this splitting is not achieved without the expense of persecutory pain; often in working with a hostile child or adult when experiencing the destructive side we may fail to recognize the underlying anxiety.

It would be wrong to imply that the paranoid-schizoid position exists only in infancy and childhood. It can persist as a major character trait in adults, and is also something to which we are all likely to revert under stress. It may help to clarify the distinction between the paranoid-schizoid position and the depressive position (which we shall discuss next) if a clinical medical officer's experience of two parents is described. He had visited their home on a number of occasions because he was concerned about their youngest child, Brett, who he thought was showing signs of mental handicap.

Eventually tests confirmed this beyond doubt, and the doctor needed to discuss the results of the tests with the parents. Brett's mother understood at once what he was saying, and began weeping; she said she had known all along that something was not right with Brett. Brett's father, however, became very angry and abusive towards the doctor. He said the doctor was 'blackening' his child and deliberately fabricating evidence. He was also angry with his wife, telling her she was spoiling Brett's chances. When his wife attempted to think together with the doctor about the best school placement for Brett, the father said they were branding his child as an idiot and he was not going to allow that.

It was apparent that Brett's father felt very persecuted by his son's handicap. He got rid of his anxiety and guilt by projecting these feelings into the doctor. He also had to keep a picture of Brett as an idealized, perfect child and could not integrate the knowledge of his mental handicap, together with the grief and mourning that would have entailed. The doctor was very concerned for Brett's father and discussed with a work discussion group the best way to help him. It seemed that Brett's father was dominated by the defences of the paranoid-schizoid position. These prevented him from experiencing any real concern about Brett's needs, because to do so would have exposed him to too much pain of a different kind.

A client in whom splitting and projection are the dominant defences against anxiety is likely to perceive the worker as attacking him in return. It is indeed difficult in some instances to avoid enacting a return of the hatred and aggression which has been projected. This aspect of the role of the worker is discussed further in Chapter 15.

THE DEPRESSIVE POSITION AND THE DEVELOPMENT OF CONCERN

In order to develop in social and emotional terms a baby needs to learn what effects his behaviour has on other people. For example, if he greedily demands more and more of his mother's time and attention, as well as more and more of her breast milk, what effect will this have on her? If he seeks to exert omnipotent control over his mother and other people in his orbit (as we saw Amy do in Chapter 10, 'Separation and control'), how does his mother experience this? Dean seemed to be becoming painfully aware of the effects of his demands on his mother (Chapter 11) and was making sometimes heartbreaking efforts to control them. A developing capacity to feel concern for what we do to other people implies leaving the divided world of the paranoid-schizoid position and moving into the unified world of the depressive position. Becoming a whole, mature human being implies accepting responsibility and concern for the pain that we may cause other people.

In listening to observations over a baby's first two years of life we were often able to see the gradual emergence of a capacity for concern for the loved mother and a wish to spare her. This often occurred first in the context of weaning (see the descriptions of Dean and Dick in Chapter 11). The term 'depressive position' implies a capacity to relate to 'whole' objects and thus see the mother as a whole and unique person. There is longing for her in her absence and a sense of concern that the infant's own activities could, or could have, harmed her. For this to happen the infant needs to be in touch with the spectrum of his feelings as a whole and to be able to bear mixed feelings ('ambivalence') towards the object. The schizoid split between ideal and bad has to come together, and responsibility taken for feelings that have been split off and projected on to others. This of course involves the risk of bringing the good into contact with the bad; and it implies concern for the good object, both as outer reality and in the inner world when it is subjected to such exposure.

Emma (Chapter 11) seemed to be struggling to reconcile the two opposites: the hard 'empty-bottle' attacking mother, and the idealized soft gentle mother. She was also struggling to reconcile her different feelings towards these two different 'mothers', and by the end of the observation it seemed as if a split had been healed.

Real concern for other people includes a desire to treat them as they would wish to be treated. This therefore implies giving a loved person her freedom; the pains and conflicts surrounding relinquishment that this entails are illustrated for us in Dick's protracted attempts to avoid holding the bottle himself and release his mother which we described in Chapter 11 'Steps in integration'. We saw how he appeared to examine his own biting impulses, possibly realizing that his teeth could hurt as well as control. There can be no 'slave mothers', bitten into submission, if the pains of the depressive position are heeded.

Implicit in the achievement of the depressive position is the growth of a good object inside (no longer 'ideal' but merely 'good') that is felt to have sufficient strength to enable the infant to tolerate the absence of an external loved person and bear separation. It also implies taking responsibility for our relationship to other people and to our internal objects, facing the sadness for damage we may have caused, bearing guilt and being willing to do what is within our capacity to put things right. If it is beyond our ability to put things right we need to be able to stand back and let others do so, if they can. As we see later in this chapter, with the example of Geoffrey ('Projective and introjective identification'), it is not necessarily easy to let 'father' decorate and restore 'mother'. We also need to try and bear what cannot be restored without resorting to a denial of the damage.

Brett's mother, in the example we gave above, seemed to be struggling with depressive anxieties, and was able to acknowledge her feelings of grief and concern for Brett.

The predominant state of mind of the depressive position is concern for others as opposed to emotions primarily related towards oneself, as in the paranoid-schizoid position. The greatest anxiety therefore centres on the well-being and safety of those whom we love in the external world, and in the inner world, while in the paranoid-schizoid position, the deepest fears relate to our own potential annihilation. Manic defences or responses are an attempt to put away or gloss over painful feelings accompanying a 'depressive' state of mind as too much to be borne. A manic response involves a denial of the truth of psychic reality (the feelings that exist inside the mind). Sometimes such a response may consist of inappropriate lightheartedness, at other times it may involve controlling other people to avoid any perception of their suffering.

The developmental achievements of the depressive position may not be reached at all by some, and perhaps it can most usefully be thought about as a state of mind that can be gained and lost on many occasions, by children and adults alike. In therapy we work with those who may not have reached a depressive state of mind, such as perhaps Nicholas (Chapter 8) or who may have lost it, such as perhaps Sam (Chapter 7). In either event the relationship with the therapist provides a further chance for giving truthful attention to the feelings surrounding integration and the development of loving concern for other people, and for inner world objects. For various reasons children may not stay in therapy long enough for the depressive position to be 'worked through'. There is pressure on the therapeutic time; parents may be satisfied with behavioural improvements; children or therapists may move away. Also sadly there is no guarantee of growth through therapy any more than in any other area of interactive relationship. But there is no doubt that we see plenty of children who can be helped to struggle with depressive pains.

Ahmed and Edward (Chapter 2) sought manic artificial cheerfulness, especially under the impact of separation at the end of the session. There was a therapeutic task here for the worker in helping them to face and work with their anxieties about damage to the object; with help they might in time be able to internalize such a capacity. In the welter of well-meaning relationships surrounding the fostering of Wayne (Chapter 1) we saw how difficult it was for both Wayne and the workers to get in touch with any depressive pain relating to his father's illness and failing capacity. Some of the pain may have been dispersed and fragmented. Helping those with whom we work to grasp depressive pain also involves the worker in painful feelings.

Depressive pains, however, can also herald growth and development. Dick (Chapter 11) already appears to be a person of character. Gillian (Chapter 9) had actually lost her mother, but towards the end of the therapeutic experience it was clear that she had good internal parental figures in her inner world. She was ready to mourn the ending of her transference relationship with the worker (see also Chapter 15). She was aware of her own responsibilities for internalizing a good relationship and how it was at risk from careless, neglectful or manic behaviour inside herself. Giving freedom to the loved person and mourning the loss of the relationship in the external world can lead to an enrichment in the internal one and set in train more advanced mental processes such as symbol formation.

> As the infant goes through repeated experiences of mourning and reparation, loss and recovery, his ego becomes enriched by the objects which he has to recreate within himself and which become part of him. His capacity to retain or recover good objects increases, as well as his belief in his own loving potentialities. (Segal, 1973).

In our work we have the opportunity of helping patients with this task, and this will be discussed later in this chapter.

The name 'depressive position' is unfortunately misleading. Winnicott (1955) calls it 'a thoroughly bad name for a normal process', his own suggested name being 'The Age of Concern'. It is in fact important to differentiate the depressive position from depression or a manic-depressive illness. The term depressive position implies neither illness nor a mood of depression. Withdrawn, low-key, passive behaviour or expressed feelings of misery do not necessarily mean that the person involved actually feels concern about other people in the external world or about his internal objects. The term depression is unfortunately often used as a blanket term to describe many states of feelings such as hopelessness, emotional poverty or failed mourning, where the subject is not in a state of mind predominantly influenced by loving concern. In such instances the depressive position may, in fact, never have been reached, or may be being avoided.

We have spoken of how one may move from a state of mind of the paranoid-schizoid position to that of the depressive position. Bion (1963) postulates a dynamic relationship between them, described by the sign Ps $\longleftrightarrow$ D. He sees the states of disintegration and integration as being in recurrent oscillation throughout life. Perhaps the observations of Dick (Chapter 11) provide an example of this, when at one moment he seemed to feel hurt and persecuted because his mother would not hold the bottle for him, and at another moment he managed to hold it himself. These fluctuations seem a necessary part of development at any stage of life. Bion suggests that change, when it happens, takes place through what he calls the 'selected fact', that is an 'emotional experience of a sense of discovery of coherence' and underlines the need for truthfully staying with a feeling of disintegration when it is present (1962a). He refers (Bion, 1970) to a letter from the poet Keats to his brothers admiring 'Negative Capability, that is, when a man is capable of being in uncertainties, mysteries, doubts, without any irritable reaching after fact and reason'. Perhaps the workers involved with Wayne and his father (Chapter 1 and above), needed to experience, or realize, how fragmented was their professional approach (with foster-placement officer, field social worker and foster-parents all uncertain of their role), before they could be in touch with the deeper concerns about the father's state of health and its meaning. It is often easier, and less painful, to follow the path of 'irritable reaching after fact and reason' in the search for an apparently tidy solution than to bear such feelings of disintegration, not knowing if they will necessarily cohere in a form that will lead to deeper understanding.

PROJECTIVE AND INTROJECTIVE IDENTIFICATION

There seems then to be a potential movement from primitive states of mind which centre on anxieties about survival of the self, to a state of concern for other people. Different ways of relating to other people reflect these different states of mind and are also reflected in them.

Peter (Chapter 11) appeared to want to be 'like' his father, and tried to emulate his father's qualities and behaviour. But he needed to 'be' father, in order not to be the real Peter who felt jealous of his sister and displaced by her. In other words we can think of him as projecting himself into a different 'father' identity to get away from the pain of jealousy; again later he seemed to feel he 'became' his baby sister when covered by her rug. We discussed projective identification as a primitive form of communication in Chapter 12; we now discuss its use in connection with a sense of identity.

In therapeutic work, too, we have the experience of clients who, wishing to feel different, 'put themselves into' us and feel themselves to 'be' the worker. This may be accompanied by putting us into the role of the child. Annabel (Chapter 8) adopted the role of the strict teacher while Dr C was made to feel he was the silly child. Of course this could be used in the session as a communication to the worker, and this aspect is discussed further in Chapter 15 under 'Countertransference'. Sometimes however the wish to *be* the adult is overriding. When Sadhna (Chapter 4, 'Emotional disturbance and school-based problems') was 'being' a little mother, the worker felt quite excluded in the session because Sadhna had taken over the adult part. Sadhna seemed to identify herself with a 'mother-worker' in a way that was not really helpful to her development. Gillian's worker on the other hand (Chapter 9) could feel that she was needed to help Gillian in internalizing a good relationship; this opened the way to a different form of identification.

Geoffrey, a 5-year-old who had been in therapy for some while, announced he was going to clean up the therapy room and be the 'painter-daddy'. He scrubbed quite hard at a number of dirty marks on the skirting board and walls and in fact made quite a good job of it. Little by little, however, it started to go wrong: he upset some of the water and the pool started to spread; he insisted on reaching higher up the wall and made a rickety structure to climb on out of chair and table and got very annoyed when the worker suggested she needed to hold it steady for him to ensure his safety; finally the whole situation collapsed when she warned him it was nearly time, and the dirty cloth ended up being flung at the door. The shaky basis of his identification was revealed. Nevertheless there was some foundation for it. The daddy who helps the mummy and cleans up for her had gone and only the angry little boy was left; but for some while he was able to identify with a helpful, supportive father and actually carried out some of the hard work.

This is an identification based on taking over father's role. Being the baby who makes the mess and has the uncomfortable feelings has been lost sight of (but returns with full force at the end of the session). Geoffrey's identification with his father was still mainly projective. It had qualities of omnipotence, self-importance and magic, and it eventually collapsed, leaving anger and chaos. When we encounter this sort of identification in our work, we need to be careful not to collude with the child or client in pretending that he really is this clever person, whilst remaining receptive to feelings that may have led him to seek to have such an identity. We also need to bear in mind that projective identification may well be based on genuine admiration of the person who is 'entered' and 'taken over' as in Geoffrey's attempt to 'be' the helpful father. (The person who is identified with can be someone external, or an internal version of him.) Projective identification used in this way consists of an omnipotent phantasy of putting parts of oneself into another person. This may be predominantly in order to have his identity, to control him or to prevent a feeling of separation, or even, for safekeeping.

As a result one can feel trapped 'inside' the object; and feelings about being shut in, or confusions of identity, can develop. Who am I? Or, perhaps: Where am I? Marcia, aged three, in a play therapy session fitted high-heeled shoes made out of Plasticine on to a little girl doll figure. At the end of the session she put this doll, together with the mother doll's clothes, away in a corner of her box. She left with a rather smug, satisfied air, as if she had made herself into the mother. But at the start of the next session she could not remember where she had left the doll, and became very perplexed and distressed; perhaps she was showing that she had lost herself in this confusing take-over of the mother's identity.

The tendency to try and acquire and to hold a pseudo-identity by means of projective identification can become a longer-term character trait, as with Sadhna, who spent her sessions 'being' the mother. It can also be a swift process, swiftly undone, as we saw when Peter collapsed in angry tears.

Projective identification, as we saw in Chapter 13 is useful as a primitive form of communication or as a vehicle for trying to put oneself in someone else's mind to try and understand their feelings. Developmentally, a more helpful form of identification springs from the internalization of helpful parents who can coexist inside along with the turbulent baby self, as in the next example.

Simon, a 5-year-old, watched his mother struggling with his baby sister; the ten-month-old little girl was crying loudly and mother looked flushed and angry. Nothing seemed right for the little girl. Then the boy said he thought she wanted her blue teddy, and went and fetched it. The little girl snatched it from him with a glare, but her crying subsided as she sucked her thumb and cuddled the teddy. Mother, flustered, laughed and said to the observer, 'That's just like his daddy; he manages to keep calm when I get in a state.' The little boy had kept a fatherly calm, but he was also in touch with his baby sister's feelings and needs, and effected a peaceful solution.

It seems to be particularly through the internalization of the feeding experiences and mother's containing function that the baby himself first acquires the capacity for laying down good experiences in his inner world. Following on this, the processes of internalization can be extended to father and others. Much of the identification that we can at any rate observe, however, appears to be projective. In small children this seems to be a necessary stage of development, gradually replaced, in favourable circum-stances, with the ability to identify with a loved and admired object, as in the case of Simon. This introjective identification, as it develops, acquires the qualities of the depressive position: the infantile parts of the self are still there and acknowledged, alongside the helpful strength of an internal parent figure.

The term introjective identification can be used in two overlapping ways. It can refer to acquiring or incorporating the characteristics of another person within one's own personality, and we know the basic personality of any individual is greatly influenced by the quality of these introjections. Some aspects of what is internalized, however, are felt to form the basis of internal objects, such as internal parents, and the second usage of the term refers to our relationship with these objects in the inner world. It is in this sense that it is probably most widely used, and how we use it here. A baby's or a child's internal objects will depend on the central figures in his external life, how he perceives them, and what he feels about them. This was discussed in Chapter 12 'Inner world and phantasy'. There were examples in Chapter 10 and 11 showing how a baby takes something in from the external world and the use he is able to make of it. Ewan found that his mother understood and helped him with his difficulties over the bath and he gradually therefore developed a capacity to manage, both at bathtime and in other situations. Dean moved on from demanding that his mother should see to his needs all the time to an attempt to spare his mother and manage on his own. This reflects an aspect of his depressive concern for her.

Introjective identification in contrast to projective identification is based on taking in. When positive, it leads to being in a good relationship with good inner objects, wishing to please them and, where appropriate, emulating their qualities.

An eighteen-month-old girl, Phyllis, was fastened in her pushchair out of reach of her mother, who was standing in a queue. The little girl could be heard starting to fret, but then talking to herself in a clear imitation of a soothing mother's voice; she had no words as yet, but the rise and fall of her voice, and the 'pretend' talking noises made quite a different sound from the fretting which had gone before. This little girl had probably had many earlier experiences of her mother actually helping her through anxieties, and she now seemed to have something like a soothing mother inside her, able to help her 'hold on' in a distressing situation for a short while at least. A baby who cries when hungry is both communicating and evacuating his bad experience; this toddler, in contrast, was aware of her troubles and even had a rudimentary capacity for making them bearable.

Introjection, like projection, is of course a recurrent ongoing process in life that affects and alters the internal world. 'The structure of the personality is largely determined by the more permanent phantasies which the ego has about itself and the objects it contains' (Segal, 1973). Of course bad experiences can lead to the internalization of bad inner objects or a good experience may be internalized in conjunction with envious, spoiling feelings. But when there is a predominance of good relationships in the internal world, the internal objects, mainly the internal parents, are felt to be the internal source of a pull towards the depressive position. This, as we saw above, is based on loving concern for one's objects and wanting to be in a good internal relationship with them. Gillian was preoccupied with internalizing a helpful, and strong, therapist, and she showed how she needed this to help her to care for her inner values.

THE POSSIBILITY OF INNER CHANGE

A human being's capacity to internalize qualities and aspects of another, through their ongoing relationship, offers the possibility for growth and change to occur through therapeutic work. One of the most fundamental aspects of this is the worker's capacity to tolerate mental pain. We saw how Colin (Chapter 7) and Nicholas (Chapter 8) used primitive ways of evading unbearable mental experience; the worker's containment of their confusion and projected distress provided a real experience for these children which they could perhaps eventually be able to internalize. Nicholas seemed indeed to be slowly acquiring the capacity to experience his feelings and think about them instead of turning them mindlessly into rubbish. As the worker thinks about and puts into words her experience of the session, the client may perceive that she has 'room' for him and that his feelings are important to someone else; he may then also develop a capacity to tolerate these feelings himself.

We also saw with Sam (Chapter 7) and Andrew (Chapter 8) how a worker's containment of the chaos of a disturbed child's inner world could enable the child to make a helpful distinction between good and bad. Until this has happened no good inner experience can stay good.

At a later stage of emotional development, the child or client may need help in bringing together feelings of hatred and idealization, in the way we have described above under the 'depressive position'. We saw how Mrs Adams (Chapter 4) was at first dominated by the need to see her little boy as idolized and idealized, or as totally bad, an example of the 'splitting' in the paranoid-schizoid position. She may have been helped to move in the direction of the depressive position and begin to have a more reasonable relationship with him, as a result of the health visitor's work (though no doubt there were to be many future fluctuations).

Many clients seem 'stuck' when they come to us for help. They may have distressing symptoms which have persisted over a long time. Betty's intractable soiling, Rupert's enuresis (Chapter 7), Gillian's learning inhibition (Chapter 9), all were outer signs of an inner inability to work through their problems. The underlying infantile feelings could be experienced anew in their relationship with their worker, who by her response is then able to offer an opportunity for change. In Rupert's therapy, for example, the overflowing bucket in the session, and the feelings associated with it that Dr M helped him put into words, became a symbol for his emotional experience of being listened to and understood, which he could internalize. It is the relationship with the worker which is central to the therapeutic process. If the infantile feelings are contained and worked through in this relationship, the client's own inner resources are strengthened; his inner world acquires some of the good capacities of the worker. Graham (Chapter 9) had found Mrs L had struggled to understand him through his defective speech, which was the vehicle for his feelings. This made him want to improve his speech, and he decided to get some speech therapy for himself.

In that sense, perhaps, the client develops the capacity to think for himself and to do some of the 'therapeutic work' himself: he begins to take responsibility for his infantile feelings and develops a belief in his own capacity for goodness. Rupert's presentation of himself initially seems to have been as an unlovable, intrusive mouse. Early on in therapy one can see his wish to reinstate good figures in his mind who would help him: the gardener who would be there when needed, the policeman who would be friendly and not aggravate him, perhaps a friendly, monitoring figure of the depressive position as opposed to a persecuting image of the paranoid-schizoid position vengefully seeking him out.

We can perhaps see a detailed example of the process of change and internalization if we look at a later sequence in Rupert's therapy. When Dr M shared her thinking with him about the nature of the overflowing bucket he responded by speaking of a nappy, and later in the session when Dr M wrote his name on the back of a picture he responded joyously 'You have given this to me.' It seems that he was in the process of taking in and having available within himself a giving and more competent figure, one with a capacity to bear and think about his misery and hatred. His relationship with this changing figure in his inner world may have made it possible for him both to want and be able to clear up the overflow from the bucket at the end of the session himself. As time went on a caring, careful parent was represented 'to watch over what he was doing' and to think about him (the making of the 'thinking hat'). These examples seem to represent both his experience of Dr M in the session and also his wish to have such a figure available to him internally when he was separated from her in between sessions. It seemed that Rupert was taking Dr M in as a good helpful figure and this in turn went some way towards restoring and recreating the good 'parent' figures of his inner world. In this way he could begin to have a sense of his own inner worth, and could find the strength to bear some of his own feelings of hatred and unhappiness.

The strength of these internalizations had to be tested out over and over again between Rupert and Dr M, especially in relation to the external separation from the therapist. He needed her to experience for him his feelings of sadness and jealousy: 'You say you're sad because I've gone'. This was particularly so around a holiday separation. The worker clearly then needs to allow time to work through the emotions associated with the ending of therapy. As we saw with Gillian the experience of separation seems to be a necessary part of the ability to internalize a good relationship, but its value depends on shared preparation.

Chapter 15

Transference and Countertransference

THE ROOTS OF TRANSFERENCE

When a client comes to a session, he brings a whole range of feelings which he may not be consciously aware of, which become expressed in play, talk or action. Bob (Chapter 4) would not have been able to speak directly about feeling repeatedly dropped or sunk from people's minds; but he was able to communicate it through his play in the session. At the end of the session he depicted anxieties about a chaotic ending in his play; these anxieties about ending and being dropped had also become relevant to the ending with the specific worker. Bob was showing feelings with an earlier origin, but which manifested themselves in the present and which acquired a new meaning in relation to the worker. This is an example of transference.

Transference relates to the client's feelings, including his own projections, experienced in relation to the worker and the setting; countertransference, which we shall discuss later in this chapter, refers to the worker's feelings aroused by contact with the client.

Freud discovered in the course of his psychoanalytic work that 'new editions of impulses and phantasies' could replace 'some earlier person by the person of the physician' and hence could be currently felt in relation to the latter (Freud, 1905). These he called 'transferences'. In reporting on the case of his patient, Dora, he showed how he had been unable to stop her breaking off therapy because he had not understood the development of transference at the time. He subdivided transferences into 'new impressions', where the content is unchanged from the past although the recipient is different, and 'new editions' which could be 'edited' in such a way so as to have a special bearing on a current relationship (ibid). It is in the re-experiencing of the emotions underlying such transferences within a new relationship that the therapeutic potential for change and growth lies. Klein showed that the whole range of internal infantile object relationships and mental processes can be transferred and currently experienced in relation to someone in the external world. Transference may be directly linked with early experiences or with much later ones and in therapy can be thought of as an expression of current phantasy.

Transference aspects of relationships can of course be, and are, experienced outside therapy. We have to remember that transference is a naturally occurring phenomenon; Freud did not invent it, he discovered it was there! Many people on reflection may perhaps agree, for example, that if they have a long wait to be served in a restaurant, their feelings about the people who keep them waiting or are being served in preference to them are stronger than the external situation actually warrants, and that some transfer of infantile feelings has taken place. Transference exists then, whether or not it is 'worked with'. Individual therapeutic work aims to provide a setting in which such feelings can be held, thought about and talked about.

A worker offers the child or client provision for open expression of feelings through play or talk within the context of a stable setting, and she offers her own thoughtful attention; it can then be possible for emotions with an infantile content to manifest themselves readily in a transference relationship. The worker becomes the person towards whom such emotions are felt and the relationship with her has transference significance. How the transference is, or is not, responded to, is likely to influence the ongoing relationship.

How can these transference relationships be used in individual work with children and young people? A worker without appropriate experience and training (Chapter 2) cannot understand or interpret unconscious symbolic material, and cannot explore detailed manifestations of her clients' transference relationship to her. But there are ways in which clients relate to workers which can be thought about and put into words for them.

THE RELEVANCE OF TRANSFERENCE IN INDIVIDUAL THERAPEUTIC WORK

We saw in Chapter 1 ('The client's initial perceptions of the worker and the setting') how, from the first contact, the setting or the worker can represent for the client something he has imbued it with: Lena felt that the place she had come to could make her feel mad; Satvinder that it could be a kind of court, with the worker on the side of the prosecution; Luke expected to be given instant skills in reading. These are examples of 'pretransference', in that the relevant feelings are present in the client before any relationship is established, and these may indeed often get in the way of establishing any helpful relationship. If the worker can become aware of these feelings in her client and put them into words this may be the first steps in the therapeutic process.

In Ahmed's fourth session (Chapter 2) he voiced his anxiety that the worker would leave. Although he was able to ask her about this, it was clear that he also 'transferred' to her the likelihood that she would become another of these 'going away' people in his life. His inner world consisted of people who deserted him. Obviously this inner world was largely formed by his real-life experiences. It would be useful, however, for the worker to put into words for him not just her own intention of staying, but also his painful feeling that new relationships would end up by being broken off, and his anxiety that she too would just go away.

When Edward (Chapter 2) asked at the end of the session whether the boats would float, he appeared to be afraid that the worker would not keep him 'floating' in her mind until the next session, despite her having clarified the arrangements for meeting with him at the beginning of their work together. He had said he got angry when sent to bed by his mother (although he also attempted to treat this in a 'don't care' way), so the worker could have made a link between his account of being sent to bed by mother and her action now in ending the session. Talking to him about the ending of this session, and his worry as to whether there would be another, could help him to be in touch with a wider range of his emotions; he might then come to feel that these had a chance of being thought about as opposed to just being denied. Bob's anxieties about being dropped (Chapter 4) were also something he experienced anew in his relationship with his worker. If a large part of the worker's role is to act as a thoughtful container for her client's communications, it follows that her absence from him may arouse considerable anxiety about her ability to keep him in mind when they are apart, as we saw so graphically in the case of Bob and also Colin (Chapter 7). It is therefore important to give recognition to a client's feelings about the worker when they are not together.

Betty (Chapter 7), by putting the messy sand on the worker, showed how she wanted her to be the same; that is, they should both be dirty; this was a transference version of Betty's internal feelings that there should be some kind of sameness between the mother and the baby. Betty actually showed in the session how she hoped to be understood and helped by the worker in this new edition of the transference (cf. 'What do you think of this then?'). Play and other activities within the setting are relevant to the transference. When Betty felt the mess had gone everywhere in the room it became for her frighteningly dirty. She seemed to connect this with the worker herself. We could say that in the transference Betty was experiencing the worker as messed up and damaged, like the people in her inner world, and hence unable to think. Betty felt that the worker could not hold on to the mess (and the unpleasant feelings), contain them and deal with them. This was not because the worker was being 'uncontaining' (in Bion's sense) but because Betty felt in the transference that she had damaged the worker by her mess. If the worker could put into words Betty's envious need for 'sameness' and her anxiety about the worker being messed up by the envy which she displayed in the session, then Betty might be able to have a better understanding of her experience of this 'new edition' of the transference with the worker. Betty's expectation was that the worker would not be able to remain 'containing'; if the worker could put this into words, while at the same time continuing to hold steady to her role as therapist, then Betty might gradually come to feel that here was someone who could bear her envy.

The relationship a child or client makes with the worker is a direct experience which they both share; it is something of which the worker has direct evidence in the session. She does not therefore have the same doubts about its truth, validity or relevance as she has about the 'history' anyone else tells her outside the session. That makes it doubly important that the client's feelings about her can be allowed to emerge and evolve uncontaminated by material she may herself introduce. If she were to insist on figuring as a friendly person by giving the child sweets (or complimenting an older client on his appearance), this would prevent her from being able to see the client's perceptions of her. Similarly, if she were to tell the client details of her own life (her marital status, children, house, holidays, illnesses), this would be an intrusion which would make it much more difficult for the client to share with her his preoccupations, projections and phantasies. If she can intrude her own personality and interests as little as possible she can learn from the client, and can in turn put into words for him his assumptions about her, and the role he ascribes to her. Since this is based on what takes place in the session, it carries conviction for the client (and worker). It also carries out a piece of therapeutic work for the client, as we described in Chapter 13, 'Containment'.

The outcome of trying to follow the transference feelings, both positive and negative, in the worker-client relationship, can be seen clearly with Gillian (Chapter 9). She had been helped not only with her symptoms in the external world and in her mourning, but in understanding that she had a developing inner world of good objects for which she was responsible. Here one can see not only how feelings were transferred in the current relationship, but how the experience became internalized. Gillian was re-establishing an inner mother who would help her to monitor her inner world; noteworthily too in conjunction with an inner father who would also have proper standards of care for the good objects of this inner world – 'Tell Dad about the danger to the goldfish.' This example shows how work in a new edition of the transference can lead to change in both the external and inner world.

THE SIGNIFICANCE OF NEGATIVE TRANSFERENCE

We spoke in Chapter 8 about negative behaviour and negative feelings, and how painful it can be to work with them. It may make the work more bearable at these moments if the worker knows that the child or client is not disliking her as herself, but as a transference figure projected from the child's inner world. Andrew related to Miss B almost as a non-person, treating her as if she would be unresponsive to him. Annabel treated Dr C as if he were nobody compared with the secretary, and she made it plain that the corridor was more attractive than Dr C's room. Nicholas subjected Mrs D to a concrete bombardment with all the contents of his box, spat at her and pulled her hair.

These are examples of directly expressed and seemingly unmistakable negative feelings. Underlying such negative expression, to a greater or lesser degree, is the client's search for, and certainly the need for, some kind of human receptacle, a container and potential thinker, who can help in bearing and understanding what is transferred (see Chapter 13). Andrew needed Miss B to give meaning to his feelings; Nicholas too needed help in understanding that someone, Mrs D, really had the capacity to receive and think about what he was bombarding her with; Annabel too may have been projecting some of her feelings of incapacity and undesirability into Dr C in order for him to think about them.

The therapists working with Jerry (Chapter 1) and Sam (Chapter 7) had to be receptacles for very negative feelings before there was any possibility that Jerry or Sam could experience them as more positive figures in the transference. Jerry needed to feel that his chaotic urges had found a home in his therapy where they were 'held' and not allowed to be totally destructive; only after this could he experience the relationship with the worker as one where good things (food, love) could be given and received. Sam seemed to need the therapist to put up with his expressions of mocking belittlement before he could move on to the expression of softer baby feelings. Eventually he was able at moments to experience her as a gentle, caring mother – for example when he asked her to push him while he sat in a pram. This seemed to be the emergence of a positive transference linked to a good mothering figure. We shall return to discuss some of these examples from the point of view of the worker's role and her use of her own feelings later on in the chapter, when we discuss countertransference. Negative emotionality expressed to the worker may be thought of as negative transference, but it may also be the basis of a communication which needs containment and has to be understood as such. It can also be an expression of full-blooded 'negative transference' where the patient sees the therapist as frightening or bad, and this too needs to be recognized. We can recall the frightened hostility directed by baby Amy (Chapter 10) against the observer; this could be called negative transference, although such terminology may feel strange used in connection with small babies. Some of Alan's response to the proposed ending by Mrs O was clearly negative transference (Chapter 9), as were Colin's murderous attacks on what he felt to be Mrs V's other children (Chapter 7): both these children saw the worker and her other relationships as something bad to be attacked or annihilated at that time. Graham's resentment about his dependence on his worker (Chapter 9), as well as his 'paranoid' feelings of being messed about by her and the hospital were a negative transference from his inner world and were noticed and worked with; the discussion of such feelings seemed to help him to feel less persecuted by outside authorities. As we saw with Satvinder and Lena in Chapter 1, some negative feelings are directed less towards the worker as a person, than as a representative of an institution or function.

The operation of transference feelings is not restricted solely to the worker and the client's direct contact with her. The client may also have strong and painful feelings about the worker's relationship with other people. Dick (Chapter 11) when about eight months old, was reported by the observer on one occasion to have remained cheerful when his mother left off feeding him in the living room to go into the kitchen (as she often did to get something); however he cried crossly when he heard her start talking to his father. This seemed to be an expression of his jealousy. Dick's apparent rivalry with the dog, and the struggles of Peter and Mary with jealousy and rivalry in family life are also described in Chapter 11. We need to relate to and think about such feelings with our clients. Once a therapeutic relationship has been established between worker and child, and the child has repeatedly experienced the help the worker can offer, the child is likely to miss the worker between the sessions; but he may also feel jealous and angry when he thinks the worker is with other people, or perhaps even that she is meanly keeping herself to herself when absent. The child is also likely to have strong feelings about any other children the worker may see in therapy. Anthony, for example, wished his worker to take his picture home and put it in her bedroom; he also wanted to investigate the boxes of other children in the playroom (Chapter 3). Rupert wanted his pictures to replace those already on Dr M's board (Chapter 7). When Dr M was able to bear Rupert's feelings of jealousy and exclusion in their relationship, this may have led to improvements in his external relationships in the foster-home, as well as helping him in his inner world.

UNDERSTANDING THE COUNTERTRANSFERENCE

We have talked about transference. How does one become aware of it? By observation and listening in the course of the session, the worker can notice and hear how she is being seen and treated. Satvinder (Chapter 1) by his surliness made his feelings very clear; Ahmed (Chapter 2) was very direct in showing his anxiety that the worker would leave. Rupert's jealousy about the others that Dr M saw was very evident. But probably it is through feelings occurring within us during the session, the countertransference, that we derive most of our understanding of the transference.

The term countertransference is used basically in two different ways. It is sometimes used in the original sense of an inappropriate reaction to a patient's material, stemming from the worker's own difficulties, but the concept has in recent years been considerably changed and widened. It is still used to refer to the response within the therapist to the patient's material, but now makes use of the nature of this response as an aid to understanding what the client is feeling and to what is happening in the session. It is in this sense that we use it in this book. Heimann (1950) refers to it as 'comprising all feelings which the analyst experiences towards his patient' and as having a major role in the work.

A worker may feel countertransference feelings as a result of something the client is relating directly to her, or as a result of a piece of play; the solemn atmosphere of the session when Gillian (Chapter 9) played with the goldfish conveyed the seriousness of her meaning to the worker, apart from the detailed content of the play itself. A worker may perceive that the client is trying to use her in some way differently from how she is offering herself. This could be true at times for both Edward's and Ahmed's workers in Chapter 2, when they were asked to go along with the children's wishes to mask their more distressed feelings. In any event the feelings would be aroused in the worker from something emanating from the client. Betty (Chapter 7) seemed to feel that her worker's containing functions were damaged by the mess she had created, so that 'in the transference' she experienced the worker as being spoiled and damaged. The worker herself was also aware of feeling useless and rejected near the end of the session, when Betty wanted to finish early 'so as to get to the café'. So the feelings Betty was evoking in the worker helped her to understand how Betty was feeling. As is so often the case, it is the countertransference that helps towards understanding the transference.

A great deal of a worker's understanding of her countertransference in the session is likely to come from her response to her client's projective identification. Gita's screams (Chapter 10) were an attempt at evacuating the bad pain from inside her, but by dint of her mother's presence and response they were also a communication. This was received by her mother and worked upon within her maternal reverie. Putting it another way, we could say that Gita, by using projective identification as a communication conveyed her pain to her mother, who experienced it in her countertransference and was then able to help Gita with it. A similar process operates in therapeutic work. A client's feelings can enter the worker, and this can happen whether the intent is to communicate, or to locate something unwanted in the therapist. The hostile bombardments and noncommunications of Nicholas and Andrew, Annabel's belittlements and Jerry's confusions were experienced by their worker in the countertransference and then, through the equivalent of 'maternal reverie', could be given meaning and perhaps understood. The workers' countertransference feelings came to them through projective identifications.

COUNTERTRANSFERENCE AND THE SETTING

In short-term work it would not be helpful to encourage the development of a deeper relationship. But it is still useful to be aware of feelings evoked in us by the client. The counselling service attended by Lena, referred to in Chapter 1, offered short-term work only. Lena in her first interview asked in an apparently casual manner, as if just a conversation opener, if all sorts of people attended. The worker found herself feeling uneasy, and yet nearly passing over the question as mere introductory small talk. She paid attention, however, to the feelings of unease within herself, and used these (with other material) to get in touch with what turned out to be Lena's real anxiety: that she had come to a service for 'mad' people. This in turn led to some understanding of Lena's fear that she might be mad, and to a discussion about whether she might seek longer-term therapy.

Some workers also have a formal role to carry which would preclude an overt emphasis on the worker-client relationship. Here, too, sensitive use of the worker's countertransference may help the client. Mr Q's work in the school support unit (Chapter 4, 'Relating to colleagues in the school setting') is an example. He was aware from discussion with Clare of some of her difficulties; he was also made to feel that Clare expected him to be especially 'soft' and kind of her. He also felt that her class teacher's requirements of Clare were 'harder' or even harsh. In discussing these feelings in a seminar, he became aware that they had arisen partly through the group dynamics of the school and partly because Clare had given him the feeling that she needed to be treated extra 'softly'. Once he could recognize that his feelings stemmed partly from his colleagues and partly from Clare, he was able to work more actively at the problems with both the class teacher and Clare herself. He thus avoided running the risk of stepping out of his role and allowing himself to be drawn into a false one of 'special therapist' for Clare.

There are always likely to be some tensions, influenced by the specific setting, which need attention if they are not to impinge on it adversely. An example could be a potential response of a colleague to an institutionally troublesome client, such as Nicholas (Chapter 8), whose behaviour was sometimes disruptive in public areas of the school. This could be taken by the worker as criticism of her management of the child, which she might feel driven to tighten at the expense of her therapeutic contact with him.

The wider setting can be relevant to the countertransference, because it can influence how a worker feels about her work. We saw in Chapter 4 how some services could sense themselves to be 'at the end of the line', when asked by society to care for clients about whom there seemed to be a minimum hope. It is difficult for workers in such settings not to be overwhelmed by feelings of hopelessness when they receive such referrals. The worker and headteacher in the school attended by Harman (Chapter 6) had managed not to succumb to such feelings.

Nursery workers as we saw with Judy (Chapter 2) and nurses in paediatric wards may tend to devalue the importance of their relationship with a child. However, it can be very helpful for a nurse to help a child to think about his feelings in the current situation. Again, the nurse may need help in order not to succumb to other people's dismissive views of her role.

In some instances the problems of a client can be so disturbing that they affect the professional workers involved, in ways that they themselves are not aware of. Being involved in a case of child abuse (see Chapter 4) is extremely painful emotionally for the worker, with a temptation to believe in some instances that one can get rid of this pain by removing the child from his home. This may be a necessary measure but in itself it must inevitably increase the child's emotional suffering. Equally, a worker could be in danger of allowing a child seriously at risk to return home because of unbearable feelings associated with taking a child away from his parents.

THERAPEUTIC USE OF THE COUNTERTRANSFERENCE

For the worker to be able to use herself therapeutically, her mental privacy with her client needs to be safeguarded as much as his privacy with her. A room in which the telephone rings, or where passing colleagues can look in, or staff come in or pass through, or a setting where the same room is not consistently available, all make it impossible for the worker to achieve the state of 'relaxed attention' of which Bion wrote. Much of what has been written in Chapter 3 about the setting is relevant here.

The worker needs to be in touch with the feelings the client brings to the session even if these are not put into words. In our work with clients we hope to learn from them about their anxieties and conflicts rather than having any preconceived theories ourselves. If parents, teachers or other colleagues give us information outside the session, the temptation to bring it in, and meet their expectations that we should somehow deal with it, becomes great. We are left with the task of trying to bear the inevitable contradiction of having what may feel to be both relevant and, at the same time, irrelevant information. It is probably more helpful to wait for material to come from the client, and only relate to material that actually feels relevant to the session. In exploratory contacts the situation may be somewhat different, but even so, when Dr G, in his wish to help and understand Lindsey (Chapter 5), approached her initially with a structured framework of questions he met with a very negative response; it was only when he was able to wait and try to experience what Lindsey was feeling, that she began to feel he understood her and could help her.

It is also important to give the client a chance to think about his experience and become aware of his feelings and not to suggest that he may be feeling something before we really have enough evidence. Even if Colin's specialist teacher, Mrs V (Chapter 7), sensed at the beginning that his 'whirling away' was to do with the missed sessions, it needed the whole session for him to disclose to her what had taken place in her absence: not just the concrete smashing of another boy's watch but also Colin's attack on his thoughts and memory of Mrs V with the giggling and the 'silliness'. If a worker is too quick to have an answer this can take away the client's chance of coming in touch with his feelings and experiencing the reality of them.

Sometimes the child or client gives the worker a mass of chaotic unconnected data that seems to have no emotional meaning. Nicholas's bombardment of Mrs D (Chapter 8) and the chaotic nature of his sessions had to be endured for some while before an underlying meaning could emerge. Sometimes the coherence and meaning (what Bion calls a 'selected fact', which we discussed in connection with Ps$\longleftrightarrow$D in Chapter 14) comes largely by an unconscious process in ourselves. If we can help a client look at an experience, as Mrs D gradually was able to help Nicholas look at his feelings about the ending of sessions and about her holiday breaks, this can enable the client to begin to think about it and hold it in his mind. It can be transformed into thoughts 'capable of growth and accretion of meaning' (Bion, 1962a).

The worker's more or less unconscious intuition can be impeded by a desire to be helpful and by a wish for results, paradoxical though this may sound, since a desire to be helpful was probably what brought us into this area of work in the first place. For example, Mrs Rogers, Kevin's mother (Chapter 10), had 'been sorted out' with a coil. It seemed that the professionals' wish to be helpful also included an element of controlling the client into using the service. This temptation exists for many people who work with disturbed children if the child runs continually out of the room during the session, for example, or tries to wreck it in other ways. (This was illustrated briefly by Annabel (Chapter 8), though the circumstances were special there, in that the rooms themselves had had to be altered.) The worker has to try and distinguish in her own mind her need to safeguard the child's session, from an unconscious desire she may have to force the child to accept help whether he wants it or not.

Being open to experiencing the emotions of another person inevitably stimulates the worker's own primitive basic feelings and also her defences against anxiety and mental pain. She may feel herself wishing to break off the therapy with a particular child because he is making her feel useless and stupid in a session; she may find herself getting increasingly angry with another child. An ability to experience these and other feelings evoked in us by our clients seems to be a necessary part of the work. Only in that way can we really be in touch with our clients' unconscious pain. Often we need to experience it in projection first before we can understand what it is. If we deny or somehow get rid of our own feelings it is not really possible for the client to be helped. A psychiatrist, for example, had been seeing a seven-year-old girl as his first introduction to individual work with children. The little girl spent much of the session in the wendy house, and made it clear that he was to stay outside, where he could not see what was going on. He used the time to write up his notes about her, but after discussing it in a seminar he began to realize that he had been blocking out an irritated feeling of being no use and of not being wanted. It was only when he let these feelings come into his mind that it became possible to reflect on whether the little girl had actually been evoking them in him.

A worker may also have to tolerate a good deal of mental confusion and chaos during a child's session. The temptation is to find an explanation to give to the child (and to herself) that would make sense of the session, as quickly as possible. When Mrs D worked with Nicholas, she told the group that she found herself on the point of repeating phrases to him about his dislike of gaps between sessions; these comments had seemed meaningful and helpful in the previous week but now felt stereotyped. She had to 'hold on' to the chaos in order to sense the feeling and quality of the current session.

In the session with Betty discussed in Chapter 7, the need for the clinical psychologist to wait patiently while the material developed was apparent. So too was the need for the worker's mind to be open to promptings from a feeling level, and to images evoked in her by Betty's play; a state of mind which we describe as 'attentive thinking with reverie'. Out of the experience of the first part of the session there eventually came a clearer communication about 'mess', which the worker could then put into words. Towards the end of the session there was a chance to help Betty distinguish between evading pain and bearing it.

Some clients may evoke in the worker a wish to be of practical help. Perhaps this was part of Mr K's problem when he was working with June (Chapter 4). She told him she felt isolated and want to get out of her home, so he arranged for her to go to a summer camp, but when it came to it, she did not want to go, and it seemed that this was not really meeting her need. Similarly Ahmed evoked in the worker a wish to cheer him up; Andrew's worker wanted to encourage him to start painting. In all these cases the burden of the child's despair and desolation evoked a natural response in the worker to avoid or evade it by an imposed cheerfulness. This is different from real hope which arises as a result of a change in the inner world.

Growth in the psyche, as we have seen, depends on the painful thought finding a container that can modify it. Through our response to their communications, we can help our clients distinguish between evasion of pain and the bearing of pain. The continual acceptance of a painful truth seems to be the common thread in the longer-term cases described (such as Rupert and Sam in Chapter 7 and Nicholas in Chapter 8); and there was some evidence in each that the worker's acceptance and modulation of the children's projective identifications was beginning to enable the children themselves to change.

If we really remain open to doubt and uncertainty, this feels dangerous, even catastrophic. We have to suffer this until we see a pattern – Bion's 'selected fact'. A new idea can come as a psychological upheaval, and it can be experienced as an attack on our existing way of life. Beginning to follow the approach we have been describing can mean unlearning or suspending earlier acquired methods of meeting other people's, or our clients', problems. But without the capacity to change, in ourselves as well as in our clients, there can be no vitality or growth.

We now return to the original meaning of the term countertransference, that is, a disturbance in the therapist herself. How is the worker to assess the feelings arising within her? To whom do they belong? Of course those fortunate enough to have or have had personal therapy will have additional equipment within themselves for monitoring their own responses. But few are in such a fortunate situation. Discussion with a group of colleagues, preferably with an experienced leader, can help in looking at the material, and thinking about where the feelings emanate; it can also help to contain the anxieties of the worker that she may be intruding some of her own problems into the work. One of the reasons that we have presented this book in the form we have is in the hope of demonstrating the usefulness of discussion.

We should like to finish this chapter, and the book, with comments from a paper by someone who has recently attended work discussion groups with us. She says that at times she has been on the brink of discontinuing seeing a child; discussion in the seminar has helped her to see that this stemmed from feelings of impatience, annoyance and dislike aroused in her by the child. Detailed discussion of his material, in the context of his life history, helped her to see that these feelings were a communication, an inevitable one, and perhaps the first major piece of information he had given her. At other times when seeing a child she had become strongly critical within herself of the child's own mother. She writes: 'I find myself struggling with the idea as to where have the feelings come from? I am never too sure if some of the evoked feelings are not from some unrecognized part of myself.' She goes on to say that the struggle to contain these feelings and not pass them back on to the child or client is greatly helped by attending a group where individual work can be discussed.

References
(See also Discursive Reading List)

Bick, E. (1968) The experience of the skin in early object relations. In M. Harris, and E. Bick (1987), *Collected Papers* (M. Harris Williams, ed.) Perthshire: Clunie Press.

Bion, W.R. (1959) Attacks on linking. *International Journal of Psycho-Analysis*, **40**, and in Bion (1967).

Bion, W.R. (1961) *Experiences in Groups*. London: Tavistock.

Bion, W.R. (1962a) *Learning from Experience*. London: Heinemann, and in Bion (1977).

Bion, W.R. (1962b) A theory of thinking. *International Journal of Psycho-Analysis*, **43**, and in Bion (1967).

Bion, W.R. (1963) *Elements of Psycho-Analysis*. London: Heinemann, and in Bion (1977).

Bion, W.R. (1965) *Transformations: Change from Learning to Growth*. London: Heinemann, and in Bion (1977).

Bion, W.R. (1967) *Second Thoughts*. New York: Aronson.

Bion, W.R. (1970) *Attention and Interpretation*. London: Tavistock, and in Bion (1977).

Bion, W.R. (1977) *Seven Servants*. New York: Aronson.

Bower, T. (1977) *The Perceptual World of the Child*. Glasgow: Fontana/Open Books.

Box, S. *et al.* (eds) (1994) *Crisis at Adolescence: Object Relations Therapy with the Family*. London: Aronson (Rev. edn.)

Britton, R. (1994) Re-enactment as an unwitting professional response to family dynamics. In S. Box *et al.* (eds) *Crisis at Adolescence: Object Relations with the Family*. London: Aronson.

Coltart, N. (1992) Diagnosis and assessment for suitability for psychoanalytic psychotherapy. In N. Coltart, *Slouching towards Bethlehem*. London: Free Association Books.

Copley, B. (1993) *The World of Adolescence: Literature, Society and Psychoanalytic Psychotherapy*. London: Free Association Books.

Court, S.D. (1976) *Fit for the future: Report of the Committee on Child Health Services*, vol. 1, cmd. 6684. London: Ministry of Health.

Dartington, A. (1994) Where angels fear to tread: idealism, despondency and inhibition of thought in hospital nursing. In A. Obholzer and V.Z. Roberts (eds), *The Unconscious at Work*. London: Routledge, pp. 101–9.

Freud, S. (1905) Fragment of an analysis of a case of hysteria. *Standard Edition VII*. London: Hogarth Press and Institute of Psycho-Analysis (1953).

Freud, S. (1920) Beyond the pleasure principle. *Standard Edition XVII*. London: Hogarth Press and Institute of Psycho-Analysis (1953).

Harris, M. and Bick, E. (1987) *Collected Papers*. (M. Harris Williams, ed.) Perthshire: Clunie Press.

Heimann, P. (1950) On countertransference. *International Journal of Psycho-Analysis*, **31**, 81–4.

Heimann, P. (1952) Certain functions of introjection and projection in early infancy. In Klein *et al*. *Developments in Psycho-Analysis*. London: Hogarth Press.

Hinton, P.E. (1980) How a ten-year-old faced her death. *Journal of Child Psychotherapy*, **6**, pp.107–16.

Holmes, J. (1994) Brief psychodynamic psychotherapy. *Advances in Psychiatric Treatment*, **1**, pp. 9–15.

Isaacs, S. (1952) The nature and function of phantasy. In M. Klein *et al., Developments in Psycho-Analysis*. London: Hogarth Press.

Jaques, E. (1955) Social systems as a defence against persecutory and depressive anxiety. In M. Klein *et al*. (eds), *New Directions in Psycho-Analysis*. London: Tavistock.

Klein, M. (1940) Mourning and its relation to manic depressive states. *Contributions to Psycho-Analysis*. London: Hogarth Press and in Klein (1975a).

Klein, M. (1946) Notes on some schizoid mechanisms. In M. Klein *et al*. (eds) *Developments in Psycho-Analysis*. (1952) and in Klein 1975(b).

Klein, M. *et al*. (1952) *Developments in Psycho-Analysis*. J. Riviere, ed. London: Hogarth Press and the Institute of Psycho-Analysis.

Klein, M. (1955) On identification. In M. Klein *et al*. (eds) *New Directions in Psycho-Analysis*. London: Tavistock Publications and in Klein (1975b).

Klein, M. *et al*. (eds) (1955) *New Directions in Psycho-Analysis*. London: Tavistock Publications.

Klein, M. (1975a) *The Writings of Melanie Klein*, vol. 1, *Love, Guilt and Reparation and other Works (1921–45)*. London: Hogarth Press and the Institute of Psycho-Analysis.

Klein, M. (1975b) *The Writings of Melanie Klein*, vol. 3, *Envy and Gratitude and other Works (1946–63)*. London: Hogarth Press and the Institute of Psycho-Analysis.

Meltzer, D. (1975) Adhesive identification. In D. Meltzer, *Sincerity and Other Works: Collected Papers*. A. Hahn, ed. (1994). London: Karnac, pp. 335–50.

Meltzer, D. (1978) *The Kleinian Development, Part 2*. Perthshire: Clunie Press.

Obholzer, A. (1994) Social anxieties in public sector organizations. In A. Obholzer and V.Z. Roberts (eds), *The Unconscious at Work*. London: Routledge, pp. 169–78.

Obholzer, A. and Roberts, V.Z. (eds) (1994) *The Unconscious at Work*. London: Routledge.

Patton, M.J. and Meara, N.M. (1992) *Psychoanalytic Counselling*. New York: Wiley.

Rutter, M. *et al*. (1970) *Education, Health and Behaviour*. London: Longman.

Rutter, M. *et al*. (1975) Attainment and adjustment in two geographical areas: I The prevalence of psychiatric disorder. *British Journal of Psychiatry*, **126**.

Segal, H. (1973) *Introduction to the Work of Melanie Klein.* London: Heinemann.

Sinason, V. (1992) *Mental Handicap and the Human Condition: New Approaches from the Tavistock.* London: Free Association Books.

Winnicott, D.W. (1955) The depressive position in normal emotional development. *British Journal of Medical Psychology* **28**, Parts 2 and 3.

Winnicott, D.W. (1964) *The Child, the Family, and the Outside World.* Harmondsworth: Penguin.

Winnicott, D.W. (1971) *Playing and Reality.* London: Tavistock.

Discursive Reading List

Anderson, R. (ed.) (1992) *Clinical Lectures on Klein and Bion*. London: Routledge.
Contributes to understanding these authors.

Boston, M. and Daws, D. (eds) (1977) *The Child Psychotherapist and Problems of Young People*. London: Wildwood House.
A description of the work of a child psychotherapist in clinical and non-clinical settings, such as schools, day-centres and hospitals.

Boston, M. and Szur, R. (1983) *Psychotherapy with Severely Deprived Children*. London: Routledge & Kegan Paul.
A moving and encouraging account.

Bowlby, J. (1951) *Maternal Care and Mental Health*. Geneva: WHO.
This well-known study describes the fundamental importance of maternal care.

Copley, B. (1993) *The World of Adolescence: Literature, Society and Psychoanalytic Psychotherapy*. London: Free Association Books.
Also discusses counselling and work with families.

Harris, M. (1975) *Thinking about Infants and Young Children*. Perthshire, Clunie Press.
Conveys a wealth of understanding.

Harris, M. and Bick, E. (1987) *Collected Papers*. (M. Harris Williams, ed.) Perthshire: Clunie Press.
A very rich book which helps in thinking about many of the clinical and theoretical matters discussed here.

Hinshelwood, R.D. (1992) *A Dictionary of Kleinian Thought* (2nd edn). London: Free Association Books.
Highly informative.

Isaacs, S. (1952) The nature and function of phantasy. In M. Klein *et al.*, *Developments in Psycho-Analysis*. London: Hogarth Press and the Institute of Psycho-Analysis.
This is a classic paper on the nature of phantasy and the inner world. It illuminates infant life and the development of emotional processes.

Meltzer, D. (1975) Adhesive identification. In *Collected Papers of Donald Meltzer* (A. Hahn, ed.) (1994), London: Karnac, pp. 335–50.
Describes the concept of adhesive identification and clarifies other processes of identification.

Menzies Lyth, I (1988) *Containing Anxiety in Institutions: Selected Essays*, vol. 1. London: Free Association Books.
This may help readers in thinking about the institutions in which they work.

Miller, L., Rustin, M.E., Rustin, M.J. and Shuttleworth, J. (eds) (1989) *Closely Observed Infants*. London: Duckworth.
A detailed presentation of infant observation together with thoughtful links to psychoanalytic theory and other modes of infant study.

Noonan, E. (1983) *Counselling Young People*. London: Methuen.
Provides a useful discussion of psychoanalytically based counselling of young people.

Obholzer, A. and Roberts, V.Z. (eds) (1994) *The Unconscious at Work*. London: Routledge.
Useful for thinking about ourselves and others in work settings.

O'Shaughnessy, E. (1964) The absent object. *Journal of Child Psychotherapy*, 1(2).
A clinical illustration of Bion's work.

O'Shaughnessy, E. (1981) A commemorative essay on W.R. Bion's theory of thinking. *Journal of Child Psychotherapy*, 7(2).
Helpful in understanding Bion's work in the context of child psychotherapy.

Rustin, M.E. and Rustin, M.J. (1987) *Narratives of Love and Loss: Studies in Modern Children's Fiction*. London: Verso.
Illuminates the depth of children's emotional life.

Salzberger-Wittenberg, I. (1970) *Psycho-Analytic Insight and Relationships: A Kleinian Approach*. London: Routledge and Kegan Paul.
Helpful in thinking about the kind of relationships discussed throughout this book.

Salzberger-Wittenberg, I. *et al.* (1983) *The Emotional Experience of Learning and Teaching*. London: Routledge and Kegan Paul.
Explores the experience of the learning process and has many applications.

Szur, R. and Miller, S. (eds) (1991) *Extending Horizons: Psychoanalytic Psychotherapy with Children, Adolescents and Families*. London: Karnac.
Provides a wide and valuable view of varied developments in such work.

Trowell, J. and Bauer, M. (1996) *Emotional Needs of Children*. London: Routledge.
Examples of application of psychoanalytic thinking in the community.

A series of short books written by a number of professionals from the Tavistock Clinic, starting with *Understanding Your Baby*, by Lisa Miller, followed by *Understanding Your 1 Year Old, Understanding Your 2 Year old*, etc., up to *Understanding 18–20 Year Olds* including *Understanding Your Handicapped Child* (1992–95), London, Rosendale Press. These short books are addressed primarily to parents, but are also useful as a background to discussion with them and also with colleagues.

Directory of Further Learning Opportunities

Opportunities known to the authors at the time of publication which are likely to have a broadly similar conceptual basis to that of this book.

1. Courses in Observational Studies and the Application of Psychoanalytic Concepts to work with Children, Young People and Families. (Various other courses may also be available at these addresses.)

Enquiries to:

Director of Academic Services
Tavistock Clinic
120 Belsize Lane
London NW3 5BA

Organizing Tutor
Birmingham Trust for Psychoanalytic Psychotherapy
96 Park Hill
Moseley
Birmingham B13 8DS

Organizing Tutor
UBHT Teaching Care
Child and Adolescent Service
Knowle Clinic
Broadfield Road
Knowle
Bristol BS4 2UH

Organising Tutor
T.S.C.Y.P.
Scottish Institute of Human Relations
56 Albany Street
Edinburgh EH1 3QR

Course Administrator
Leeds Community and Mental Health NHS Teaching Trust
Southfield House
Clarendon Road
Leeds LS2 7PJ

Organising Tutor
Merseyside Psychotherapy Institute
c/o Dept. Child and Adolescent Psychiatry
Alder Hey Children's Hospital
Eaton Road
Liverpool LI2 2AP

Organising Tutor
The Oxford Observation Course
c/o 12 Rectory Road
St. Clements
Oxford OX4 1BW

2. Other varied opportunities. Enquiries to:

Consultant Child Psychotherapist
North Devon Family Consultancy
Barnstaple Health Centre
Vicarage Street
Barnstaple, Devon EX32 7BT

The Secretary
The Bridge Foundation
12 Sydenham Road
Cotham, Bristol BS6 5SH

Principal Child Psychotherapist
Iddesleigh House
Child Adolescent and Family Consultation Service
97 Heavitree Road
Exeter EX1 2NE

Principal Child Psychotherapist
Herefordshire Psychoanalytic Psychotherapy Group
Child, Adolescent and Family Guidance Centre
Health Centre
Gaol St.
Hereford HR1 2HU

Principal Child Psychotherapist
Thorneywood Child and Adolescent Psychiatry Unit
Porchester Road
Nottingham NG3 6LF

Head Child Psychotherapist
Plymouth Child and Family Consultation Service
Erme House
Mount Gould Hospital
Plymouth
Devon PL4 7QD

Course Director
Winnicott Centre for Children and Families
Torbay Hospital Annexe
187 Newton Rd.
Torbay TQ2 7AJ

Consultant Child Psychotherapist
Child and Family Centre
Treliske Hospital
Truro, Cornwall TR1 3LQ

Index